PRAISE FOR *ANTS AMONG ELEPHANTS*

A *Shelf Awareness* Best Book of the Year

⊚ ⊚ ⊚

"Sujatha Gidla's *Ants Among Elephants*, which records the life of a Dalit family in the central Indian state of Andhra Pradesh and spans nearly a century, significantly enriches the new Dalit literature in English . . . Defiant in the face of endless cruelty and misery, and tender with its victims, she seems determined to render the truth of a historical experience in all its dimensions, complexity, and nuance. The result is a book that combines many different genres—memoir, history, ethnography, and literature—and is outstanding in the intensity and scale of its revelations . . . Gidla's book achieves the emotional power of V.S. Naipaul's great novel *A House for Mr. Biswas.*"

—Pankaj Mishra, *The New York Review of Books*

"A remarkable family history . . . *Ants Among Elephants* may well be eye-opening not just for non-Indians—who will recoil in righteous horror from the intimate details of caste discrimination—but also for many Indians, for whom the lives of Untouchables take place out of sight . . . In this book of nonfiction one reads of real people fighting real cruelty with real courage and grace."

—Tunku Varadarajan, *The Wall Street Journal*

"With her luminous command of fine details, Gidla manages a difficult and admirable task: she takes a tremendously personal memoir and renders it with such clarity that it tells the broader story of a place and an era."

—James Norton, *The Christian Science Monitor*

© NANCY CRAMPTON

SUJATHA GIDLA

ANTS AMONG ELEPHANTS

◎ ◎ ◎

Sujatha Gidla was born an untouchable in Andhra
Pradesh, India. She studied physics at the Regional
Engineering College, Warangal. Her writing has
appeared in *The Oxford India Anthology of Telugu
Dalit Writing*. She lives in New York and works as
a conductor on the subway.

ANTS AMONG ELEPHANTS

ANTS AMONG

AN UNTOUCHABLE FAMILY AND

ELEPHANTS

THE MAKING OF MODERN INDIA

◉ ◉ ◉

SUJATHA GIDLA

FARRAR, STRAUS AND GIROUX | NEW YORK

Farrar, Straus and Giroux
175 Varick Street, New York 10014

Printed in the United States of America
Published in 2017 by Farrar, Straus and Giroux
First paperback edition, 2018

The Library of Congress has cataloged the hardcover edition as follows:
Names: Gidla, Sujatha, 1963– author.
Title: Ants among elephants : an untouchable family and the making
 of modern India / Sujatha Gidla.
Description: First edition. | New York : Farrar, Straus and Giroux, 2017.
Identifiers: LCCN 2016052857 | ISBN 9780865478114 (hardback) |
 ISBN 9780374711382 (e-book)
Subjects: LCSH: Gidla, Sujatha, 1963– —Childhood and youth. | Gidla, Sujatha,
 1963– —Family. | Dalits—India—Biography. | Families—India—Biography. |
 Teachers—India—Biography. | Poets—India—Biography. | Revolutionaries—
 India—Biography. | Caste—India—History—20th century. | India—Social
 conditions—1947– | Kakinada (India)—Biography. | BISAC: BIOGRAPHY &
 AUTOBIOGRAPHY / Literary. | HISTORY / Asia / India & South Asia. |
 SOCIAL SCIENCE / Discrimination & Race Relations.
Classification: LCC DS422.C3 G54 2017 | DDC 305.5/688092254—dc23
LC record available at https://lccn.loc.gov/2016052857

Paperback ISBN: 978-0-374-53782-1

Designed by Richard Oriolo

Our books may be purchased in bulk for promotional,
educational, or business use. Please contact your local
bookseller or the Macmillan Corporate and Premium Sales
Department at 1-800-221-7945, extension 5442, or by e-mail
at MacmillanSpecialMarkets@macmillan.com.

www.fsgbooks.com
www.twitter.com/fsgbooks • www.facebook.com/fsgbooks

1   3   5   7   9   10   8   6   4   2

FRONTISPIECE PHOTOGRAPH: Sujatha, Rathnamma,
Prabhakara Rao, Babu, Manjula, and Anitha in 1966

IN MEMORY OF MY GREAT-GRANDMOTHER
MARTHAMMA

◉

FOR ALAN

ANTS AMONG ELEPHANTS

INTRODUCTION

◎ ◎ ◎

MY STORIES, MY FAMILY'S STORIES, were not stories in India. They were just life.

When I left and made new friends in a new country, only then did the things that happened to my family, the things we had done, become stories. Stories worth telling, stories worth writing down.

I was born in south India, in a town called Khazipet in the state of Andhra Pradesh.

I was born into a lower-middle-class family. My parents were college lecturers.

I was born an untouchable.

When people in this country ask me what it means to be an untouchable, I explain that caste is like racism against blacks here. But then they ask, "How does anyone know what your caste is?" They know caste isn't visible, like skin color.

I explain it like this. In Indian villages and towns, everyone knows everyone else. Each caste has its own special role and its own place to live. The brahmins (who perform priestly functions), the potters, the blacksmiths, the carpenters, the washer people, and so on—they each have their own separate place to live within the village. The untouchables, whose special role—whose hereditary duty—is to labor in the fields of others or to do other work that Hindu society considers filthy, are not allowed to live in the village at all. They must live outside the boundaries of the village proper. They are not allowed to enter temples. Not allowed to come near sources of drinking water used by other castes. Not allowed to eat sitting next to a caste Hindu or to use the same utensils. There are thousands of other such restrictions and indignities that vary from place to place. Every day in an Indian newspaper you can read of an untouchable beaten or killed for wearing sandals, for riding a bicycle.

In your own town or village, everyone already knows your caste; there is no escaping it. But how do people know your caste when you go elsewhere, to a place where no one knows you? There they will ask you, "What caste are you?" You cannot avoid this question. And you cannot refuse to answer. By tradition, everyone has the right to know.

If you are educated like me, if you don't seem like a typical untouchable, then you have a choice. You can tell the truth and be ostracized, ridiculed, harassed—even driven to suicide, as happens regularly in universities.

Or you can lie. If they don't believe you, they will try to find out your true caste some other way. They may ask you certain questions: "Did your brother ride a horse at his wedding? Did his wife wear a red sari or a white sari? How does she wear her sari? Do you eat beef? Who is your family deity?" They may even seek the opinion of someone from your region.

If you get them to believe your lie, then of course you cannot tell them your stories, your family's stories. You cannot tell them about your life. It would reveal your caste. Because your life is your caste, your caste is your life.

Whether they know the truth or not, your untouchable life is never something you can talk about.

It was like this for me in Punjab, in Delhi, in Bombay, in Bangalore, in Madras, in Warangal, in Kanpur, in Calcutta.

At twenty-six, I came to America, where people know only skin color, not birth status. Some here love Indians and some hate them, but their feelings are not affected by caste. One time in a bar in Atlanta I told a guy I was untouchable, and he said, "Oh, but you're so touchable."

Only in talking to some friends I met here did I realize that my stories, my family's stories, are not stories of shame.

◎

NO ONE INFORMED ME THAT I was untouchable. It is not the kind of thing that your mother would need to tell you. What I was told was that we were Christians.

Christians, untouchables—it came to the same thing. All Christians in India were untouchable, as far as I knew (though only a small minority of all untouchables are Christian).

I knew no Christian who did not turn servile in the presence of a Hindu.

I knew no Hindu who did not look right through a Christian man standing in front of him as if he did not exist.

I accepted this. No questions asked.

I saw the grown-ups in my family scrambling to their feet, straightening their clothes, and wringing their hands when a certain bowlegged, cross-eyed, drooly-mouthed Hindu man passed in front of us.

I saw our Hindu neighbors passing us by without even registering our presence.

Accepted. No questions asked.

I knew the cross-eyed, drooly-mouthed man was fucking my aunts (both of them), making children with them, but not marrying them because they were Christians.

I knew a Christian boy who was pushed in front of a train for falling in love with an uppercaste girl.

Christians are lowly. Hindus are superior. Christians are weak. Hindus are powerful.

I understood. I accepted. That was the natural way of things.

The questions started when I was fifteen and someone took me and my sister to see a movie. Then they came in a flood that would not stop for years. In a way, they still haven't.

In the movie a rich girl falls in love with a poor boy. The girl's powerful family intimidates the poor boy's family into forcing him to stop seeing her. The girl, not knowing what her family has done, goes searching for the boy. When she can't find him, she gives up and agrees to marry a nice, well-educated, wealthy man.

No surprises here for an Indian moviegoer. The shock came at the wedding scene. The heroine wears a white gown. Not a sari like a Hindu bride. A white, Western-style gown with a veil, like they wear at Christian weddings.

My blood froze. My brain went numb. I couldn't breathe.

The rich girl was Christian! And I recalled that in the scene where the poor boy's family was threatened, his father had on his chest the cross-thread worn by all brahmin men.

This movie, in sheer defiance of the laws of nature, portrayed Christians as rich and powerful and—most amazing of all—scornful of brahmins, the highest caste of all.

It is simply not possible to convey what this meant to a fifteen-year-old untouchable Christian girl.

Were there really Christians like this?

Why had I never seen them?

Why had no one ever mentioned this before?

My questions found no outlet. It was too shameful to bring up the subject of our inferior status, even among my own folk. I never thought to ask anyone. I wouldn't have known how to put the words together.

Four years later, at nineteen, I left home to enroll in a postgraduate program at the Regional Engineering College (REC) in Warangal. There were only fifteen RECs in the whole country. Students from other states and even other countries went there to study. That was the first time in my life I saw people from outside my home state of Andhra.

Being a small-town girl, I was afraid of betraying my curiosity about all the strange and modern things I saw at the college. I saw girls with short hair. I saw girls in sleeveless blouses. I even saw some girls wearing pants. Some wore lipstick and tweezed their eyebrows. I saw girls secretly smoking. I learned the concept of boyfriend-girlfriend. And of course all of these girls could speak English.

It was here that I first saw in real life what I had seen in that movie: Christians who looked down on even high-caste Hindus.

But what could I ask them? I was ashamed to bring up the subject. I finished my program without ever finding out what the difference was between them and me.

After Regional Engineering College I went to yet another citadel of engineering education. I went to Madras to attend the Indian Institute of Technology. IITs are the most elite, most cosmopolitan technical institutions in India, the Indian equivalents of MIT and Caltech. I was a research associate in the department of applied physics working on a project funded by the Indian Space Research Organisation.

In the ladies' hostel, my eyes were dazzled by the sight of the other girls. They were all so beautiful, rich, happy, charming, high-class. I felt as if I were surrounded by movie heroines, but with brains. And in the hostel I saw many more of those elusive superior Christians.

One thing I noticed quickly: they all came from the southern state of Kerala. That movie I had seen, I found out later, had been made in Malayalam, the language spoken in Kerala, and dubbed into my own native language of Telugu.

These Kerala Christian girls lived in the same wing of the hostel as me.

Jessie's beauty was otherworldly. She was always flanked by two brahmin girls, her loyal sidekicks.

Supriya Abraham, when she descended to the ground floor to go to the mess, was like a star from the sky deigning to visit the earth.

The brahmin boys who fawned over these Christian girls would look at me in disgust. In my town, Christian girls were called crows, pigs, scavengers. One boy in my neighborhood used to call me and my sister "shit lilies."

I wanted to make friends with these Keralites. Wasn't I a Christian like them? But they shunned me just as any Hindu would. I was deeply hurt, more deeply than when it happened with the Hindus.

But I was determined to find out why I was different. Jessie was kind, one of the only girls who would talk to me. Her room and my room were on the same floor. I tagged along with her to church even though by then I already didn't give a damn about God.

I asked to see photos of Jessie's family. They were obviously wealthy. I started probing, asking questions. Jessie explained, "We are brahmins." She told me her family came from a brahmin caste in Kerala called Nambudiris. Nambudiris are so high in rank that they look down on all other brahmins.

"Why did you become Christian?"

She explained that among the Nambudiris, in ancient times, the eldest son inherited all the property, and only he was allowed to marry. The rest of the sons inherited nothing and had to find lower-caste mistresses or remain celibate.

When Jesus' disciple Thomas traveled to Kerala, some disgruntled younger Nambudiri sons left Hinduism altogether and were baptized by Thomas.

"So we are brahmin Christians," Jessie told me.

But I refused to believe her. Is that all it took? Some Christians decide to claim brahmin heritage and everyone believes it? It was too far-fetched.

When I came to America, I met more Kerala Christians. By this time I was brazen. Every time I met one, my first question would be "How come you have high social status whereas we don't?" They all told me the same story: they were brahmins converted by Saint Thomas.

"When?"

"Fifty-two A.D."

So what is the relation between religion and caste? Between caste and social status? Between social status and wealth? Between wealth and caste? I thought about these things incessantly.

I decided to find out how *my family* became Christians. I called my mother. That was when she began to tell me the story of our ancestors.

◎

MY MOTHER AND HER ELDEST brother have facility with language, insight into people and social conditions. He became a famous poet (under the pen name Shivasagar), while she could never get herself organized to sit down and write. Both have the ability to captivate. And both had much to tell about the things they had seen and participated in. When I came along wanting to know more, they were overjoyed.

Growing up, I had heard my mother reminiscing about her beloved eldest brother, who had disappeared years ago and gone underground.

My uncle K. G. Satyamurthy, who was known as SM, was a principal founder in the early seventies of a Maoist guerrilla group recently declared by the government to be the single greatest threat to India's security.

When I was eight years old my mother took me and my brother and sister to a movie about a young man who had organized a rebellion against the British to stop them from encroaching on the forests and displacing the poor tribals (those living in primitive tribes in the vast forests of the country, as more than 8 percent of the people in India still do today). On the way my mother told me, "It is a movie about a man much like your uncle."

Another time she took us to a movie featuring a song that took its lyrics from one of my uncle's poems.

As I grew older, I kept asking to hear more about this mysterious man. And my mother would tell me stories about his cleverness, his charm, his beauty, his ardor, and his cunning.

When I first started looking into the story of my ancestors, I knew I had to get in touch with SM. He was still in hiding but was now at least reachable. Being older than my mother and more in touch with earlier generations, he knew even more about their history. He told me much more than I could fit into this book, fascinating stories that I hope to present someday. And naturally he had his own story to tell.

By the time I contacted SM, he was a fallen angel. He liked the idea of someone's writing about his glorious bygone years.

The stories he told were full of detail and colorful expressions in our native language. I did not want to lose anything, so I bought a little tape recorder that I could connect to a phone line.

SM loved telling me these stories. But more than anything else, SM longed to lead the masses in another struggle. Every time some young admirers would come to him saying, "Sir, we want to start a new party. Would you be the leader?" he would run off with them to a jungle somewhere, inaccessible by phone. This happened three, four times. It was frustrating to track him down. Each time it would take weeks or months before I could get back in touch and persuade him to give me some time on the phone.

So I asked him if he would promise to spend time with me if I came to see him in person. He agreed.

I flew to India along with my closest friend, equipped with my recorder and microphone, a hundred blank tape cassettes, and a stack of notebooks.

Traveling with my mother, we took a train to Vizag, a city in Andhra, where we met SM and the young man who was acting as his assistant. Ever since SM turned twenty, he had never been able to live without a personal aide to carry his things, clip his nails, and so on. He didn't even know how to shave himself.

There he was, waiting for us, small and frail with copper skin, silver curls on his head, high cheekbones, and big hooded eyes. His arms and legs were sticklike and his belly rounded, like a famine victim's, as my mother had always described him.

We booked adjacent rooms at a hotel. Each morning for three weeks my friend and I woke up, washed, changed, had breakfast, and carried our equipment over to SM's suite.

He would be ready and waiting for us, lying in bed dressed in a neatly pressed shirt and pants. His assistant sat by the bed with a pen in his hand. I would clip the mic to SM's shirt collar and he would begin. It was serious, dead serious, like Lenin dictating the party program to his comrades.

He had arrived with his assistant carrying all the books and documents SM needed as supporting material. If he was telling me such and such a thing happened under British rule, he had a book to prove it. If I ever asked him something he wasn't sure of or lacked evidence to back up, he would ask the young man to make a note. Sometimes my mother would jump in and say something.

He talked for four or five hours at a stretch. Just to keep track of what he was saying, jot notes, and ask for clarifications was exhausting. It must have been five times more strenuous for him.

At the end of the three weeks he gave me a surprise parting gift. It happened that SM was working on his autobiography. He gave me copies of all the written material, telling me, "Use it freely."

I came home with a suitcase full of papers and books, a list of more books to look up, and all the tapes and notes.

There was so much material. I jumped in headlong. But as I worked, I always needed more details. Get SM on the phone. Again the same problem: he was off somewhere trying to start a new party.

On a second trip I visited all the places where my family's story had taken place. I spoke to people my subjects had known, including some relatives living in remote villages I had never before seen. They were all excited to take part. One man even showed me a small book he had written about his village. I used material from these interviews as well, and the people I met corroborated the stories that my mother and uncle had told me.

Of all the people I spoke to, only my mother understood the kind of book I was writing. She knew what I needed to hear about and would tell me anything I wanted to know.

SM, when asked about himself, would only talk about his political life, his life in the movement. I would try asking what it was like for him when his first child was born. He did not care to answer. When I asked how it felt to be separated from his children when he went underground, he told me he did not remember. That may have been true. He was like that. The movement was his life.

The most frustrating person to interview turned out to be my mother's other brother, Carey. Carey was director of physical education at Kakatiya Medical College in Warangal, in northwest Andhra. When I went to Warangal to speak to him, I found him full drunk. He was slurring his words so badly I could not understand a thing. And his niece was grinding lentils in the next room, and a few feet away the maid was slapping wet clothes on a stone slab. In the hot afternoon air the noise of the grinding and the washing was maddening. Unlike my mother and SM, these people had no idea of the value of what I was trying to do. I consoled myself with the thought that I could play the tapes back at slow speed and try to figure out what Carey was telling me.

Back in New York, I listened to my tapes and could not make out a single word. I wanted to strangle Carey with both my hands.

He agreed to talk to me on the phone, but he was too self-conscious and always too drunk to be of any use. Carey was in some ways the most fascinating of the three siblings. He never knew what fear felt like. He was utterly immune to corruption. But sadly he was the least articulate.

And many things he was unwilling to discuss. When I tried to ask about his famous sexual conquests, he would scold me: "Why are you doing this? Why are you writing this book? Why are you dredging up this ugly stuff?" I tried to tell him that in America sexuality is not something to be ashamed of. He couldn't believe it.

I know it wasn't easy for him to look back on many things. He would say, "Abba! What degrading poverty it was." And he was bitter. Many times he criticized my mother and SM. He felt he was the only one who had lived up to the ideals of their youth.

I came up with an idea. I should try catching him early in the morning before he got too drunk. Because of the time difference, this meant I had to stay up late and go to work in the morning with little sleep.

But before I could get anywhere with him, Carey died. He may have been killed. No one in his family would tell my mother anything, probably because they didn't want to have to deal with an investigation.

Compiling the material for this book has been a race against death. The people I needed to speak to were old, many of them also impoverished and in poor health. Getting everything I needed from them before it was too late became an obsession of mine. Nancharayya, David John, Rani, Graceamma, Manikya Rao, Lilly Flora, Carey—they all died before I had a chance to finish talking to them. Every time my mother would tell me the latest news, I was inconsolable.

My mother thinks I've developed an attachment to the people I am writing about. She thinks I am grieving their loss. But what I am really grieving is the material that is lost forever.

When these deaths come, they traumatize me. I cannot speak or eat or sleep. I cannot stand or sit up. When Nallamma, a peripheral figure in the story, died soon after I spoke to her, it nearly killed me. No one could understand. When friends, not knowing how I felt, tried to coax me out of bed, I turned violent.

Another time, when I heard Carey's high school friend Pulla Reddy had had a stroke and lost his ability to speak, I was speechless. I sent a check for $200 so he could get physical therapy and some other care. I thought of all the things for him to lose the use of, why should it be his tongue, the one part that mattered most for my purposes. I didn't need him to dance, I didn't need him to lift anything. As I saw it, I had been cursed most cruelly. In the end he could speak a little, but I had no heart to hear him struggle. When he died, the news was kept from me.

And then my father's aunt Dyva Vathi. She fell. Lost her memory. Her memory!

Finally I closed my ears to such news. My mother, out of concern for my feelings, has told all the relatives to never mention a word to me about death or illness.

I know SM had a stroke a couple of years ago, is blind in one eye, cannot move. I was relieved when my mother told me he had not lost his speech. I tried to call him. But the daughters who took over his care had cut off his phone privileges.

So I went to see him in person. He could speak, but I could not understand anything he said because all his teeth had fallen out.

The small stroke should not have incapacitated him so much. His daughters told me they had to wait three days to take him to a doctor. Three days? I didn't understand. They explained they wanted to take him to the doctor who would see him for free, an admirer of his, who was out of town. So they waited.

Sure enough, his memory was affected. Nothing was left for me there. One of his daughters has removed the TV from his room and prohibited newspapers and visitors. In those conditions he won't last long. I know I am never going to see him again.

I stopped inquiring about his health, his condition. I don't want to know more. I avoid looking at Telugu news online for fear of coming upon an obituary.

As of this writing, I do not know if this book's principal subject is alive or dead.

April 15, 2012

PRELUDE

◉ ◉ ◉

WHEN I ASKED MY MOTHER and my uncle about our ancestors, they started with their grandparents' generation, the earliest one they'd known.

Venkataswami and Atchamma, their grandfather and grandmother, were born in the late 1800s in Khammam district, within what later became the state of Andhra Pradesh, where they lived as part of a nomadic clan. Their clan did not practice agriculture. They subsisted on fruits, on roots, on honey, on whatever they could catch or snare. They were not Hindus. They worshipped their own tribal goddesses and had little to do with society outside the forest where they lived.

When the British cleared the forests for teak plantations, my great-grandparents' clan was driven out onto the plains, where the civilized people,

the settled ones, the ones who owned land and knew how to cultivate it—
in a word, the Hindus—lived. The little clan, wandering outside the forest,
found a great lake and settled around it. There was no sign of human life
for miles and miles. They took up farming. The land around the lake was
fertile and gave them more than they needed. They called their new settlement Sankarapadu, after one of their gods.

But soon the civilized people took notice of them. They were discovered by an agent of the local zamindar—the great landlord appointed by
the British to collect revenue in that area—who saw the rice growing in
their fields and levied taxes, keeping the bulk of what he extracted for
himself.

But that was not enough for this agent. He and his family and his caste
people moved nearby and set about stealing the land by force and by cunning. They loaned the clansmen trivial sums at usurious rates to buy small
necessities such as salt, seeds, or new clothes for a wedding. Unable to pay
off these debts, the villagers gave up their land acre by acre. My ancestors,
who had cleared and settled the area, were reduced to working on their
old fields as laborers.

This is what has happened to tribal peoples in India who try to settle
down and cultivate land since time immemorial. It still happens to this
day. What set Sankarapadu apart was that the Hindus who usurped all the
fields around it did not settle there themselves. That's because the village
is surrounded by fetid swamps filled with poisonous snakes, scorpions,
and thick swarms of mosquitoes. The landlords settled on safe and elevated ground several miles away in a village called Polukonda.

In the forest, my great-grandfather's clan had had no caste. But in Hindu
society everyone is assigned a place in the caste system. Certain castes traditionally own land, and others have to work for those who do. For those
who must work, the caste you are born into determines the kind of work
you do. There are priestly castes, carpenter castes, potter castes, barber
castes. The more impure a caste's traditional occupation in terms of ritual
law, the lower its status.

When the people of Sankarapadu entered Hindu society with no caste
of their own and the most impure occupation of all, that of landless labor-

ers, there was no question where their place would be: at the bottom, as despised outcastes. Outcastes are also called untouchables because they are supposed to be so ritually unclean that the slightest contact with them will defile even low-caste Hindus. Untouchables cannot share meals with others, much less intermarry with them, and are made to live apart from the rest of the village in a segregated colony on its outskirts. Sankarapadu became the untouchable colony of Polukonda, albeit an unusually remote one.

But my great-grandfather and his fellow villagers were still new to the caste system. Their spirit was not yet broken.

When a young burglar of the outcaste Yanadi tribe was on the run from the police, the villagers gave him shelter. They knew it was the sacred duty of Yanadi clansmen to violate private property—a system with which the Yanadis had never made peace.

When police came looking for the young outlaw, the villagers, not knowing what police were, beat them up and chased them away. The next day a hundred policemen descended on the village. They destroyed what little the villagers had, molested the women, and arrested the entire male population.

The villagers did not know what to do. They did not know about jails, bail, courts, or lawyers. By luck, some Canadian missionaries active in a nearby town learned what had happened. They sent a white lawyer to defend the villagers and win their release. In gratitude, the villagers started to give up their old goddesses and accept baptism. They began sending their children to attend the schools set up by the missionaries.

Untouchables had long been forbidden from learning to read and write. But when the missionaries arrived, they opened schools that, to the horror of the Hindus, welcomed even the untouchables. Although these schools were the only institutions offering modern education, caste Hindus often refused to send their children, unwilling to let them sit side by side with untouchable students.

The missionaries tried to accommodate these local customs. Sometimes they would make the untouchable students sit on the floor, reserving the benches for caste students, as they did in my school. They even opened what the missionaries themselves called "caste schools," where no untouchable students were admitted. Even so, these godly people made hardly any converts among caste Hindus.

My great-grandfather had six sons. The youngest was my grandfather, Prasanna Rao Kambham. (The surname Kambham was taken by the clan from the Khammam region they had left behind.) When Prasanna Rao's family converted to Christianity, his three eldest brothers were already too old to overcome their fear of reading and writing. They did not dare attempt something so far outside their place. They lived out their lives as coolies, while their three younger brothers, including Prasanna Rao, went to the mission school, where they were trained as teachers.

At this school the boys and girls were kept strictly separated. They never even saw each other except on Sundays, when they all went to church. Peering across the aisle, Prasanna Rao noticed a girl named Maryamma and fell in love by sight.

But he was not allowed to talk to her. To express his interest he first needed to speak to her parents. After a prolonged inquiry, Prasanna Rao learned that Maryamma's mother lived in a village in the same district called Parnasa. Her name was Marthamma.

Marthamma was a poor untouchable widow. Some years before, she and a group of other women had been laboring in the fields and singing as they worked when a missionary woman overheard them. Impressed by Marthamma's voice, the woman went up and asked her to accept Jesus and come and sing in the church. But Marthamma said no. She had too much work to do to feed her children.

To make ends meet after her husband died, Marthamma pounded rice for caste-Hindu women in her village and gleaned grain left behind in the fields. But still she and her children did not have enough to live on.

In desperation, Marthamma decided to ask for help from the missionaries. She was granted an audience with one Mary Selman. When they met, Marthamma recognized her as the same woman who had asked her to come and sing. Miss Selman offered her a job as a "Bible woman"—one who goes from village to village to preach the gospel. Her three remaining children were enrolled in the mission school. Marthamma accompanied her children in the classroom. There she learned to read as her children's classmate.

When Prasanna Rao traveled to Parnasa to speak to her about Maryamma, Marthamma was delighted. He was tall, handsome, educated.

The young couple married and went off to work as teachers in a small mission school in a village called Adavi Kolanu. They were still poor, but despite this they were living a kind of life their parents could never have imagined. Maryamma and Prasanna Rao, unlike their parents, had been raised in the Christian faith and educated from childhood. Now they were teaching others. The parents of the children they taught looked up to them. All of this gave them a new outlook, a new feeling of hope. You could see it in the way they held themselves, in the way they dressed.

Untouchable men and women were traditionally forced to wear loincloths. The missionaries taught untouchables how to make themselves look respectable. Maryamma dressed in a sari and a blouse, and Prasanna Rao wore pants and a shirt in the Western style. They both took pride in their appearance.

Soon Prasanna Rao and Maryamma had a baby, a boy they named fondly G'nana Satyamurthy, which means "wise figure of truth." As he grew up, he would be known as Satyam.

He was born in July. When December came, his parents started looking forward to Christmas. Their new son's first Christmas.

On Christmas Day, Maryamma went into the village (where no untouchable was allowed to live) to buy spices for the holiday feast. She was wearing a new sari that the missionaries had given her as a Christmas present and a flower-print blouse she had stitched herself out of the fabric of a cast-off dress. Some uppercaste men standing outside the store, infuriated to see an untouchable daring to wear decent clothes, insulted her crudely.

Maryamma ran back home in tears. Prasanna Rao's friend Samson, the village canoeman, went to the church, where the whole community was gathered, and told them what had happened.

When the untouchable Christians of Adavi Kolanu heard how their teacher had been treated, their Christmas was poisoned. They called off their celebrations and decided to demand an apology from the caste Hindus.

The caste Hindus were also determined. They intended to remind the untouchables of their place. The two groups gathered in the village square. Violence was in the offing.

Just then, a small brahmin, a disciple of Gandhi's, intervened. "Kill me first before you kill each other," he challenged them.

To kill a brahmin is the sin of sins. First the untouchables backed down, then the caste Hindus.

The nonviolent brahmin then counseled the untouchables to never again try anything that might provoke the caste Hindus. This was the way his idol, Gandhi, always resolved caste disputes.

Prasanna Rao and Maryamma could not stay in a village such as Adavi Kolanu, under the thumb of the caste Hindus. They decided to move two hundred miles away to Visakhapatnam (Vizag to the British), one of the few large cities in Andhra.

In Vizag the couple found jobs in Christian schools. Big, spacious schools surrounded by high compound walls. Though founded as caste schools by the missionaries, they had recently been opened to untouchable students under the influence of the freedom struggle, and already untouchables made up the majority of students and teachers. Prasanna Rao and Maryamma's salaries were ten times their former ones.

As soon as they arrived in the new city, Prasanna Rao threw their luggage in a corner of their room, grabbed his five-year-old son's hand, and ran out to show him the ocean. For a tiny boy who had spent his whole brief life inland, what a stunning sight it was! The lighthouse, the white dunes, the big ships and little boats. The waves!

Satyam by then had a little brother whom Prasanna Rao named William Carey (after the founder of the Baptist Mission to India). Soon he would have a sister, Mary Manjulabai, whom the family called Papa, meaning "baby."

Not for nothing was Satyam named the wise one. He knew that his parents had only convinced the landlord to rent them a portion of his house by telling him they were among the few caste Hindus who'd converted to Christianity. To keep up that charade they stopped eating beef, which in India is eaten only by untouchables and Muslims. Satyam knew the landlord was suspicious of their story but also needed tenants with good jobs. Sometimes he was nice to Satyam and Carey and gave them papayas; other times he bellowed at them like a bull ready to charge.

Tuberculosis is a disease of the poor. When Prasanna Rao's orphaned niece came down with it, he brought her home with him from her village and took her to King George's Hospital. The girl responded well and recovered completely.

But Maryamma, who caught the girl's infection, did not. On October 5, 1941, she died. Her death brought the family's brief period of happiness to an end. Satyam was ten, Carey seven, and Papa only four years old.

One afternoon not long after, their father bathed them and dressed them up in their best clothes. He had them sit on the steps of the school where their mother used to teach. "Just wait here, like good boys and good girl," he told them.

Hours passed, night fell. Their father did not come back.

Overburdened by grief and by the debts he owed the moneylenders for his wife's medical care, Prasanna Rao ran away, abandoning his children to the care of their aunt, who took the two boys, and their grandmother, who took Papa.

At school the teachers were telling stories of a villain named Hitler. The world was at war. Vizag, with its natural harbor, was a target for Japanese bombing. The beautiful beach where the children used to go to with their mother was now occupied by British soldiers. There were warships in the harbor.

On Easter Sunday 1942, their aunt took Satyam, Carey, and Papa to the burial ground to clean their mother's grave and lay jasmine blossoms on it, singing sad Christian hymns.

The next day, at one o'clock in the afternoon, the children heard the sirens go off, followed by earsplitting blasts. They felt the city shake. The Japanese were dropping their first bombs on the harbor.

Their aunt gathered all the children and fled. The whole city seemed to be fleeing at once, transformed into one vast terror-stricken mob. Everyone was running toward the railway station.

The children were taken to stay with their uncle Nathaniel, who lived in the countryside in Marthamma's home village of Parnasa. Nathaniel, unlike his sisters, had not had the good fortune to go to school. He lived outside the village and worked as a coolie for the railroad, carrying rocks in an iron basket on his head. None of his ten children went to school.

When Satyam and his siblings first arrived, Nathaniel's children hid behind straw heaps, too shy to meet their cousins from the city. By and by, they came out to play. One cousin, Kamili, followed Satyam day and night. She was fascinated by this boy who wore knickers and a shirt, who knew how to read and write. She took him to the meadow where she grazed the family buffalo. Full of pride, she introduced him to her friends, the other girls who brought their families' buffaloes there.

The children, left to their own devices, left the buffaloes to theirs. The girls surrounded Satyam and asked him about the city. He told them the story of the *Ramayana*, which he had learned in school, and together they acted it out. The girls all adored him. They climbed date trees to pluck fruit for him; they made up little rhymes fondly poking fun at him. Kamili was in love with Satyam, but he loved one of her friends.

Satyam would always notice an older boy glaring at him from across the meadow. "Why is he not grazing with you?" Satyam asked the girls. They explained that the boy was *golla*. Gollas are a cattle-herding caste—a low caste, but even the lowest of caste Hindus are superior to untouchables. Satyam learned that untouchable buffaloes were not allowed to graze in the same meadows as the caste buffaloes.

One day the golla boy came charging into the untouchable meadow like a ram and lunged at Satyam. Satyam, born with high-arched feet, was never able to run. The boy threw him down and kicked him in his ribs while the terrified girls looked on helplessly. "You untouchable son of a bitch! Who told you that you could wear knickers?"

In the evening when Nathaniel returned home from work and heard what had happened, he scolded his nephew. "You want to go to the meadow? Then wear a loincloth. You want to wear your knickers? Then stay home!" That's how things were in a village.

Because he could not go to the meadows with his friends, Satyam started visiting a young couple who lived out on their own, even farther from the village than the other untouchables. When his aunt found out, she asked him to stop. "They are *madigas*," she told him. "Those people are filthy."

There are many untouchable castes. They all have to toil on the fields of caste Hindus, but they are distinguished by the tasks they are called on to perform in addition. *Malas* such as Satyam and his family were village servants made to do whatever menial work was needed. Madigas haul away dead animals from the village and use the hide to make leather. Malas see themselves as superior to other untouchable communities such as the madigas. To the caste Hindus, though, they're all untouchable, all despicable.

Satyam stayed away from the golla boy. But despite his aunt's admonition, he continued to go to see the young madiga couple and soon became their only friend. Their isolation, their beauty, their fascinating work, and the parental attitude they showed toward him all drew him to their hut.

At the end of the summer, the family had to decide what to do with Maryamma's children. Marthamma was summoned to Parnasa to discuss the matter with Nathaniel and his eldest son. Marthamma was determined to honor her daughter's dying wish: "Educate my children." Since Parnasa had no school, Marthamma offered to take the children to a place that did and look after them there. She enrolled them in a government school in Gudivada.

When Kamili heard that Satyam was going away, she threw herself in the dirt and cried. Marthamma scolded her granddaughter: "Get up, get up! It's not like your husband is leaving you!"

Kamili never went to school. Her father married her off to a fellow track coolie at the age of thirteen.

In Gudivada, Marthamma rented a single bare room for the four of them in a hut in Mandapadu, the mala colony of that town.

Satyam brooded ceaselessly. His mother was dead, his father was gone. First his aunt took him and his siblings in, then his uncle, and now his grandmother. Would they settle here? Or would there be another move? Another guardian? What would happen to him and his brother? To his little sister, who had barely known her mother? Who is going to teach her how to comb her hair? They were living in a one-room hut with holes in the roof, sleeping on the floor.

He looked around for answers. The Mandapadu malas he lived among were all poor like his family, most of them being landless agricultural laborers. But they did not all suffer passively. Many were attracted to the independence movement—some supporting Gandhi and his Congress Party, others the Communist Party. Both parties wanted to drive out the British colonial rulers; the Communists wanted to go further and overturn the whole social system. Then there were God-fearing Christians who looked only heavenward for salvation.

Satyam's own uncles disagreed about independence. Uncle Nathaniel was skeptical: "If we drive the white devil out, the Hindu devils will massacre us." Uncle John, who had earlier supported British rule, switched his allegiance to Congress: "Independence is the solution."

Under Marthamma's influence, Satyam decided to leave everything in the hands of "our Lord savior." That summer he read the Bible cover to cover. Piously he washed his hands each time before touching the Holy Book.

But in August 1942 Gandhi called on the British to "quit India." Gandhi had been a principal leader of the nationalist agitation for more than two decades. Never in all that time had he taken such a militant tone.

Now that it seemed as if something was finally going to come of all the talk Satyam had been hearing, he embraced the nationalist cause. For over two hundred years, the British had ruled his country and stolen its vast wealth. Freedom from that rule would naturally change everything, including his family's situation. He'd heard that the white lords lived in bungalows, ate bread they sliced with knives, and wiped their mouths with cloth. When they left, surely all Indians could live like that.

Gandhi called for "open rebellion" to back up his demand. The Indian people had been waiting for such a call. But they did not heed Gandhi's strictures to keep the struggle nonviolent. When British troops fired on protesters, they fought back. Young activists attacked police stations, cut telegraph lines, burned post offices, derailed trains carrying war supplies.

Satyam, eleven years old, longed to take part in these acts of rebellion.

He searched high and low for those daring heroes. But alas, within twenty-four hours of Gandhi's speech, all known Congress supporters had been locked up.

Gandhi, in prison himself, deplored the destruction. He relied on the threat of mass resistance to weaken the British hold on power and persuade them to hand it over to native elites. But the last thing he wanted was for the masses to arm themselves and take power in their own hands.

When Gandhi called off the Quit India Movement, Satyam lost respect for him. Satyam dreamed of contributing his own blows against the empire. At times he felt his body had been taken over by the ghost of Bhagat Singh, a revolutionary anti-imperialist martyr hanged by the British. Satyam scrawled *Quit India!* inside abandoned buildings and defiantly walked on railway tracks, which was forbidden in those days out of fear of sabotage.

Despite his disillusionment with Gandhi, Satyam was not drawn to Congress's main rivals, the Communists, because they did not join the Quit India Movement. Satyam asked his Communist neighbor why not. The boy explained, "We must support the British in the war. They are allies with U.S.S.R."

"But why should we care about U.S.S.R.?"

"Because it is the country for all poor people in the world."

Satyam wasn't convinced. His family was poor and so were all his neighbors. Because of this poverty his mother had died, and his father had gone away. Everyone said it was the white lords who were looting India of its wealth and impoverishing the country.

Satyam supported Congress because Congress opposed the British. But his hero wasn't Gandhi; it was Subhas Chandra Bose, who had led a militant faction in Congress. Unlike Gandhi, Bose held that the British could not be pressured to leave India willingly but had to be forced out. To this end, he sought help from Britain's imperialist rivals: Nazi Germany and Japan. He raised an army in Singapore—the Indian National Army—to liberate the subcontinent. He would later die in a plane crash before his plans could be realized. But he remained an idol to the restive Indian masses.

Satyam bought a cheap, mass-produced portrait of Bose in the bazaar. One night he and Carey snuck into Satyam's classroom and tacked it on the blackboard. This was Satyam's act of sedition.

The next morning, the teacher demanded to know who was responsible. Satyam kept quiet. "Whoever it was," the teacher announced, "I salute you! I am proud to be your teacher." In those times, even some teachers in government schools were brave enough to express nationalist sympathies.

But the repression of the Quit India Movement meant Congress activists were lying low. It took Satyam a long time to find any. When he finally met them, it was by sheer chance.

Since barber-caste people will not touch untouchable hair, Marthamma used to take Satyam and Carey to a "Christ barber": a Christian trained in haircutting by the missionaries to serve their fellow untouchables. But the Christ barbers were not professionals. They cut hair in their spare time, working for free and without proper equipment. Satyam was tired of being ridiculed by his classmates for his poorly cut hair.

A caste friend from school insisted on taking him to his own barber, Veeraswami. Veeraswami, a fervent nationalist, believed all Indians, caste and outcaste, must come together to fight the British. Satyam had finally met a bona fide activist. Veeraswami not only cut Satyam's hair, he gave him political lessons and kept him supplied with seditious reading material. As young as Satyam was, Veeraswami talked with him seriously and introduced him to the like-minded people who congregated in Veeraswami's shop.

One day a tall, fine-looking man appeared at Satyam's family's doorstep. Dressed in a trench coat and boots, the man was a strange sight in that slum. Among the children, only Satyam recognized him. It had been four years since the family had seen or heard from him. Their father had come back.

When Prasanna Rao had run away to escape his debts after Maryamma died, he'd joined the military. The British sent him to Iraq.

Sitting on his father's lap, Carey lit up. "*Nanna, Nanna*, did you have a rifle? Did you fight in the war?" No, his father told him. Because he could read and write, they made him a clerk. He kept accounts.

It never occurred to the children to resent their father for abandoning them. They were proud that he had traveled abroad and seen the lands of the Bible, and proud that he returned looking like a movie star in his stylish clothes with a suitcase full of treats they had never seen: butter and jam and biscuits. Prasanna Rao and his children spent a joyful month together before he had to return from leave.

When he went away this time, he promised never to desert them again. He didn't even have to leave the country: the war was over. From then on he wrote a letter home every week, and every month he sent a money order for forty rupees in the name of his wise son. His salary in the military was seven times what he'd made as a teacher in Vizag.

After the war ended in 1945, the Labour Party came to power in Britain. The new government recognized that it was no longer possible to maintain direct colonial rule over the subcontinent. The best hope for protecting British interests there lay in transferring power to the Congress Party. The political prisoners rounded up during the Quit India agitation were released (except for Communists), and elections to form native governments in the provinces were announced. The British viceroy would stay in power in the center for the time being.

In preparation for these elections, Congress held their own elections for party leadership. Satyam, now fourteen years old, was voted treasurer of the Gudivada Youth Congress. He was the only mala to hold office on the town committee.

When his Congress friends came to see him in the home his grandmother had recently purchased in the new untouchable colony of Slatter Peta, she proudly referred to him as "ma Jawallalu" (our Nehru). Carey and Papa idolized their brother, bragged about him to their friends, and made all his ideas their own.

In his final year of high school, Satyam led a student strike. The strike demanded an end to the "detention system" that required graduating students to pass an exam at their own school before they'd be allowed to sit for statewide final exams some two months later. The policy was seen by students and parents alike as unfair and oppressive. When agitation against it broke out across Andhra, Satyam led the struggle in Gudivada. He gave the strike a political character, turning it into a protest against British rule. He stole his father's military shirt to dress up a straw effigy of imperialism that the students set on fire in the center of town.

The strike lasted a month before the government gave in and abolished the detention system. It was a sign that the old colonial structure was giving way.

Satyam's friends all intended to go to Hindu College in Machilipatnam, forty-two kilometers from Gudivada. Because it was a government college, the fees were nominal. Satyam would have been able to stay in the harijan hostel, a free hostel set up for untouchable students who could not afford rent and food in towns where they went to school, away from their homes in villages. He could have had meals, books, soap, oil, and tooth powder, even a small stipend to spend on such things as magazines or cinema tickets, all provided by the government.

But instead he chose Andhra Christian College in Guntur. Guntur was twenty-five kilometers farther from home, and being a private institution, it had higher fees and no harijan hostel. But to the Kambhams, A.C. College seemed the obvious choice. Satyam preferred it because it was much more fashionable and prestigious. Prasanna Rao and Marthamma preferred it because it was a Christian college in a Christian town. Guntur is where the missionaries found their first converts among Telugu people. The Christian community there is the oldest in the region and is therefore considered among Christians in the area to be purer in its beliefs and practices, as though the faith somehow gets diluted as it spreads. Called *sampradaya kristavulu* (old or traditional Christians), they are a prosperous and highly cultured community, the product of the mission schools and hospitals that have long both served them and afforded them employment. Among these venerable institutions, A.C. College has pride of place.

The day Prasanna Rao brought his son to enroll in college, they went around the campus together, walking the hallways with fear and awe. When they entered the main lecture hall, Prasanna Rao, overcome with gratitude and humility, fell to his knees. He prayed out loud, right there in the empty lecture hall, with his hands clasped in front of him, his voice trembling, and tears wetting his face. He thanked the Lord Jesus for lifting his family out of filth to bring them to this noble institution that had such magnificent halls.

Satyam began his college life in a small shared room in a hostel called the Higher Hall. He ate his meals in a mess attached to the hostel. Every morning as he walked across the campus to the lecture hall, the majestic clock tower seemed to be looking down at him as a father might look at his son with benevolent patronage. Whenever he strolled out of the campus to get a cup of tea, he would be amused to see the ancient watchman pacing back and forth furiously in front of the gate, barking out edicts, convinced that the responsibility for maintaining all this greatness rested on his own hunched shoulders. It was a beautiful campus full of clever-looking people. Satyam had never before seen even one person who looked so clever.

Satyam did not know any of his classmates, but that did not worry him. Few of the arriving students, except those from Guntur, knew each other yet. Satyam expected to join the Student Congress here, as he did in high school, and looked forward to forming friendships there. He planned to run for office in the student union. He and his new friends would probably spend their summer holidays in nation-building activities, perhaps contributing labor to construct dams or to organize libraries in villages that did not have one.

Shortly after he enrolled, students started preparations to celebrate the day India would become an independent country. For weeks Satyam worked side by side with the other students, day and night. He felt a sense of camaraderie with his classmates even though he had still made no friends.

At midnight on August 15, 1947, the day that Satyam had been dreaming of these last five years came at last. He could not sleep that night. In the morning he washed up carefully and put on his best clothes. He left his room early, not wanting to miss anything. Students from colleges all over the district, joined by thousands of municipal workers, thronged to take part in the celebration on his campus. The crowds swelled like a river in monsoon.

Standing shoulder to shoulder, the students and workers sang in one voice:

A different world,
a different world is calling us.

It will be the confluence of
the sacrifice of Jesus,
the compassion of the Buddha,
the teachings of Muhammad the prophet,
and above all the glorious dharma
of the Aryan Upanishads.

As one religion
and one dharma,
a different world is calling us.

As he joined in the singing, Satyam's eyes filled with tears. British rule was over, but the real work of independence still lay ahead. "They are leaving," he thought. "But we will have to build this nation."

In their speeches the politicians, intellectuals, and trade-union leaders all talked of *bhavi bharata pourulu*—"future citizens of India." Who were they? They were him. Young men such as himself.

The celebrations went on all day. As he watched the dances and dramas and competitions, Satyam realized that in all those crowds of students, he knew no one well enough to talk to. They were all dressed in their best, and what a difference there was between his best and everyone else's. The girls wore fine saris and the boys all had on nice Western shirts and trousers. Beside them, in his white cotton *lalchi* (a traditional men's shirt) and pyjama, Satyam looked out of place.

For weeks he had worked side by side with the other students, day and night, to help prepare these celebrations. But the solidarity he had felt was no more. Now that the common enemy was defeated, the differences between him and the other students came to the fore. He noticed he was not included in any of the performances.

The celebrations continued into the evening. The program included a fancy-dress contest. A girl dressed up as a Lambadi—a member of an impoverished tribe in Andhra whose traditional costumes, like those of Gypsies in the West, are remarkably colorful and ornate—won the first prize. "Would a real Lambadi woman get this admiration?" Satyam asked himself as the girl—the darling daughter of a rich Hindu family—got up before the applauding crowd to receive her prize.

As he looked on, a short, chubby dark boy Satyam had never before seen came up to him and introduced himself. He had a strange question for Satyam, one that Satyam had no answer to: "Do you think this independence is for people like you and me?"

ONE

⊙ ⊙ ⊙

"MATTER CAN NEITHER BE CREATED nor destroyed," the lecturer told the junior Intermediate students.

Satyam, sitting in the last bench, muttered, "What does it matter to me?" He used to be fascinated by all the new things he learned in the physics class. But he hadn't eaten in a long time.

His father had stopped sending money. It seemed that Satyam was expected not merely to survive without food, but to study and get his degree in this condition.

The problem of how to support Satyam while he was in college was one Prasanna Rao had spent years planning with care. In the military, Prasanna Rao stinted on everything and each month put away a large share of his salary. By the time he left his job there, he had saved up a solid five thousand rupees—an unimaginable sum in his community.

He knew exactly what he wanted to do with that money. He was going to buy some land and use the money he raised from the sale of its produce on his son's education. That way, in a few years not only would he be the father of a college graduate but also the owner of a piece of land.

Prasanna Rao had been raised in a village. And in villages, a man may be educated, he may wear a shirt and pants, he may even have a job with a good salary, but the real prestige lay in owning land. Among untouchables, owning even a small piece of land is rare.

So with his savings Prasanna Rao bought two and a half acres of land. He borrowed and bought two acres more. The rate of interest on the loan was high, but the land he had bought was so fertile he expected to be able to pay off the debt in no time.

Prasanna Rao also found a job teaching in a government school. With his salary and what his land would produce, he would surely have more than enough money to put his son through college. And that son would surely become a doctor.

Man makes his plans. God has his own.

Season after season, Prasanna Rao would see his land turn green with beautiful, tender plants that bent and swayed under the weight of golden rice. But just when the crop was ready to be reaped, the stream that nourished his land—the Budameru—would flood and wash away his hopes.

Prasanna Rao's debts, like water-soaked logs, got heavier and heavier, sinking his family deeper and deeper into poverty. Soon they could not afford two meals a day. Carey and Papa were too young to endure starvation, and Prasanna Rao, as the sole breadwinner, needed to preserve his own strength to provide for the family. So the brunt of their sudden poverty was borne by the son who was away at college. Unable to spare anything for him, Prasanna Rao sent Satyam neither money nor explanation.

Satyam was in a painful predicament. He knew no one at A.C. College, no one in the entire city of Guntur, whom he could turn to for help. He did not pay the mess bill for July. He was given a month's time, but when he failed to pay the following month, the administration added his name to the list of delinquent students posted at the entrance of the mess hall for all the world to see. To avoid running into his classmates he started going to the mess just before it closed, after everyone else had left. Even then, every time he walked in, the manager would look at him as though to say, "You don't pay bills and you show up to eat?" Satyam skipped meals as often as he could.

Poverty was nothing new to him. All his life he had been poor. In Slatter Peta the difference between his family and the rest of the malas was small. They were all ants. It mattered little if one was a bit bigger than the others. But here at A.C. College, Satyam was an ant among elephants. No other student was in his situation. He suffered from hunger, but even more from loneliness and shame.

At home, as poor as they were, the Kambham family lived within the limits of what they had. They never thought to want more. They simply lived the way they had always lived. When they made egg curry, a man was served half an egg. In their family, that's what a man ate. They never thought of fruits unless they saw some on a tree, or unless someone was sick. When Satyam's mother was sick and dying, every so often Prasanna Rao would buy her a grapefruit. Their idea was that nature designed grapefruits for the sick. When the children asked to share it, the grown-ups told them, "There is medicine for your mother inside that grapefruit, and all of the medicine is in one single section of the fruit. From the outside we can't tell which one has the medicine in it, so we have to let your mother eat the whole thing."

But now Satyam was all alone in a strange town with no one to ask for help. His family had made a mistake in sending him to A.C. College. They had been greedy. They wanted too much for their own good.

◎

SATYAM WAS ASHAMED THAT HIS classmates might have seen his name posted at the entrance of the mess hall. He had no money for books or lab records or term fees or exam fees. He couldn't afford to dress the way students were supposed to, in shirt and pants. The strap of his thongs was broken and secured by a safety pin that kept coming undone. So he stopped going to classes.

With nothing better to do, he started reading newspapers at the college library. After finishing the papers, he would wander into the stacks.

The A.C. College library, located above the lecture hall, had a large collection of Telugu literature. Satyam had never been particularly interested in Telugu literature. What he had seen of it in his high school textbooks had bored him. Classical Telugu poetry was of two kinds: *puranas* (mythological poems in praise of the gods) and *prabandhas* (courtly poems in praise of the rulers). They were written in a highly formal dialect that borrowed heavily from Sanskrit. To most Telugu speakers, including Satyam, it was all but unintelligible.

While looking through the stacks in A.C. College library, Satyam discovered a new kind of poetry that took as its subject matter neither gods nor rulers. It was about ordinary people and contemporary life. The verse, Satyam found, was free of the strict and complicated metrical rules that marked the older forms. The language was modern colloquial Telugu, easy to understand and yet beautiful. Satyam read the *Navayuga Vythalikulu* (Harbingers of the New Era) anthology of Muddu Krishnudu. It was the first anthology he had ever seen, a selection of modern Telugu verse. Much of it was love poetry. Reading it, Satyam felt new sensations stir inside him.

> Like a canoe,
> the moon drifts
> across the sky.
> In it is my beloved.
>
> Why that tender smile?
> What for that white sari,
> those white jasmines in her hair?
>
> And for whom,
> those beckoning hands?
> They beckon me to join her.

Satyam looked up at the moon. He saw riding in it a girl in a shimmering white sari, beckoning to him. He wished he could make out her face. Was it his cousin Kamili? Or Suryakantham, his childhood friend?

He went on to read every modern poem in the library. Poems by Joshua, Devulapalli, Nandoori, Duvvoori, Thripuraneni, Karunasree, Gurajada. These were pioneers of *navya sahityam*, "new literature," as the movement he had chanced upon was called. While on the floor beneath him lecturers lectured and students studied, Satyam read. He read *eda-peda* (left and right). He learned to hide in the library when it closed at night and even slept there sometimes.

The father of navya sahityam was Gurajada. His most famous poem was one he wrote in 1910 called "Love Thy Country." Two lines in this poem had a great impact on the political consciousness of Telugu speakers:

A nation is not the soil.
A nation is the people.

Two simple lines and yet so powerful. It was as though Gurajada was explaining what a nation was to the many for whom this was a modern and abstract notion. These two lines followed Satyam wherever he went.

Satyam read poetry as though he were preparing for an exam. If he didn't know the meaning of a word, he would look it up in dictionaries or ask people he thought might know. He copied his favorite poems into a notebook. In his room, he would sit up into the night, reciting from his notebook as tears welled in his eyes. Sometimes he would wake before dawn, make up a tune, and sing softly to himself the lines he had learned by heart.

His roommates, who had always looked at him strangely and left him alone, became curious. What was he doing, staying up all night? When he went out, they sneaked a look in his notebooks. They found the poems he had copied and some of his own that he'd started to write. Soon after, a boy from the next room came to him with a request: "Would you write a love letter for me?"

Before long, a procession of boys was asking Satyam to write for them lyrical messages to the girls they admired. As a love-letter writer, Satyam finally began to achieve recognition among his classmates.

◎

THE BRITISH HAD LEFT INDIA, but at A.C. College the English principal, Sipes, refused to leave. The word was that different factions of untouchable Christians were vying by stratagem and violence for control of the vast property owned by the Lutheran mission, including A.C. College. Sipes had to settle the quarrel and appoint a successor before he could leave.

In the meantime Sipes continued to rule A.C. College like his own private colony. He insisted on continuing to hold detention exams to decide who could sit for their finals. The students were angry. This was supposed to be a free nation now.

Satyam, who hadn't been going to classes, had not heard of this grievance. He only knew when the library opened, when it closed. On his way to the library he noticed groups of students gathered in front of the administrative building.

"What is going on?" he asked.

"Strike. We are fighting against detention."

Satyam felt a wave of nostalgia. He stayed for the rally, but only as an onlooker.

The next day, finding the library closed on account of the strike, Satyam went back to observe the protest. Hundreds of students had boycotted classes. Satyam saw girls taking part alongside boys. Lecturers joined in support. They all shouted slogans. Satyam was moved. He joined the crowd, chanting along with the others:

"Down, down, Sipes!"

"Down, down, detention!"

Throughout the day, the strike leaders made speeches one after the other. During a lull, Satyam seized his chance. He got up on a wall to speak, exhorting the students not to be scared of the police, to stand strong until they won. As he finished, he saw one of the strike leaders, a short round dark boy with smiling eyes, the same boy Satyam had met on the evening of the independence celebration, making his way toward him with a big grin. He congratulated Satyam on his speech and seemed genuinely pleased to see him taking part in the strike. His name was Manday Pitchayya.

Encouraged by Pitchayya, Satyam gave his speech every day as the strike wore on. Finally Sipes called in police to break up the protests, as they had the year before in Satyam's high school.

But these were not colonial police. They were the police of a newly independent India. Yet, Satyam noticed, they didn't hesitate to use force. When students lay down to block the gate, the police simply trampled on the students' bodies. And when the police raised their lathis and let them fall on the students' backs and heads and shoulders and shins, the students ran for their lives. Some were seriously hurt, with broken limbs or blood running down their faces. When the police had cleared the area, the ground was strewn with placards and sandals. To this day such scenes are common in India whenever police attack a student demonstration.

After a month of relentless agitation, the administration gave in and abolished the detention system. The sense of belonging that Satyam had felt during the strike was short-lived. When students went back to their classes, he retreated into loneliness and poetry. But Pitchayya kept in touch with him. He would visit Satyam in his hostel room. He seemed to like Satyam despite his impoverished appearance. Pitchayya was the only person on the campus who did not seem to notice Satyam's shabby clothes and broken footwear. Satyam learned Pitchayya was an untouchable like himself, though not a Christian. His mother was a poor widow who owned two acres of land. In addition to working her own tiny plot, she worked for wages on the land of others.

Pitchayya looked around Satyam's room, noticed a stack of poetry books, and asked, "Do you like reading this stuff?"

Satyam caught a touch of sarcasm in Pitchayya's tone but did not know how to reply.

Pitchayya then asked, "Have you ever read the *Abhyudaya*?"

"What's that?" Satyam asked. The word *abhyudaya* means "progress." That was all he knew.

Pitchayya pulled a magazine out of his pocket and showed him. "You can read this, but be very careful. Don't let anyone see it." Satyam hadn't heard those words since the end of colonial rule.

That night he couldn't put the magazine down. Not 150 miles from where he was sitting, a struggle was raging in the countryside. It wasn't being fought against foreign rulers, but against a native king and native landlords. And this time it wasn't Gandhi and Congress who were leading the struggle, but the Communists.

In the pages of the magazine Pitchayya had given him, Satyam first learned the story of the Telangana struggle, which was then still unfolding. He was shocked by what he read. Telangana was a neighboring region— just across the Krishna River from Andhra—yet had neither been under direct British rule nor under that of the new Indian government. Rather, it had its own feudal sovereign. Nothing much was known about it outside its borders: no news ever escaped this realm. The situation there, as Satyam learned for the first time through the Communist propaganda he was given, was fantastic, grotesque, totally anachronistic—like something out of an old folktale.

◎

O BROTHER AND SISTER, MOTHER and father, this is the story of Telangana.

Once there was a king who ruled the kingdom of the Deccan in southern India. The Deccan was a realm of silk and pearls and diamonds and gold.

This king was the lord of the untold riches of the Deccan. To this very day, to the moment these words are being written, no richer man has lived on earth.

The king's pearls could overflow an Olympic-size pool. His gold could fill a five-story building. He had treasure houses loaded with rubies, emeralds, and priceless sapphires. He had great trunks full of diamonds. The world's fifth-largest diamond was used in his study as a paperweight.

The city of Hyderabad, built as a token of the great king's love for his queen (Hyder Mahal), was one of the most beautiful yet modern cities on the subcontinent, with its palaces, gardens, and bazaars; its clean, wide roads; its hospitals and universities.

The king was a man of passion who worshipped beauty and pleasure. The royal palaces of Hyderabad were filled with beautiful princesses from Persia, Turkey, Egypt, and Arabia—his wives and mistresses. They bathed in rosewater and wore crushed pearls on their skin.

The king was a lover of the arts. During his reign, famous architects from east and west converged on his royal court. They designed architectural marvels for the royal city—forts, mansions, palaces, bridges, theaters, and grand monuments. Every night banquets were held on tables a mile long.

Poets, scholars, musicians, painters, and sculptors came from all over the world to seek the monarch's patronage. They invented new styles, new forms. The king himself was a great scholar, a master of four languages, and a composer of sublime verse on the subject of unrequited love.

Hyderabad was no mere city. It was paradise on earth. Its monarch was no mere monarch. He was the monarch of monarchs. He was His Exalted Highness Sir Mir Osman Ali Khan, the Nizam of Hyderabad and Berar, Prince Asaf Jah VII.

Now how was all this possible?

Let us grant that this king—the prince of the great Asaf Jahi dynasty that was ruling Hyderabad and Berar, the Nizam as he was known in Urdu—was the great-great-great-great-great-great-grandson of the first caliph, the prophet Muhammad (peace be unto him).

Let us even agree with the mullahs that he was appointed by Allah himself to rule the earth.

But, even so, how was it possible for anyone to be blessed so much in excess of any other human being ever born?

◎

IN THE KINGDOM OF THE Nizam was a young couple who had a little son.

They woke him up one morning to get him ready for a trip. His mother bathed him and fed him with her hand. She dressed him in his best and they set out on the road.

"Amma," the little boy asked his mother, "where are we going?"

She told him they were going to a fair where there would be toys and sweetmeats. As she said this, her eyes filled with tears.

They walked through the alleyways, passing the mango grove and the streets of the village. Finally they came to the *dora's gadi* (landlord's fortress). They kissed their son and held him in their arms one last time.

Then a door beside the main gate opened. The child was put into the hands of someone belonging to the dora's household. The door closed upon them.

The couple turned and walked away. Their son would never come home to them.

O brother and sister, mother and father, this is no folktale set in a distant past. It was real life in Telangana in 1947 when Satyam came to know of it.

Under the *vetti* system, every untouchable family in every village had to give up their first male child as soon as he learned to talk and walk. They would bring him to the dora to work in his household as a slave until death.

There were systems of servitude in every part of India, but none was as ruthless as the vetti system in Telangana, the heartland of the Nizam's kingdom of the Deccan. Just as the mention of the castle of Dracula made the villagers of Transylvania tremble, the dora's gadi struck terror in the hearts of Telangana peasants. It was a symbol of tyranny, slavery, and cruelty, a place of torture, rape, and murder. No one wanted to go anywhere near the dora's gadi if he or she could help it.

It wasn't just untouchables who were subjected to inhuman treatment under the rule of the doras. Every caste suffered. Under the system of vetti, everyone was forced to provide goods and services to the dora on demand and without compensation.

The potters had to make pots for the dora's household. The weavers had to make clothes for him and all the members of his family and their retinue of servants and slaves. The cobblers had to make them shoes. The carpenters had to fashion and repair the tools of the dora's fields and make improvements on his houses. The toddy tappers, who distill palm sap into country liquor, had to keep the dora's glasses full.

The villagers who did not have anything to give the dora had to provide him free services. The barbers had to cut the hair, shave the faces, and bathe and massage with oil the bodies of all the male members of the dora's family. The washer people had to wash clothes for the dora's household and rub his feet until he fell asleep. The diggers had to build embankments on the dora's lands. Those who had no special skill had to labor in the dora's fields, to carry things for him, to do any work he gave them.

When the dora and his family had to go somewhere, they often traveled in palanquins. The men of the *besta* (fisherman) and *boya* (stonecutter) castes were forced to bear the dora's palanquin on their shoulders, carrying the dora from village to village. Other times the dora might travel by horse or bullock cart. When he did, a man of the washerman caste would have to run before the horse as a path clearer and another behind as an escort.

These lowly service castes weren't the only ones who suffered under the vetti system. Brahmins had to perform ritual services for the dora. Grocers had to keep him supplied with provisions. If an item was out of stock, a merchant was expected to procure it specially for the dora—all for free.

The whole village was the dora's, along with everything in it. If anyone so much as picked up a twig from the ground for his hearth, he could be fined and beaten.

All the women in the village belonged to the dora, too. If he called them while they were eating, they had to leave the food on their plates and come to his bed. Untouchable girls were chosen at a young age to live in the house of the dora, where they served as concubines for him and his relatives and guests. When the dora's daughter got married and went to live in her husband's village, these slave girls went with her as part of her dowry like pots, pans, and other chattel.

At the head of the doras stood the Nizam. His regime was their regime. Wealth from the dora's estates flowed into the treasury of the Nizam's government in the form of taxes. Some doras received their lands from the Nizam in exchange for maintaining his troops.

The Nizam himself was not merely the doras' overlord, he was the greatest dora of all. Ten thousand square miles of land spread throughout his realm were set aside to meet his personal expenses.

The impoverishment of his subjects was the source of the Nizam's riches. The splendor of his court had its corresponding cost in human blood and human dignity. The gardens and monuments, the learning and fine arts, the banquets and moonlit dances—all that delighted the senses and elevated the spirits of the Nizam and his court—required the suffering and degradation of millions of human beings.

◎

EVEN THE WEALTHY MIDDLE CLASSES in Telangana were oppressed under the Nizam's regime. The rich peasants were squeezed by competition with the doras for land and labor. The merchants didn't like having to supply things for free. Educated professionals, in particular, resented the lack of basic democratic rights, especially the right to use their own language and to practice their religion freely. For while the Nizam was Muslim and spoke Urdu—the language of Muslims in India— the great majority of his subjects in Telangana were Hindus who spoke Telugu.

Under the Nizam's rule, Urdu was the only medium of instruction allowed in schools and universities. Urdu and English were the official languages of the court and public administration. Only those literate in Urdu were able to get government jobs or conduct official business, while the use of Telugu was suppressed.

Under these conditions, some adventurous Hindu youths—brahmins and reddys, the sons of merchants and rich peasants, who had some means but no future in the kingdom of the Nizam—turned to an organization that came to be known as the Andhra Maha Sabha (AMS)—the Andhra Society. Founded by urban, middle-class professionals, the AMS stood for the promotion of Telugu culture. They wanted to win civil liberties for Telugu speakers under the rule of the Nizam.

Their demands were small. They wanted the right to print newspapers and books in their own language. The right to speak Telugu in public, to organize Telugu literary associations, to celebrate Hindu festivals freely.

But the Nizam would not relax his iron fist. And the direct agents of the British crown were no more sympathetic. In a meeting with Sir Richard Chenevix Trench, a British army officer and high official in the Nizam's executive council, and J. E. Armstrong, the Hyderabad police commissioner, some AMS leaders tried to explain that their organization was not a political organization. They merely wanted to spread knowledge by establishing libraries. And who could object to the spread of knowledge?

Mr. Armstrong replied, "Sir, I know from my experience in Bengal what a library movement means. It is nothing but a revolutionary movement."

British demands to maximize revenues were the source of Telangana's misery. These demands could only be satisfied by the cultivation of cash crops. But the sandy soil of Telangana had never been fit for anything but subsistence farming. To grow tobacco and cotton required large-scale irrigation. It required the eviction of small peasants from their family plots to assemble vast tracts of land. It required gangs of servile labor to work these plantations.

So under a series of so-called land reforms encouraged by the British, a class of great landlords, or doras, was created. These doras were made owners of lands so vast they commonly spread out over several villages, lands that had formerly been cultivated by hundreds or thousands of individual families. The small peasants and low-caste artisans evicted from these lands were turned into dependent laborers. And the untouchable laborers were enslaved. Although based on traditional caste hierarchies, the vetti system was not a traditional system. However antiquated it appeared, it was unknown before the end of the nineteenth century. Like chattel slavery in the Americas, it was a modern product of the capitalist world market.

The British supported the Nizam in his suppression of Telugu libraries and any other measure he found necessary to maintain his autocratic rule. His rule was their rule, too. Long ago, in recognition of the Nizam's dynasty's help in crushing the great native uprising of 1857, the British had conferred upon the Nizams yet another title to add to the already long list they bore:

F.A.B.G.

Faithful Ally of the British Government

◎

THE MILITANT EDUCATED YOUTH WHO joined the AMS had a different outlook from that of the older, city-dwelling members. For one thing, they had grown up in the villages as the sons of rich peasants. They knew the conditions in the countryside. For another thing, many had traveled outside Hyderabad and seen the nationalist movement firsthand. They knew that a tiny association of middle-class professionals such as the AMS, however noble and enlightened its positions, could not achieve reforms on its own. That required mass support.

The younger members therefore called on the AMS to take up social questions of concern to the surrounding rural population. They wanted the AMS to agitate for a ban on child marriage, for compulsory primary education, for a lower tax rate on the peasantry. The older membership of the AMS didn't disapprove of such causes, but the tone of the younger members and some of the tactics they proposed were not at all to their liking.

Soon the younger members found an ideology that suited their appetites. They made contact with the Andhra Communists. Communists could not organize openly in the Nizam's autocracy, where even meetings of literary discussion groups had to be cleared in advance with the police.

The younger members within the AMS gave the Communists political cover to operate in Hyderabad. Meanwhile, the Communists gave their supporters in the AMS more than ideas. They sent personnel and material support. The Communists built the AMS into a Hyderabad unit of the party in all but name.

With the help of the Communists, the AMS was transformed into a different kind of organization. Membership fees were reduced from one rupee to one anna, a sum all but the poorest could afford to part with. A membership drive in the countryside recruited 100,000 new members.

Thousands of them flocked to the 1944 AMS conference. They decisively outnumbered the supporters of the old, moderate leadership, who walked out in revulsion. The new mass party championed social reforms such as the abolition of vetti, ownership rights for peasant proprietors, and the lowering of agrarian taxes.

The demands of the AMS were radical, but not too radical. They did not include a call to abolish the Nizam's tyranny. In time, that would change.

And certainly nothing in their program called for seizing the doras' vast landholdings and distributing them to peasant cultivators.

But that, too, would change.

The new Communist leaders of the AMS had swollen its membership rolls through mass recruitment of poor peasants. But they did not set out to do anything with the AMS branches they'd founded except spread propaganda. They had no plan to organize mass actions to fight for the reforms they talked about.

But the tens of thousands of poor, illiterate peasants had had a different idea when they handed over their hard-earned membership fee. They thought they were buying their freedom with one anna. They thought the little paper receipt they got in return for this fee was a passport out of vetti servitude.

Acting on this conception, they soon put the AMS—and the Communist Party, for by now there was no practical distinction between the two—to the test. The masses called their leaders' bluff. Starting with a poor peasant woman named Ailamma.

Ailamma and her family, washer-caste people, were vetti slaves of one of the cruelest doras in Telangana. Only after they performed their vetti duties in the dora's household and his fields were they allowed to work on their own meager two acres of land.

When a *sangham* (local chapter) of the AMS was set up in their village, Ailamma's husband and son were among the first to join. But the dora sent his goondas to round up the sangham leaders and drag them to his gadi, where they were tortured. Ailamma's husband and son were imprisoned there.

Meanwhile, Ailamma's harvest came to hand. She had no one to help her bring it in. She knew that once she reaped the crop, the dora's men would come and loot it.

So Ailamma went to the sangham leaders to ask for men to stand guard while she reaped. The leaders—poor peasants and vetti slaves like Ailamma herself—had never thought of using such tactics. Their activity was limited to signing up new members and submitting petitions. But they listened to Ailamma's plea. Inspired by her courage, twenty-eight youths volunteered to form a cordon around her as she reaped. When the dora's men arrived, they saw the sangham youths armed with slings and sticks. Not being used to resistance, they turned away. Ailamma reaped her crop and the youths helped her carry it home safely.

The dora could not let this go. His rule was based on fear. If one woman could defy him, what was to stop the others? He sent his men to throw stones at the sangham leaders' houses, knowing this would provoke a protest march to his gadi. There his goondas, from hiding, opened fire. One sangham member, a cattle herder named Doddi Komurayya, was hit in the stomach. He fell to the ground, dead.

But the sangham members did not run in fear. They raised a cry: "Blood for blood!" The goondas fled for safety behind the gadi's high, fortresslike walls. The people of the village surrounded the gadi, chanting, "Blood for blood!"

As the news spread to other villages, a crowd of two thousand gathered on the spot. They fought off a troop of two hundred goondas sent to disperse them.

The next day, not one tree remained in the dora's mango grove. And not one wall was left standing in the courthouse where the sangham leaders had been tortured.

This was the beginning. The struggle spread from village to village. In village after village the dora was forced to flee and his lands were divided up among the villagers. Within weeks as many as four hundred villages had been liberated by peasant governing committees.

These peasant governing committees formed village defense forces. It wasn't just men who joined. Children twelve years or older were allowed to fight, and women also. Women, those slaves of slaves, who had never had a say in anything. Small, frail, weak, voiceless, inferior women. They, more than men, were eager to take up weapons.

The Communist Party had planned none of this. It took them by surprise.

The peasants themselves, not the party, embarked on the path of mass struggle. When that struggle broke out, they asked the Communists for leadership. The Communists were content to organize these militants into defensive formations wielding sticks and stones against their enemies. To these weapons the peasants added spades and hammers, sickles and axes, large pestles used for pounding grain. At home they kept reserves of chili powder on hand and cauldrons of boiling oil or water to throw in the face of invaders. These primitive methods had surprising success against the doras' goondas, who were ill trained, poorly armed, and cowardly.

But they were useless in fighting off the Nizam's police and army. When these forces moved in over the following months, even the heroism of the peasant militants could not make up the difference. The doras returned. The uprising was practically extinguished.

The will to fight and die was not enough. To survive, to advance, the struggle needed leadership. It needed coordination. It needed training. More than anything, it needed guns.

It was only a year after the struggle started that the Communist Party began to provide these things. They regrouped the scattered remnants of the peasant resistance and began to recruit offensive guerrilla units at the district and regional level. Only then, after much hesitation, did the Communists allow the fighters to seize guns and train them to use them.

The Communists, finding themselves at the head of a mass struggle, finally agreed to lead it. But to do so, they had to adopt the movement's basic aim.

What the peasants had wanted from the beginning, when they'd first come together to defend Ailamma's crop, and had been acting on ever since, at their own initiative, was to seize control over their own means of life. They wanted land. They forced the Communists to take up this fight, to raise the slogan "Land to the tiller!"

By the time the Communists came around, it wasn't only the police and the army they had to fight. The Nizam had let loose an even dirtier force—the genocidal Razakars.

The Razakars were a Muslim-chauvinist, pro-Nizam militia. With India's independence on the agenda, the Nizam feared that the new government would invade and hold a referendum to force him to cede power. Hindus made up 90 percent of his subjects. The purpose of the Razakars was to slaughter and terrorize as many Hindus as possible before a vote was taken. They were recruited from among the poorest Muslims under the slogan "We are the rulers."

Trained as paramilitary shock troops, these Razakars, or "volunteers," unleashed systematic violence upon Hindus as well as secular-minded Muslims, subjecting whole villages to orgies of murder, torture, looting, arson, and rape. They especially liked to stab a man in the rectum with a long sword, twist it around inside him, and pull it out with such force that his guts fell out in a heap. They wrapped people in dry hay and set fire to them, watching them roast alive. They spread-eagled babies and nailed them to walls.

And so the Deccan came under the spell of demons. Under the three-pronged attack of the police, the army, and the Razakars, Telangana became a death camp, a cemetery, a ghost land.

But the poor peasants kept fighting.

They wanted freedom from bondage. They wanted land. They wanted dignity.

The touchables and the untouchables. The Hindus and the Muslims. The men and the women. The young and the old.

With their sticks and slings and chili pots and as many rifles as they could steal, they fought on. By August 1948, their revolt had spread to more than three thousand villages.

A red dragon was making its way across the kingdom of the Nizam.

⊙

PITCHAYYA, SATYAM SOON REALIZED, WAS a Communist Party member. Being a student was only a cover for his party work, which included recruiting new members and sympathizers from the college. Pitchayya introduced Satyam to two men who, like him, had been inspired by Pitchayya's accounts of the Telangana Armed Struggle. These were Manikya Rao and Hanumayya, two young lecturers at the college.

Meeting these men made Satyam feel lucky to have chosen to go to A.C. College after all. Had he gone to Hindu College, he would have had no dearth of friends—his old high school friends had all ended up there—and plenty of opportunity for political activity as a leader in the Youth Congress. But the new friends he made at A.C. College were worth more than his old ones. He looked up to them, and they opened a new world for him.

Hanumayya came from the low *vaddera* caste. He was a brilliant philosophy lecturer, and like Satyam he had a great love for Telugu literature, especially poetry.

Manikya Rao was an untouchable Christian from Guntur, one of the "traditional Christians" the town was known for. His father was a reverend, not a two-bit pastor like the ones Satyam had known in his childhood who preached in makeshift churches with no furniture or toured the villages, collecting eggs, vegetables, and dung cakes for their services. Manikya Rao's family was highly educated, highly cultured, and well-off compared to other untouchables. At the age of twenty-three, Manikya Rao had read the Bible, both Old and New Testaments, from cover to cover twenty-three times. Now that he was a Communist, he would never look at that book again. Handsome and well built, he was as good a volleyball player as he was a mathematics lecturer.

Though older than he was, these men treated Satyam as a peer. And like Pitchayya, neither of them minded Satyam's poverty. Hanumayya came from a poor family like Satyam's own, while Manikya Rao was too noble to judge anyone by wealth or social status.

After Pitchayya introduced Satyam to Hanumayya and Manikya Rao, the three of them saw less and less of Pitchayya. After all, he was a party member and had important work to do. Only once in a while would he come around to check on his recruits. He would ask them what they were reading and suggest new books for them.

But Satyam started meeting Hanumayya and Manikya Rao regularly.

In the evenings, the three friends would sit on the lawn in front of Satyam's hostel and talk about philosophy. Manikya Rao would initiate these discussions. Hanumayya would give explanations since he was the philosophy lecturer. Satyam's role was to ask questions. Their talk would touch on various topics, including problems of ethics and metaphysics, but their reflections invariably led them to questions of political philosophy. Questions such as What is communism? What is socialism? Is there a difference?

Hanumayya explained that there were two types of socialism: utopian and scientific. Utopian socialism was based on the idea that equality is a just and compassionate thing, whereas scientific socialism (also called communism) was much like physics or chemistry or maths. Two plus two is always four—no justice or compassion is involved in this determination. Likewise, when human societies, in their development from cave-dwelling clans, finally reach a certain historical stage, their members inevitably come to share equally in what is produced.

Satyam found Hanumayya's exposition of scientific socialism appealing, but Satyam had a lot of questions. If history is inevitably developing in the direction of a socialist society, why does one need to *fight* for it? Hanumayya explained that even though the progress toward socialism was a natural evolution, every transition from one stage to another caused a lot of violence and disruption. The old privileged classes did not want to make way for a new class coming to power. It was something like birth pangs. Though it's natural for a woman to give birth, it is still painful.

Satyam was amazed by this way of thinking—that one can look at society, the people in it, the things they do, in the same manner as a natural process that can be studied in a science lab.

Hanumayya explained to Satyam and Manikya Rao about how the struggle between classes in society is reflected in something called ideology—in ideas and culture. Under the right conditions, the spread of certain ideas could in turn spur social change.

This line of thinking made Satyam reflect on how the culture around him was changing. He thought of the novelist Chalam, whose books were causing a sensation in Telugu society. Chalam was the first to reveal the shocking fact that women have physical desires and take part in sex not only for the sake of their husbands. Chalam also pointed out that women have brains and need to think for themselves. He wrote:

Woman too has a body; it should be given exercise.
Woman too has a mind; it should be given knowledge.
Woman too has a heart; it should be given experience.

His books were considered worse than pornography. But, like pornography, many people who were quick to denounce them in public were keen to read them behind closed doors.

Chalam was naturally associated with communism. After all, he was as bold and revolutionary, as attractive and revolting. Everything exciting and progressive that was happening in those days in the arts or social life was associated with communism. Still, the Communist Party denounced Chalam. Under communism women may be equal to men, but that didn't mean Communists condoned promiscuity.

Satyam agreed with the party about Chalam. Upon reading his novels, Satyam shuddered to think how he could ever look at Marthamma or Papa with the same eyes that had read that book. But he liked the idea of treating women as thinking creatures. And Chalam's style enchanted him.

But for Satyam the writer who best spoke for the spirit of his times was the revolutionary poet Sri Sri. It was Sri Sri who became Satyam's idol.

Sri Sri was not a Marxist who wrote poetry in support of his politics; he was a poet who took up Marxism for the sake of his writing. In the struggles of the oppressed and the hope for a new, egalitarian social order, Sri Sri found inspiration for the kind of poetry he wanted to write.

Sri Sri was the one who had written "A Different World," which Satyam remembered singing at the independence celebration. But though the poem had been adopted as an anthem for the nationalist movement, the author was actually writing about a truly new and better world like the one that Satyam longed to see. When armed peasant struggle in Telangana broke out, Sri Sri's poems gave voice to the aspirations of the movement.

Sri Sri's poetry was revolutionary not just in theme, but in form. He abandoned traditional versification, producing free verse with a strong colloquial rhythm. Chalam wrote that Sri Sri "broke the back" of classical meter and diction in Telugu verse.

And Sri Sri went further than any other in making contemporary everyday experience a subject of Telugu poetry. One of his poems begins:

Little doggy,
Matchstick,
Bar of soap—

Don't look down on them.
They are all full of poetry.

Piece of bread,
Banana peel,
Plank of wood—

They go on staring back at you,
Demanding that you find their depth.

Sri Sri was invited by the student cultural clubs of A.C. College and Hindu College to speak on modern poetry. On the day of his speech, when word got out that the poet was resting in a room on campus, Satyam snuck past a throng of young admirers lined up outside and tiptoed inside to stand by the bed. He stood and gazed at the poet's unusually wide forehead and marveled, "This must show how intelligent he is! And no wonder, if he writes like that."

That evening the auditorium was full. Hundreds stood for lack of seats, and hundreds more gathered outside the door in the hope of catching the great man's words.

Sri Sri's oration lacked the thunder that was in his verse. He mumbled disconnected sentences. The students turned to one another in disbelief. Everyone wondered if he could be an impostor.

Sensing the restlessness in the room, Sri Sri told a story: "There once was a famous sculptor. When invited to deliver a speech on the art of sculpture, he pulled the veil off one of his sculptures and said, 'This is my speech.'"

Then Sri Sri recited a long poem beginning "Poesy, O Poesy." When he reached the end, he announced, "This is my speech." The audience was silent, mesmerized.

Before he left, Sri Sri promised his fans a new poem to be called "Maha Prasthanam" (The Great Journey). "It will be very long," he said. "The length of a full-length mirror." Some months later, when Sri Sri's new book came out, Hanumayya, who had introduced Satyam to Sri Sri's poetry, gave Satyam the money to buy it. He raced out at once to a bookshop. That night he read the poem over and over, a hundred times. When the sun came up, he fell asleep exhausted like a wounded soldier expiring on the battlefield.

Hanumayya wanted to write essays, plays, and poetry in support of the revolution. Manikya Rao, on the other hand, was interested in organizing struggles.

And Satyam, the youngest, shared both the older men's interests and yet was more ambitious than either. He planned to combine in himself Sri Sri and Lenin. Write like Sri Sri. Fight like Lenin. A pen and a gun. Every time Pitchayya came to see Satyam, he asked the same question: When can I go to the guerrilla front? Each time Pitchayya told him the time had not come yet.

◎

SIX MONTHS AFTER SATYAM ENROLLED in A.C. College, on the afternoon of January 30, 1948, a seventy-eight-year-old Gandhi was making his way to a prayer meeting propped on the shoulders of his teenage grandnieces. He was weakened from days of fasting for an end to the communal violence resulting from Partition, the division of British India into the independent states of India and Pakistan. Someone ran out of the crowd, pulled a pistol from his jacket pocket, and shot the old man three times. Gandhi fell to the ground, uttering the name of a Hindu god: "Hare Ram!"

Gandhi's killer was a Hindu—an early member of the fascistic Hindu-nationalist Rashtriya Swayamsevak Sangh (RSS) who believed Gandhi had betrayed all Hindus by agreeing to give up a portion of the subcontinent to the Muslims.

At the news of Gandhi's death, people built memorials to him in hundreds of thousands of cities and towns and villages across India, wherever they could find two stones. If they didn't have time or means to carve a bust, they just went looking for a round stone that resembled his head. They set up shrines and performed *poojas* (Hindu rites).

Students at A.C. College gathered on the campus and sang a song written by the great Congress poet Thenneti:

Pitchollu
Mana meeda
Pistollu.

Manishinani cheppakoy
Manni champestharu.

Matha pitchha,
Mada pitchha,
Rajullo
Rasa pitchha.

(The crazed men
Trained on us
Their pistols.

Don't tell them, brother,
That you are a man,
A human being.
They will kill us.

The madness of communalism,
The madness of lust,
The depraved craze
Of the rulers.)

The Communist poet Sri Sri wrote:

In the valley of tears
A ray of compassion.
O Mahatma,
What is the truth?
What is the falsehood?

Despite the antipathy Satyam had always felt for Gandhi, even when he was a Congress supporter, he now felt a kind of sadness he had never before known.

But his grief did not last long. The next afternoon when he ventured out of his room to get a cup of tea, he saw a huge commotion in front of the campus gate. A large crowd had gathered and were all looking up at a crazy man who had climbed the electric pole. It was the beggar who used to beg in front of the campus, wearing a Congress topee on his head and bearing in his hand a Congress flag. He was a disciple of Gandhi and now, filled with overwhelming grief, he was ready to touch a live wire and kill himself. The students and staff gathered below, pleading with the beggar not to do it. The drama went on for hours. In the end the crazy beggar came down, and from that day on he did very well in his profession.

In a few days Gandhi's bones were turned to ash and the ashes divided and distributed in equal portions to all the states of the Indian republic. In accordance with Hindu rites, the ashes were to be sprinkled into the waters of sacred rivers. Satyam and his two friends decided to watch the absurd spectacle. They took a ticketless train ride to Vijayawada, where the government of Madras had organized a mass ritual on the banks of Krishna River. The crowd was so vast one couldn't hope to get a look at what was going on. When Satyam's train was going over the bridge that spanned the river, he had a brilliant idea. He pulled the emergency chain. The train stopped for several hours, giving them a fine view of the chief minister carrying the little pot of ashes on his head toward the river as the brahmin priests around him chanted mantras.

Satyam's sister, Papa, was in Parnasa with her grandmother when the news of Gandhi's assassination came. Although Papa had only just turned eleven, she was vigorously anti-Gandhi. She admired Bose, mostly for his looks. She was impressed by his light skin, round chin, red lips, and fat baby-face. She thought Gandhi old, ugly, and—"Why doesn't he wear proper clothes?"

As for Marthamma, she didn't like Gandhi either. She preferred Nehru, who for her was the personification of aristocracy. Because of these feelings, neither Marthamma nor Papa cried. But one thing Papa discovered was that if big leaders died, she got a holiday.

◎

SATYAM AND HIS FRIENDS WERE still waiting to receive assignments from the party. For reasons they did not understand, they hadn't even been taken in as members yet. For the time being, their talents and enthusiasm had no outlet.

A.C. College had a beautiful auditorium with room for a thousand people. Its stage was equipped with curtains, professional lighting, and a sound system. The college cultural association supplied costumes, makeup, and props to students who wished to put on performances under their auspices. Hanumayya decided to write a play to be performed in this venue—one with a political message. Manikya Rao would direct it.

The play told the story of a king who oppressed his subjects, faced a revolt, and was made to flee—a thinly veiled retelling of the Telangana struggle. Since at that time respectable girls weren't coming forward to act, Hanumayya insisted that Satyam play the heroine, a lowly peasant woman who stands up to the king. "Only you are so beautiful," Hanumayya told Satyam. "Only you are suitable for the role." Satyam was then still seventeen. Neither tall nor short, he had thin limbs, thick, curly hair, and big, tragic eyes. Satyam hesitated, but Manikya Rao and Pitchayya and Satyam's other friends all urged him on. The play was a big hit—mainly, everyone agreed, thanks to Satyam's performance. The way he smiled and moved, people said he looked more feminine than any girl on campus.

Satyam and Hanumayya came to dominate the cultural program at A.C. College. They performed a dozen more plays, many based on the Bengali novels sold in kiosks outside campus for two rupees each. Satyam and Hanumayya looked for Telugu works that they could adapt for the stage, preferring out of both practicality and national pride to draw on sources in their own language. But just about the only novels written in Telugu at that time were short, sleazy ones with titles like *Three and a Half Kisses*, which sold on moving trains for only one rupee each.

Through his acting, Satyam became known to all three thousand students on campus. Girls admired him for representing their sex so well and so favorably. The popularity he earned satisfied his longing for recognition for the first time since high school.

But his deepest wish was to go to Telangana to take up arms against the doras and Nizam. He kept asking Pitchayya to put in a word to the party on his behalf.

◎

A FULL YEAR AFTER INDEPENDENCE, the tricolor flag of the Indian republic had not yet replaced the banner of the Asaf Jahi dynasty over the Nizam's Kingdom of Hyderabad Deccan.

Hyderabad was surrounded on all sides by Indian territory. Yet against all logic, the Nizam refused to join India. He declared his kingdom an independent state.

India gave him time to reconsider. Meanwhile, the Telangana Armed Struggle continued to spread, despite the atrocities of the police, the army, and the paramilitary Razakars.

On September 13, 1948, the Indian army finally undertook a direct invasion of Hyderabad. In a shockingly short time the Asaf Jahi army was defeated. The Razakars surrendered. The Nizam had been deposed.

The 224-year-old dynasty was no more.

There was jubilation in Telangana. Many of the peasant guerrillas came out of hiding. The feudal order had been destroyed at last. The guerrilla heroes finally put down their precious rifles and went home to celebrate, to reunite with their families.

But the Indian army did not put down its guns. It immediately turned them on the peasants.

This had been its real mission all along. The Nizam was annoying to India, but a popular uprising against landed property was intolerable.

While the operation to oust the Nizam had taken only four days, the occupation of Telangana went on for three years. Over two thousand fighters and their family members were killed. Three hundred thousand tortured. Fifty thousand arrested. Thousands more detained in concentration camps. Thousands of women were raped. Under the guns of the Indian troops, peasants were evicted. Under military and police security the doras came back to their *paraganas*, and the land that the peasants had seized from them was returned. The Telangana struggle was finally crushed and, but for the abolition of vetti, its gains reversed.

◎

PITCHAYYA WAS THE NUCLEUS AROUND which the group of three friends at A.C. College had formed. He had brought them together, told them what was taking place in Telangana.

Then Pitchayya, one day, disappeared.

The three friends quickly concluded, "He's gone U.G."—underground. When a member took up work in aid of the armed struggle, he had to break off prior associations without notice to evade the police.

Along with Pitchayya, many other things disappeared. There were no more political discussions on the lawns of A.C. College. No more issues of *Abhyudaya* to read. No more Communist books for sale. No more meetings of the literary club such as the one at which Sri Sri was presented on campus.

The Communist Party was outlawed. Their offices were shuttered. Their publications banned. No one could utter a word about Telangana. It was said that these measures were necessary to keep order in the wake of Gandhi's assassination eight full months before—even though it was not a Communist who had killed Gandhi, but a Hindu fascist. In fact, these measures were the reflection within Andhra of the vicious repression going on in Telangana.

The campus was now closely watched. No one was allowed to enter the hostels who did not belong there. The watchmen observed their duties to the letter. They wouldn't even let the police enter the hostel without written permission from the principal.

Pitchayya would reappear on campus once every few months. He said he was now living in Madras to keep out of reach of the police. There he was doing menial work for party leaders and living on money he got from his mother.

Pitchayya had no trouble entering the Higher Hall. The ancient watchman, the most vigilant watchman of them all, was friendly with Satyam and never barred his visitors. Simply because Satyam would say hello and ask after his children. No one else would do that.

On these unannounced visits, Pitchayya would give the three friends reports on the progress of the armed struggle. How the Communist villages of Elamarru and Katooru were under the iron boots of the Malabar Police. How peasants in those villages were rounded up and arrested by the hundreds, how women there were raped.

About the rapes, Satyam noticed, Pitchayya would go into the greatest detail. He would start out saying, "This was no ordinary rape—no, sir!" Then he'd describe how the saris were ripped off, how the blouses were torn open, how the women were pushed to the ground. After listening to a few of these reports, Satyam noticed that Pitchayya showed a certain excitement at the thought of the rapes, which he was unable to conceal. It made Satyam recoil.

Satyam would press Pitchayya to introduce him to one of the underground Communist leaders. Satyam imagined these heroes looked fierce, like panthers: tall, lean, muscular, dark, with fiery eyes, a long mustache that curled up at the ends, a rifle slung over one shoulder, a cigarette burning between the lips. But Pitchayya always put him off.

After some time, Pitchayya stopped visiting. The three friends would never see him again. Now that their only link to the party was broken, they would get no more reports on the struggle. But they remained devoted to the movement. They continued to operate, as best they knew how, as an A.C. College party unit. Since their political activity through plays was now restricted, they decided to lead a struggle of their own.

Manikya Rao organized a conference in Guntur to discuss the demand for reservations for untouchable Christians. Reservations were a form of affirmative action to counter the effects of centuries of caste oppression. The untouchable leader B. R. Ambedkar had fought to include the right to reservations in the national constitution he drafted. Under these provisions, a proportion of government jobs and seats in government schools were reserved for untouchable candidates. But untouchable Christians were excluded from this policy as a sort of penalty for having left the Hindu fold. The rationale was that when untouchables convert to a religion that does not recognize caste, they are untouchables no longer and have no need of reservations. Manikya Rao hoped to organize prominent Christian figures who could launch a movement to demand reservations for the untouchables left behind by this discriminatory government policy.

With Satyam at his side, Manikya Rao convened scores of religious leaders. He brought Roman Catholic and Protestant clergy together with teachers and principals from Christian schools.

That conference set in motion dozens of further gatherings but failed to encourage any outright agitation. The religious leaders were loath to take any action that had the slightest air of militancy—that just wasn't the Christian way of doing things. Instead they issued statements and passed around petitions. This protracted process eventually succeeded in winning a modest reform: Christian untouchables were awarded a 1 percent reservation in institutions and agencies of the state government. At the national level, untouchable Christians and Muslims continue to be denied the advantages of reservations in education and government jobs to this day.

Although both Manikya Rao and Satyam were untouchable as well as

Christian, neither of them felt any personal stake in the question of reservations for untouchable Christians. They took up the struggle simply because, as Communists, they wanted to do something for the oppressed, and they happened to be familiar with this cause.

When Satyam and his brother and sister were little, their father tried as hard as he could to shield them from the terrible reality of caste. Whenever he took them to the countryside to visit relatives, he would take a long, circuitous path to avoid running into caste people before whom they would be forced to take off their shoes and fold their hands and bend their waists.

In Gudivada, Satyam, Carey, and Papa excelled in school and had many caste friends. They preferred not to think of themselves as untouchable. Even when reminded that not everyone shared this perspective, they chose not to dwell on it. Satyam's best friends in high school were the Pinnamaneni brothers, the sons of a wealthy *kamma* landlord. Their father had set up an opulent house in Gudivada for his sons to stay in while they went to school there. Satyam and other friends were often invited. While others went in through the front door, Satyam was made to go in through the back and warned to disappear if the boys' father ever made an unexpected appearance. One had to respect other people's customs, Satyam reflected, and thought little of it.

In college Satyam became more self-conscious of his caste, but he was a Communist now. As a Communist one was supposed to think only in terms of class and not of caste. When the class struggle was won, discrimination based on caste would disappear. As a Communist, Satyam saw himself as an uplifter of untouchables, not as an untouchable fighting for his own rights. He would continue to take this attitude as long as he remained in the movement.

◎

AT THE END OF SATYAM'S term at college, as his classmates prepared for their final exams, Satyam didn't know what to do. He had attended no more than ten classes in two years. He had no books to study. He thought of trying to borrow some, but who would lend him textbooks at exam time? Everyone was studying all day, drinking tea and staying up to study late into the night. Satyam spent his time sleeping and reading poetry.

He decided to attempt his exams without preparation. But the principal called him in and told him it was out of the question. Satyam had no record books from his science labs, no sign-offs from his lecturers. So he was not even eligible to sit for exams in physics, chemistry, biology, or zoology. That meant he would fail Intermediate and couldn't go on to medical school. "I hope you don't mind," the principal told him. "If you want, take your English and Telugu exams."

On the last day of exams, all of Satyam's classmates were running here and there, packing their things into iron trunks, rolling up their bedding, buying train tickets home. Satyam had nothing to pack and no money for a ticket. And how could he, the first in his family to be admitted to college, return to them in failure? They wouldn't even recognize him. He had changed so much. He was malnourished. So he stayed in the hostel even after everyone else had left the campus.

He ate little and slept through the day, waking up at odd hours. The single set of clothes he had was in tatters. He told himself he lived like this because he didn't care for convention. He saw himself as being like the great Dr. Johnson, the man who wrote the dictionary single-handedly. Hanumayya had told him how Johnson, though brilliant, was "irregular" and sat on a three-legged chair. He slept whenever he liked, dressed however he liked, ate whatever came to hand. All he cared for was reading and writing. Satyam read all the time and dreamed of becoming a writer.

But what he most longed to do was take up a rifle and join the fight in Telangana. The words of Avanti Soma Sundar's song "Veera Telangana" (Heroic Telangana) were always on his tongue:

Khabad-dar!
Khabad-dar!
Nizam Padushah, hey!

Nizam Padushah, hey!
Khabad-dar!

(Look out!
Look out!
Nizam, king of the world,
You better look out!)

But Satyam didn't know how to go about joining the party. Every time he asked, Pitchayya had just put him off. Satyam never understood why the party was so reluctant to accept his membership.

What he didn't know was that the party was in crisis. When the Indian army turned its guns on the Communists, the betrayal left the leadership divided and confused—they had no time for new recruits.

Seeing their young friend in such bad shape, Manikya Rao and Hanumayya gave him money for bus fare. "Go home, man, go back to your family."

But Satyam still couldn't face his father and siblings. So he set off to Sankarapadu, where his poor, ignorant, doting uncles and aunts and cousins lived. They at least still thought he was great.

His cousin Vijayamma was in Sankarapadu for summer holidays. When she saw Satyam, her face lit up. She cried, "Oh, college man is here! I guess after college he'll get a great job and make fistfuls of money. I wonder if the sight of small people like us will reach his eyes."

Vijayamma was bursting with news for Satyam. When no one was looking, she pulled him aside.

Vijayamma, nineteen years old, had some schooling, but none past high school. Thanks to the generosity of the Canadian Baptist missionaries, she was given a job teaching in a mission school. The mission head, a madiga man named Isaac, had been left in charge when the Canadians went back home.

Isaac was a light-skinned madiga. Everyone thinks all untouchables are dark, but many of them, especially madigas, are as light skinned as brahmins. Light-skinned Isaac had married a brahmin Christian girl. There

were a number of brahmin Christians at that time as a result of child mar-
riages among brahmins. When brahmin girls widowed in their teens got
pregnant, either through a secret affair or after being raped by relatives,
the family would dispose of the offspring by leaving them at Christian or-
phanages, as Isaac's wife had been. Every eligible untouchable Christian
boy dreamed of marrying one of those orphan brahmin girls. So when
Isaac, a favorite of the missionaries, wanted to get married, he chose a brahmin girl. She worked in the mission hospital in the village of Gudlavalleru
as the head doctor, despite not having a medical degree. When Isaac was
given charge of the mission, he moved its headquarters to Gudlavalleru
for her sake.

Isaac and his wife had a daughter named Flora. The family lived in
a mansion previously occupied by the white missionaries. Because she
was unmarried and poor, Vijayamma was allowed to live in a hut on the
premises. She and Flora were around the same age and became friends.
Flora confided in Vijayamma—but that did not mean that Vijayamma was
free to see Flora in her family's mansion whenever she liked, nor was
Vijayamma permitted at any time to enter through the front door, or to sit
on their sofas or at their dining table.

Flora attended A.C. College. Once when she came home on vacation,
she told Vijayamma how she admired one boy in her class, how talented
he was as an actor, and how if only he studied a bit, he would surely become a doctor. That boy was Vijayamma's cousin Satyam. One day Flora
suggested that Vijayamma invite Satyam to Gudlavalleru.

Hearing Satyam's name in Flora's mouth, Vijayamma built up fabulous dreams in her mind. It made perfect sense to her that this girl had
fallen for her handsome and talented cousin. Who could resist his charms?
Vijayamma envisioned herself and her family becoming part of Isaac's
family, the core of the Canadian Baptist mission empire.

Back at home in Sankarapadu, Vijayamma told Satyam that Mr. Isaac's
daughter wanted to see him as soon as possible. Vijayamma couldn't use
the word *love*—that would have been too obscene—so she said obliquely,
"To her, you mean a lot of *this*."

Satyam remembered Flora. She was that healthy-looking tall, fair girl with long, thick, curly hair. But in college Satyam had only had eyes for one girl, a dark-dark girl with white-white teeth and smiling wide eyes named Ahalya who reminded him of his childhood friend in Parnasa, Uncle Nathaniel's daughter Kamili.

Satyam had never noticed Flora, but now that Vijayamma had told him what Flora had said, Satyam recognized her true beauty and charm. She had all high-caste features. Her skin was fair. Her nose, he saw now, was not like the typical snub noses of his people. It was definitely a caste nose. But Satyam was most struck by how healthy she looked. She was healthier than any kamma girl, even. And she was elegant. Even though her father was rich, she had quite simple tastes and didn't flaunt her wealth; she wore less gold than girls much poorer than she.

After summer holidays Vijayamma went back to her job and Satyam returned to campus. But now he couldn't stop thinking about Flora. When the poem of the girl in the moon came into his head now, it was Flora, with her glowing face, whom he saw in a jasmine-white sari beckoning down to him. He decided to take a bus to visit his cousin Vijayamma in Gudla-valleru and hopefully see Flora, too.

As he entered the compound gate that morning, he saw, surrounded by green trees and beds of colorful flowers, the great white mansion where Flora lived. In front of the mansion was a garden with a fountain in the center. Satyam had never seen anything like it outside of the movies.

But Satyam had not yet been invited to this fine house. He went instead to the tiny, palm-thatched hut in back of the mansion where Vijayamma lived with her few possessions. She had a straw mat to sleep on and a pillow and a sheet; an earthen water pitcher and a few earthen pots; a hearth and a small oil lamp; a few pieces of clothing; and a Bible.

Vijayamma was happy to see Satyam. She told him that Flora would send word when and where to meet. Until then they would have to wait. They waited until noon, when Flora sent a servant to fetch Vijayamma. Vijayamma came back with a message for Satyam: he could come to the house at three o'clock exactly, when no elders would be present. Flora's stepmother (her own mother had died) would be at the hospital and her father would be at the school.

At three, Vijayamma brought Satyam to see Flora. She was waiting in front of the house, smiling courteously. Vijayamma slipped away quietly, so that Satyam and Flora could talk alone.

The two of them turned and made their way toward the house. The main entrance, Satyam saw, was not an ordinary front door. It was a *simhadwaram*, an entrance like that of a temple with elaborate friezes carved into the frame and two lions guarding the way. As they approached, Flora politely asked him to come through a back door instead. Satyam knew she didn't mean to insult him. One has to respect other people's customs.

Inside, the cool, spacious rooms—each room could accommodate two huts the size of the one Satyam's family lived in—were filled with mahogany furniture: cupboards, armoires, sofas, tables, chairs, even a polished grandfather clock. Translucent white lace curtains covered the windows and the doorways, and lace cloths were draped over the tables.

Flora asked Satyam to sit down. She called a servant and asked him to bring tiffin (snacks) and tea for her guest. The tiffin was *kyma* (minced goat meat) served with bread. Satyam had never before eaten bread. Flora was living exactly the kind of life he imagined the white lords to live, the kind of life he used to think independence would bring him and his family. The bungalow, the bread, the napkin to wipe the mouth.

Once they were served, Flora did the talking. "You are so fine in the dramas," she told her guest.

Satyam was too shy to speak. He pretended to concentrate on eating.

"On the stage you're more beautiful than any girl." Flora went on praising him in her delicate voice. "The way you smile, the way you carry yourself, the way you gesture with your hands, the way you adjust the sari end and twirl it in your fingers. The girls in the ladies' hostel, we all learned that from you."

After the meal, Flora had to go out to her stepmother's hospital. "Can you stay at your cousin's?" she asked. "Please do."

"She wants me to stay!" Satyam thought. With his brain buzzing like a tuning fork, he returned to Vijayamma's quarters.

He waited. Two days passed, then three, then four. No word from Flora. They gazed at Flora's house, helpless and unsure what to do. Vijayamma grew anxious that Flora's parents weren't leaving her free to arrange another meeting. Vijayamma was scared the whole affair was going to fizzle out because of them.

Frustrated, Satyam considered going to the house on his own. But Vijayamma said no. "People like us cannot dare. Wait for her to send word—it's the only thing we can do."

There was no question of inviting Flora to Vijayamma's home. How could she visit a poor hut like theirs? Where would she sit—on the dirty sheet drawn across the straw mat? What could they offer her? They had to face the fact that they had no control over the situation.

Satyam stayed for a full week with no word from Flora. Then he went back to Guntur.

He knew one thing: Flora loved him. And why? He knew that, too. Right after independence many movies were made about the rebellious daughters of rich, evil men falling in love with a champion of the poor. Satyam aspired to be such a hero, and Flora must have seen that promise in him. He longed for a chance to show her what he was capable of.

◎

IN JULY 1949, NEW STUDENTS began arriving at the A.C. College campus. Satyam had noticed that some of them looked much too old to be college students—twenty-five, twenty-six years old.

One evening Satyam was visited by one of those new students, who introduced himself as Duggirala Moses. He said he'd heard about Satyam from Pitchayya. Moses explained to Satyam that the old-looking new students were Communist Party sympathizers and civil rights activists from Khammam district in Telangana fleeing the police and military repression.

Moses had a party task for Satyam. He wanted Satyam to help start a monthly magazine. Satyam could not believe his ears. It was the very chance he had been looking for. A chance to prove himself not just to the party but also to Flora.

Hanumayya would be the editor, and financing would come from a man who owned a popular tailoring shop just outside campus. The man came from a poor untouchable family, but in recent years as an idea of fashion had developed among Telugu people for the first time—men wanted their collars "like this" and women wanted their blouse sleeves "like that"— his business had started making money. A Communist sympathizer, he agreed to front the money for this publication.

Since the Communists could not safely publish in the name of the party, they sought to get their line out through people such as Hanumayya and Satyam—people who weren't associated with the party in the eyes of the police. Hanumayya would write the editorials but otherwise give full responsibility for the contents and design to Satyam.

Satyam and Hanumayya decided to call the magazine *Keka* (Scream). To illustrate the title, on the cover of the first issue they printed a photograph of a skeletal young man dressed in nothing but a loincloth, his belly distended from hunger, stretching out his hand and crying out for alms. The emaciated model was Satyam himself.

For the first issue, Satyam badly wanted to write a poem, but he couldn't come up with anything he liked. So he stole a poem by the revolutionary poet Narayana Babu, changed a few words, and printed the poem under his own name. But when everyone congratulated him on how good it was, he couldn't bear to deceive them and confessed.

The inaugural issue was fairly well received, though some complained about the design and Hanumayya's editorials. So for the second issue Satyam improved the design and wrote the editorials himself. He even wrote his own poem this time.

For his first article, Satyam decided to write about the black American boxer Joe Louis, who had just retired after an unprecedented twelve-year reign as heavyweight champion. Only in A.C. College, through his friendship with Hanumayya, had Satyam started to learn about the world outside India. When he read somewhere about Joe Louis, Satyam was surprised because he hadn't known that there were people in America who weren't white. Hanumayya explained that black people in America were kept in poverty and ignorance and fear.

So Satyam was inspired to write the essay that became the centerpiece of the second issue. It began in pompous high-Telugu style with the line "Durbhara jeevitha vidhanam lo nundi pravirbhavinchina maha ma-hudu Joe Louis" (Rising like a brilliant comet from the wretched depths of life came the greatest of the great men, Joe Louis).

Satyam didn't know any of the details of Joe Louis's career or what he had done that was great. All Satyam knew was that Louis had wrestled or something and won the first prize. What mattered was that he was a black man who had overcome his oppression and achieved great things.

For the second article Manikya Rao suggested that Satyam write some-thing criticizing the corruption of the new native leaders of the Christian missions in Andhra. When the Canadian missionaries left India after inde-pendence, leadership passed into the hands of their native favorites (who were in some cases their own illicit children). While the foreign mission-aries had built and fostered a Christian community in Andhra, their suc-cessors looked only after themselves.

Satyam loved the idea. He chiseled away at his article like a sculptor of fine figurines. He gave it a nice alliterative title: "Gudlavalleru Kalava Pakkana Gudlagooba" (The Owl by the Side of the Gudlavalleru). Owls are not associated with wisdom in India. They're thought of as nighttime predators, symbols of darkness and evil. The Gudlavalleru was the canal that passed through the village where the Canadian Baptist mission was based, and the "owl by the side of the Gudlavalleru" was none other than the new head of the mission—Flora's father, Isaac.

◎

THE EXAM RESULTS CAME OUT. Satyam had of course failed hopelessly. But it didn't bother him too much: Flora was back on the campus. One of Satyam's friends from Slatter Peta was Flora's roommate in the ladies' hos-tel. She told him Flora had come back to pick up her certificates so she could apply to a medical college. She would be leaving in a couple of days.

One morning Flora was out walking. A car came out of nowhere and struck her. She was thrown forward and lay on the ground in a puddle of blood. Satyam saw the accident and came running. He took Flora into his arms. She was still breathing but just barely; only if she got to a hospital in time would she have a chance. Satyam rushed her there himself. The doctors saved her life. Satyam didn't leave her side. Day and night, he nursed her back to health. Flora couldn't help but fall hopelessly in love with him . . .

In Satyam's fantasies, Flora nearly died hundreds of times.

He decided to write her a letter. It was all about the moon and the stars and the cool breeze. Nothing about his feelings for her in so many words, but she would know what he meant. He waited for her along her route. When she came by, he called out to her and handed her the letter. She took it and walked on without a word. Satyam had not expected her to stop and speak to him. Modesty prevented that. The important thing was that she had accepted his letter.

Now he waited to hear from her. But no word came. The hurt was unbearable.

At last he heard from his friend that Flora was taking a train the next day to try for a seat in a medical school in some other town. That evening he put on his slippers and went to the railway station with a copy of the second issue of *Scream* to show her the article he had written on her father. It was his last chance to see her.

He saw Flora standing on the platform with her friends. When she saw him approach, she stepped forward to meet him. Softly but firmly she told him, "Look, Satyamurthy. Your caste and my caste are not one. You are Christians." She meant mala Christians, untouchables. "We are brahmins. You are have-nots, we are haves. You are a Communist. My father is for Congress. How in the world can there be anything between us?"

Just like that. How clear her thinking was, how plainly she let him know how things stood!

She added one more thing: "One day I'm afraid you, as a poor man and a Communist, will burn down our bungalow." Satyam then realized that Flora must already have read his article on her father's embezzling of mission funds.

The train arrived. Flora departed. Satyam went home in a daze.

He understood, finally, that Flora had never had any romantic plans for him. She had all along seen that such a match was impossible. She had only wanted to meet the actor whom everyone admired onstage and tell her friends she knew him personally.

Satyam saw Flora again. She was walking in front of him—so healthy, so upright, so confident. No, it wasn't a girl at all. It was a lion. Maybe it had strayed from the simhadwaram of the house where Flora lived. What a magnificent creature it was, how elegantly it moved! What grace! Its hind parts, the part the tail grows out of, the part the shit drops down from, moved along with the rest of its body. Wherever the lion moved, its ass moved, too. No, that was Satyam: he was the lion's ass.

In reality, he never saw Flora again. Only in his nightmares.

◉

AFTER FLORA LEFT CAME ANOTHER crushing blow. *Scream* had to be shut down.

Hanumayya saw what was going on. The families, friends, and even acquaintances of known Communists were getting fired or even jailed. Hanumayya, who came from a poor family, did not want to risk his job. He quit as manager and disassociated himself from *Scream*. The ladies' tailor also stopped funding the magazine. With no funds and no manager, *Scream* died out.

The folding of the magazine affected Satyam more than Flora's rejection. A great chance to prove himself, to make use of his talents, and to show his worth to the party had slipped out of his hand.

Just as Satyam began thinking of going home to his family, Moses, the student who had asked for Satyam's help with the magazine, unexpectedly invited Satyam to meet an underground party leader.

The first meeting was at a tea stall. The man, Turumella Govindayya, was in his early twenties and neither as tall nor as muscular nor as dark as the underground leaders of Satyam's imagination. He didn't even carry a rifle. But he *was* a real underground leader, not merely a student organizer. Satyam never learned the man's exact position in the party, but he seemed to have some standing, perhaps on a district level.

Govindayya was a mala, but no ordinary mala. He was a mala *dasari*—a member of the priestly subcaste. Since brahmins won't defile themselves by offering their services to untouchables, untouchables need hereditary priests of their own, their own untouchable brahmins, and these are the mala dasaris. Govindayya bought Satyam a cup of tea and gave him a report on Telangana. He told him of a few spectacular victories the people's army had won in attacking police stations and making off with stores of weapons. Then he told of the repression, how many people had been lost. Satyam took a chance and asked if he could join the guerrillas. Govindayya replied that he would talk to the leaders above him. He never said why he'd arranged to meet Satyam in the first place. It looked to Satyam as if he was being sized up.

Govindayya met Satyam a couple more times. The safest place was at Satyam's hostel. As always, the watchman admitted Satyam's visitor. When Satyam asked about joining, he was told the party had stopped recruitment. But one evening Govindayya sent word that he had an assignment for Satyam. Not in the field of battle, but in a role that was no less important. Satyam went as instructed to an abandoned, dilapidated house in a remote corner of town to meet Govindayya and a man whose name he was not told.

They asked Satyam, "Would you like to live here?"

The remote house was the scariest place Satyam had ever seen in his life, filled with cobwebs and dust. Little plants were growing out of the walls. But still he answered without hesitation, "Yes."

Govindayya once again described the gains that had been achieved in Telangana. He told Satyam about the land distribution, the abolition of debts, the establishment of a people's government. The region was already liberated. There was no need for more armed struggle there. The red troops were crossing the Krishna River to spread the revolution to Andhra.

What the party needed now were secret dens in Andhra to allow the underground leaders to come and go. Satyam's assignment was to live in this safe house and take care of it—keep it clean and receive visitors when they came. He would also act as a courier, passing on secret messages. Satyam was thrilled. Govindayya told him it was an important task, and dangerous. If the police ever learned of his role, he was sure to be shot. Satyam was prepared to take that chance. At least in this way he could make himself of use. They told Satyam they'd need to meet once more in a few days to arrange the details; Satyam would hear from them soon. For the next few days, as he waited to be summoned again, Satyam was too excited to sleep.

Then news came from Moses that the party had no use for Satyam after all. No explanation was offered.

What had happened was that one of the party's top leaders had left his underground den and disappeared. No one knew where he was. His former comrades feared he would talk to the police and tell them about the party's underground activities. The party members were afraid that if he did, they would all be hunted down and killed. Since this leader knew of the plans to extend the network of secret dens into Krishna district, these plans had to be abandoned.

Satyam wasn't told any of this. He understood simply that no one needed him. Not even if he was ready to risk his life.

Then he received a letter from his father. Prasanna Rao was now living with Papa, Carey, and Marthamma in a new village called Telaprolu. The rich landlords there paid Prasanna Rao handsomely to tutor their children. At last the family was doing well.

Prasanna Rao wrote that Satyam shouldn't feel ashamed for not having completed his studies. His father asked that he just come home.

TWO

⊚ ⊚ ⊚

TELAPROLU IS A RICH VILLAGE dominated by the landlord caste of reddys. Before the 1950s, in the eyes of the landowning castes, education was worth nothing. An educated man was noble but useless. These castes measured a man's worth by how many acres of land he had, how many cows or buffaloes he kept, how high his cattle-fodder pile was, how large a house he lived in, whether he slept in a four-poster bed, and how much gold was hanging from his wife's appendages.

As soon as the British left and power was transferred to the natives, the reddys and the kammas were swept up in enthusiasm for education. In the changing society, training in maths and science could prepare one's children to become doctors and engineers. And training in English could get them into the civil service, until then the exclusive domain of the brahmins. After independence, government careers meant not only wealth from bribes but prestige and political power—for the caste as a whole as well as for the individual.

So in 1951, when the reddys of Telaprolu decided to educate their children, the district government obligingly set up a school in their village.

The school needed good teachers—nothing less than the best would do for the landlords' children. But the best teachers then were untouchable Christians. Thanks to the work of missionaries in the coastal districts, untouchables were second only to brahmins in education.

So when the three new teachers arrived in Telaprolu, a problem arose. Where should they live?

The Telaprolu *malapalli*—its colony for untouchables of the mala caste—was so far away from the school in the middle of the village that if the teachers lived there, they would be late to work every morning. And the teachers themselves did not want to live in the malapalli. As salaried people, they could afford to live a little more decently than other untouchables. But as untouchables, they were not allowed to rent a house inside the village.

So the three Christian teachers went to the school committee and appealed for permission to rent the vacant lot next to the school building. The committee, after discussing the matter with the reddy elders, granted their request. They could have a place in the village to live—segregated, but on the inside.

In a vacant lot under tamarind trees, the Christian families erected small mud-and-thatch huts. No one from the village gave them a hand, not even the *upparis*—the digging caste—whose own colony was right next to theirs.

◎

WHEN PRASANNA RAO WAS POSTED to the new district school in Telaprolu, he decided to bring his children from Gudivada and naturally expected Marthamma to join him there. But she refused to come.

Marthamma had become a bitter woman back when Prasanna Rao was looking for a piece of land. His plan was to buy the land near his own village and lease it to his brother Nallayya. Marthamma wanted him to buy land near her own village instead and lease it to her son Nathaniel.

Marthamma argued, "It was I who had to leave my job to raise your children, send them to school when you ran away from home." She asked: "Did that Nallayya raise your children? Did any of your brothers come to take care of them?"

For his part, Prasanna Rao, the mildest of men, never argued back. All the same, he wouldn't for a minute consider buying land in his in-laws' village. It was an outrageous suggestion. What kind of a man buys land in his wife's village?

In fact he deeply resented his mother-in-law for the way she'd been raising his children. When he was in the military, he thought he was sending her more than enough money to provide for them decently. Yet when he came home several years later, he was shocked to see them living like a coolie's children.

What had she done with the forty rupees he'd sent every month? It was a mystery to him. If when he came to visit he bought thirty kilos of rice to last thirty days, Marthamma ran through them in five days.

Prasanna Rao's interest was in his own children, while Marthamma was interested in the well-being of all of her grandchildren. When she'd set up house in Gudivada for the purpose of educating Prasanna Rao's children, she'd brought along two of her son Nathaniel's sons—one of whom had been working as a semibonded laborer—to "help raise Prasanna Rao's children." From then on, at least two of Nathaniel's sons always lived in the house, fed and clothed and sent to school with the money Prasanna Rao provided.

But what could Marthamma do? How could she see her son's children live in slavery while sending her daughter's children to schools and colleges? Her mother's heart would not allow it.

To Prasanna Rao, Marthamma had been raising his children in poverty. When she refused to join him in Telaprolu and went off to live with Nathaniel instead, thinking, "I will see how this Prasanna Rao will raise his children without me," Prasanna Rao let her go, thinking, "I will show this Mrs. Marthamma that I can very well raise my children on my own." He brought the two children to Telaprolu.

◉

THE CHRISTIANS' HUTS WERE TINY. Prasanna Rao was a six-foot man. The roof of the hut he built was a good foot lower than he was tall. To enter the hut, he had to bend himself double. In that cramped space, which barely accommodated his body, he lived with his two younger children. Every morning he woke up before they did and lit the hearth and made coffee. With a cup of coffee in each hand, he woke up Papa and Carey. As they drank the coffee and got ready, he would make rice and curry to eat when they returned for lunch. Then *adara-badara* (in a rush) they would all run off to school.

Prasanna Rao was then in his thirties. He always dressed neatly in a full-sleeved shirt tucked into pleated trousers and secured with a nice belt. With his handsome features, groomed hair, and courteous demeanor, he was a special sight for the villagers. When they saw him in the street, they stopped and gaped. "Abbo, Masteroo! Very handsome! What dignity!" In school, he was instantly popular with his students.

His reputation as an excellent teacher soon spread throughout the village. The reddys had land and wealth and power but no education. Even for those who could read and write, English was hopelessly beyond them. How could they help their children with their homework? They all wanted Prasanna Rao to give their children private tutoring.

He seized the opportunity with both hands. Students would come to his house after school. He charged only a small fee—only five rupees per head every month—but he had so many private students that he was soon making ten times his regular teaching salary. In addition to fees, the grateful reddys sent gifts to his home—milk, curds, butter, fruits, nuts, vegetables, pickles, cobs of corn, buttermilk, coconuts, honey, jaggery, sugarcane, fish, and many other things. In Telaprolu, Prasanna Rao and his children lived in plenty, as they had never lived before. There was nothing they needed.

With this kind of income and no need to buy food, another man would have saved the money and bought land. But after his bad luck in Sankarapadu, Prasanna Rao didn't want to gamble. The land he'd bought to supplement his income had only made the family poorer. He remembered too well the starvation they'd had to endure for the past three years. So he spent all of his salary to provide things for his children. Every day he would go to the bazaar and buy delicacies and sweets for them. For the first time in their lives, Papa and Carey had fine clothes and new books.

Not since her mother's death, when she was only four years old, had Papa lived with a parent of her own. Now for the first time she could remember, she felt as if she was in her own home. She no longer had to fear her grandmother's scoldings and beatings. She didn't feel as if she was living at the mercy of others. "This is my house," she could say. "This is my father."

Prasanna Rao, conscious perhaps of having neglected his children in the past, showered them with love. Papa was his favorite. She was thirteen years old now and already wearing half saris—an intermediate step to full saris that girls normally take at age sixteen. Taking after her father, she was growing like a beanstalk. Yet every evening when Prasanna Rao returned home, he would lift her in his arms like a baby—Papa, who had never before known a parent's love. Carrying her around like that, he would sing her lullabies. He was twelve years late, but better late than never. He didn't know any real lullabies, so he sang her hymns from the Andhra Christian hymnbook.

In the three years that his children spent with Prasanna Rao in Telaprolu, he made up for having deserted them, and then some.

But with the cooking and housework, life was terribly hard for him. Especially when the monsoon season came and he had to get up at four in the morning to light the hearth. The wood would be damp and it would take a long time to start the fire. A man of heft, he would have to get down on his elbows and knees in front of the little three-brick hearth, bending low with his bottom hoisted way up in the air, and blow, blow, blow through an iron tube for over an hour. By the end of it, his lungs would ache. He had to walk a quarter mile to draw water since he wasn't allowed to touch the nearby caste well. He carried it back in heavy iron buckets. He would take one bucket in each hand and make a dozen trips back and forth from the well. The family needed water for everything: cooking, drinking, taking baths, cleaning, washing. When Prasanna Rao cleaned the dishes, he had to scratch loose with coconut fiber and brick powder the food stuck to the bottom of his earthen pots. When he did the washing, he had to beat the soaked clothes against a stone and then rinse them and dry them and fold them.

Because he was living in the caste area, he had no one to help him. If he had been living in the malapalli, he would have gotten all kinds of help. The untouchables of Telaprolu and even the surrounding villages were proud of their "Masteroo." But Prasanna Rao was determined to shield his children from the wretchedness and disease and shame of the malapalli. And his children themselves were no help to him. They didn't know how to cook or clean. Marthamma had always done everything for them.

Prasanna Rao would return from school to lead his private classes without a moment's respite. Then late in the evening he cooked for his children and fed them. No sooner had he fallen asleep than it was already 4:00 a.m. and time to wake up and fetch the water and get the fire started.

He lacked one indispensable thing in that traditional society: a woman's presence.

Papa took the initiative. When school holidays came, she told her father, "Give me bus fare to go to Parnasa."

In Parnasa, Marthamma's situation was not at all good. Her son's family, for whose sake she had robbed Prasanna Rao all those years, did not reciprocate her concern for their welfare. Nathaniel did not have much say in how his mother was treated. His wife, who was in charge of family affairs, did not care for her mother-in-law. She saw her as an unwanted burden.

In Prasanna Rao's house, Marthamma had been the master. Whatever she said was a verse from the Vedas. Living with Nathaniel, she had tasted the ordinary lot of a widow. There she was treated with contempt.

When Papa appeared at the doorstep, Marthamma took her in her arms. In each other's embrace, grandmother and granddaughter wept for a long time.

When they recovered, Papa wiped her tears and made the little speech she had rehearsed on the bus: "Ammamma, you did so much for us. Without you we would not have survived. Why abandon us now? Please come back to us." Marthamma followed her willingly.

With Marthamma taking over for the second time the family responsibilities her daughter had left behind, Prasanna Rao put his mind to his work. Night and day he engaged students. He was making more money than he'd ever dreamed of and spending it freely on his family. In place of scarcity, Marthamma now had abundance to manage.

Now that their life was a chariot of flowers, it was time to bring back the eldest son, the one who'd left and never returned. Prasanna Rao sent him a letter: "Come home."

◎

THREE YEARS EARLIER, WHEN SATYAM had gone off to college, it was as if the whole Kambham clan were sending a soldier into battle. Now he was returning to his family wounded and defeated.

The day he was to come back, they prepared for his arrival as if for a special guest. Marthamma cooked a lunch with three different curries. The night before she'd made curds. Prasanna Rao went to the bazaar and brought home bananas and sweets. Carey fetched a bucket of water for his brother to wash up. Papa placed a clean tumbler next to the bucket. She lowered the cot where their father slept at night and spread a clean sheet neatly over it for her brother to sit on.

When Satyam walked in and they saw him for the first time since he'd left for college, they were shocked. He looked like a famine victim, with sticks for arms and legs and a big pot for a belly. His skin was pale; his eyes looked yellowish. His beard had never been trimmed.

Prasanna Rao finally found his voice. "Okay, come, wash up and eat something."

No one could think of anything to say until night fell and Satyam went to sleep. Then they sat together and made plans to restore his health.

Marthamma said that goat's milk would quickly strengthen Satyam's body. The next day Prasanna Rao went to the bazaar and bought a goat. He finally had the means to follow the advice the doctor had given him nineteen years earlier when Satyam was born: "Give your son some milk every day."

In the morning as Satyam sipped his coffee, Carey clipped the overgrown nails on Satyam's fingers and toes and shaved his beard. Papa boiled water and Carey bathed his brother, gently scrubbing his delicate body. Papa laid out his clothes. They did everything for him. Carey and Papa would fetch water for him, bring him a towel. They served him food and washed his hands after he'd eaten.

This marked the beginning of Satyam's lifelong physical dependency on others. He never learned to shave. He couldn't clip his own nails or even bathe himself. First his brother and sister would do all such things for him, and then his wife, and finally his political followers. If he wanted a pen, he would say, "Someone, bring me a pen." But even writing was too much for him: he preferred to dictate. It's astonishing that anyone could go on living like that. It takes a lot of effort to be so helpless. But Carey and Papa loved to pamper him. They simply adored their brother.

In Prasanna Rao's house, no one ever said a word about the college debacle. Prasanna Rao didn't ask his son when or if he planned to retake his exams.

After a few weeks under the family's care, Satyam's health was nearly restored. Since his father had more private students than he could handle, Satyam offered to help. Prasanna Rao was by then known all over the *taluka* (district subdivision). Parents from other villages would send their sons and daughters to Telaprolu for tutoring. Some had to walk five to ten miles; others came on bicycle.

Prasanna Rao assigned his students in Ampapuram, a nearby village, to Satyam. He would ride his bicycle and get there early in the morning. He'd finish class by 9:30 a.m. Then he would race back to Telaprolu and wait outside the library for the doors to open at ten.

◎

TELAPROLU WAS KNOWN AS a great Communist center, and the Vemana Library was its beacon. The local Communist leaders had stocked it with Telugu literature and all the writings of Marx and Lenin that had been translated into Telugu. With around a thousand volumes and some thirty or forty dailies, weeklies, and monthlies housed in two modest rooms equipped with wooden benches, it was not as big as a city library, but for Satyam it was perfect. For two years he went there daily. He read every book in its collection, from the medieval Telugu epic *Manu Charithra* to the latest poems of Sri Sri.

In the library, he read the novels of Chalam and Kodavatiganti Kutumba Rao, and many Bengali novels in Telugu translation. They were the first works of Indian literature to depict romantic relationships realistically. He read them looking for answers. In his dreams every night, Satyam found himself racing to the station to catch a train. As he stood there panting, he would see the back of the train already pulling out. Every morning as he woke up gasping, his first thought was of Flora. He wondered, if he'd done this instead of that, would she have come to him?

When the library closed, Satyam would go home and lie in a corner with a book in his hand. Or he would read sitting on the banks of the Eluru Canal or stretched out on the little bridge that went over it. He read up in the branches of a pipal tree. He read as he wandered through a mango grove.

When his eyes got tired from reading, he would lie on his belly in the grass and watch a herd of goats swimming across the river to the other side, where there was more grass to eat. One day, just like that, a poem came into his head:

Ee
Eethaku
Aa
Methaku
Saripothundi.

(For
This swim,
That grub
Is just enough.)

At the riverside, he would listen to the songs of the canoemen and canoewomen as they pulled themselves across:

Your mother and my mother
They went to Karempoodi.
Come and pound the spice,
O Lambadi Ramdasa!

My sari's turned all yellow,
The yellow of new motherhood.
Where do we hide the baby,
O Lambadi Ramdasa?

Let's drink the wine of Seethampeta.
Let's climb into a canoe.
Let's elope to a faraway town,
O Lambadi Ramdasa!

◎

SITTING IN THE LIBRARY, HOLDING the latest issue of *Telugu Swatantra* in his hands, Satyam could not believe his eyes. He read that story, his story, his first published story, over and over. It read even better in print. The editor had changed the original title, "Siksha Smriti" (literally "Penal Code," but the word *siksha* means "education" as well as "punishment"), to "Father and Son"—losing the pun. But no matter.

In the story, a young man, the son of a village teacher, wants to go to college. His poor father doesn't have the money to send him.

One day the young man leaves home and boards a train to Bombay. There he finds a job. He starts sending money to his poor father back in the village. Every month his father receives a money order but never a note from his son. The young man never asks after his father's health, nor does he write to tell about his own. When his father writes letters, the son ignores them.

Finally the old man boards a train to Bombay, holding a scrap of paper on which he's written out the "from" address that appears on the money orders. With great difficulty, he finds the office where his son is employed. He sends word to his son and takes a seat to wait. At last his son comes out. But his son will not speak to him, not one word.

The old man understands it is a matter of crime and punishment. His son is penalizing him for having failed to fund his education. The father goes home and lies down on his cot to die, muttering, "I can punish you, too, Son."

The publication of "Father and Son" resolved for Satyam whatever resentment he'd felt toward his father for not sending money while he was away at college. It worked like a medicine to heal the wounds left by the hardships he had faced.

At A.C. College, Hanumayya had whetted Satyam's intellectual curiosity. In Telaprolu, Satyam set out to learn directly, through his own study, from Marx, Engels, and all those great men. He also read *India Today*, a political history of India under colonial rule written by R. Palme Dutt, a British Communist of Indian origin. Satyam was not going to be an ordinary party member who followed what the leaders said. He was intent on becoming a theoretician.

Kattamanchi Ramalinga Reddy, a well-known poet and social reformer, wrote a book called *Analysis of the Philosophy of Poetry* in which he makes fun of the style and content of traditional Telugu literature. Satyam wrote an essay criticizing this book, which he titled "Analysis of the *Analysis of the Philosophy of Poetry*." He pointed out that Reddy merely attacked the form of classic Telugu literature without recognizing that its character arose from the feudal society that produced it.

This work of Satyam's never saw publication. It was rejected by *Telugu Swatantra*, the journal that had printed his short story. *Telugu Swatantra*'s founder, a man known as Gora, was an anti-Marxist social reformer like Kattamanchi himself.

Undaunted, Satyam wrote another article a few days later and sent it off to a magazine called *Shanti* (Peace), where it appeared in the next issue. Based on a report on the economic condition of the West that Satyam had read in an English-language version of a magazine from the Soviet Union called *New Times*, Satyam's article predicted there would soon be a global depression and, as a result of this crisis, a third world war. A few years later he came to recognize (as he saw it) the faulty understanding of Marxism that had led him to this wrong conclusion.

At the age of twenty, Satyam had already written several of his best-known poems—poems inspired by the rhythm and imagery of Sri Sri's verse as well as the verbal grandeur of the reactionary brahmin writer Viswanatha Satyanarayana. A poem of Satyam's called "My Penance" was published in *Visalandhra*, the organ of the Andhra Communist Party:

> This night is
> A bird that flapped its terrible wings
>
> This night is
> Venom spewed by
> The fanged demon
>
> From this night
> From this earth
> Towards the light
> Of a new world
> Towards the sweet
> Morning light
>
> This is my penance
> For the meek and the oppressed
> And for the lowest of the low
>
> This is my penance
> A fearsome march
> Against the evil and the cruel

In Telaprolu it was thought that Satyam must be a saint or a sage. He sat under the tamarind tree in the lot beside the school just like Buddha under the pipal tree. Always reading, writing, thinking. This son of Prasanna Rao, failed student though he was, became for his father a source of great pride.

⊚

BY THE TIME SATYAM ARRIVED in Telaprolu, the Communists who had built the library were nowhere to be seen. They had all gone underground.

Satyam knew what had been going on in neighboring Telangana. He'd heard that, as the Indian army advanced, the guerrillas took their rifles and fled into the jungles of Warangal to the north. Those who didn't escape were captured or shot dead.

The army then occupied the area and carried out what the government called its "pacification program." This meant that whole villages were razed and Communist sympathizers there rounded up and sent off to concentration camps. Where roads had been dug up to aid the guerrillas, Indian soldiers buried peasants alive in the trenches and forced the survivors to build new roads over these mass graves. The Nehru government's atrocities in Telangana were even worse than the Razakars'.

And they were not confined to Telangana. Many people from Andhra, especially Krishna and Guntur, had gone to fight alongside the peasants of Telangana.

The Nehru government dispatched a special battalion of the army, the dreaded Malabar Police, to Krishna district in order to root out Communists and their supporters. By the time Satyam arrived in Telaprolu, scores of Communists there had been arrested and one shot dead. The Communist leader in the village, Senagala Viswanatha Reddy, had gone into hiding. A senior cadre in nearby Buddhavaram, a kamma man named Paparayudu, was shot dead shortly after Satyam arrived.

But Satyam knew in his heart that the Telangana fighters would soon be back to liberate Krishna district and the entire region.

How did he know? He'd read what had happened in neighboring China, where a great leader named Mao Zedong had led his peasant army on what was called the Long March. They retreated only to return one day, stronger than ever, to complete the revolution and establish a Communist society.

The armed peasants of Telangana, too, must have made a tactical retreat to evade Nehru's forces. Soon they would return. With that hope Satyam bided his time.

Then came the news that even without Communists to lead them the landless masses of Telangana, defying the army and the doras, were organizing strikes and winning hikes in wages. Some of these struggles were even led by women.

This news inspired Satyam to try to raise the consciousness of the agricultural laborers in Telaprolu, the largest and most wretched section of whom were madigas. But whenever he tried talking to them, they got nervous and made some excuse to leave the scene. The madigas of Telaprolu remembered what had happened to one of their own a few years earlier, a man named Noble.

Noble was born to a poor, landless couple. Educated by missionaries, he became a schoolteacher. Everyone called him Noble Masteroo. When he learned that poor men and women in neighboring Telangana were rising up against the landlords, this frail dark young man said farewell to his wife and five small children and went off to join the guerrillas.

The Malabar Police made an example of Noble, who was the only madiga among the Communists of Telaprolu. He was taken to a deserted area where they tortured him for days. Then they tied him to a tree and shot him dead.

His illiterate wife was left with no income. She and her five children were penniless.

⊙

AS A MALA, SATYAM COULD not simply walk uninvited into the madiga *goodem*—the colony for untouchables of the madiga caste—and talk to the people there. That would be taken as suspicious or threatening.

So every evening when he set out on the road leading to the madiga goodem, he always stopped along the way in the low-caste colony at a tea stall owned by Ramachandra Rao.

Ramachandra Rao liked talking politics with the low-caste men who gathered at his tea stall. He was a Congress man, a firm anti-Communist. But he wasn't a Gandhian. Like Satyam, he had been a great admirer of Subhas Chandra Bose, the leader whose portrait Satyam had tacked to the blackboard in his high school, the one who led a militant faction in Congress in opposition to Gandhi. That year, when Rao organized a memorial meeting for Bose, he decided to ask Satyam to speak. He was so impressed by what he heard that he invited Satyam to give political classes to his customers. One time Satyam said to him, "Listen, I am a Communist and you are an anti-Communist. How can there be friendship between us?" Ramachandra Rao laughed and told him, "You are the kind of Communist I like."

Among the customers at the tea stall were a couple of madiga youths who ventured out of their colony to spend time there, Sulaiman and Rama Rao. As Sulaiman was not in the habit of wearing a shirt, everyone knew of his remarkably thick growth of chest hair. He never knew anger and was never seen without a smile. Rama Rao's manner was so familiar that no one who came across him ever stayed a stranger with him for long. He always put castor oil in his wavy hair and combed it back neatly. Satyam befriended these two men and through them was finally welcomed into the madiga goodem.

They introduced him to another madiga, a thief named Subba Rao. Subba Rao was only a small-time thief, but he had the air of a big-time bandit. He wore his thick mop of hair in the style of a current cinema hero. When he was amused, he laughed like a villain, but mostly he affected a faint, sensual smile like a movie star surrounded by adoring fans. He had two wives. His first wife got up early in the morning to pluck tamarind leaves, putting them into a bamboo basket. She spent the rest of the day going from hut to hut in the two untouchable colonies of the village to sell the leaves for pinches of rice. A hard day's work yielded enough for four servings. When she got home, she cooked the rice and made a curry with tamarind leaves and carrion beef—the same meal day after day for years, but Subba Rao never tired of it. After eating with his first wife, he took what was left over to share with his second wife, with whom he spent the night, waking up the next morning entwined with her long after his first wife had left for the tamarind grove.

Subba Rao took to calling Satyam "Comrade Noble," and Rama Rao's wife would say sadly, "Here is another Noble getting ready to be shot."

One day the police grabbed Subba Rao and locked him up for a theft somewhere far away. The madigas were all illiterate and utterly without resources. They couldn't think of raising bail or hiring a lawyer. When Satyam got in touch with civil liberties activists in Vijayawada and had Subba Rao released, Satyam came to be seen as a hero, a magician who knew how to get people out of the hands of the police. The madiga laborers began to regard him as a leader.

◎

WHEN THE TEACHER ASKED FOR a volunteer to use the English word *while* in a sentence, Papa raised her hand. The teacher knew she was one of the few students he had who was capable of answering such a hard question. But even so he was surprised by what she said: "The Koreans are harvesting while the Americans are bombing them."

The teacher put his hand to his chest and swooned. The answer was not merely grammatically correct, it was creative. The contrast it drew between American aggression and the peaceful labor of the Korean people made a meaningful statement. And that a student of his—a girl, at that— knew anything of international politics was entirely unexpected.

The teacher did not know it was all her brother's influence.

Normally a man like Satyam would turn to male companions to discuss politics or literature. But whenever Satyam was thinking deeply about something, he longed to tell it to his sister. "Too bad, *amma*, too bad you were born a girl. Otherwise, we could spend every minute together." Women and girls were expected to stay at home unless they had a specific reason to go out.

Papa and Carey would pick up the books their elder brother left strewn around the house. Imitating him, they got into the habit of reading novels, although they never developed the slightest appetite for abstract thinking or poetry.

Papa and Carey were especially drawn to the novels of Sarat Chandra, a Bengali author whose works were being translated into Telugu. Sarat's novels typically featured a heroine who supported her weak husband, cared for her failing in-laws, and set her husband's wayward younger brother on the right path. These books were modern in their depiction of a strong-willed female character, though she used her strength not to assert herself but rather to endure her unhappy fate. She strained to prop up the very thing that was crushing her, the patriarchal family.

Papa and Carey each formed an ideal of life from these novels.

Carey longed to deliver a prostitute from her wretchedness by marrying her and making her a respectable woman.

Papa dreamed of becoming an exemplary wife, daughter-in-law, and sister-in-law. Above all, she would be honest. She would do nothing that needed to be kept secret from anyone in the world.

Now that Papa was living in her own home at last, loved and cared for by her own father, with nice clothes to wear and plenty to eat, she felt grateful to her family. Whereas earlier she had wanted to spend all her time playing with her school friends, now she liked to be at home with her father and brothers. She did work around the house without anyone forcing her, helping her grandmother cook and clean. She washed dishes, heated water for baths, served her father meals when he came home.

◎

PAPA WAS HELPING HER GRANDMOTHER wash clothes in the backyard when it started to rain. Marthamma called out to Papa, "Come quickly and take these dry clothes inside!" Prasanna Rao, who'd been chatting with the other two Christian teachers, said goodbye to his colleagues and rushed inside to place pots under the known holes in the roof.

The breeze became a violent wind, and the light rain turned into a torrential shower. Satyam and Carey came running home to take shelter. Hours passed without respite. The family watched as night seemed to fall in the early evening. Coconut trees swayed hysterically in the engulfing darkness.

The wind shook the palm roof of the hut more and more forcefully until the pole supporting the roof began to rattle. Marthamma screamed, "O Yammo!" (O Mother!). Prasanna Rao grabbed onto the pole in a desperate attempt to keep it in place. The whole family held on to it like life itself.

Around midnight their eastern wall collapsed—the mud construction simply melted away. Their home was now more of a hazard than a shelter. Leaving the roof to fly off where the wind would take it, they fled. Outside, there were no lights as far as they could see, just water and wind.

Over in the brahmin quarters, poor brahmins were taking shelter and comfort in the homes of the better-off. Some went inside the Rama Temple. Throughout the village, families of each caste helped others from the same caste.

But no one offered to take in the Christians, whose primitive huts were all swept away. The three Christian families left behind all their belongings and ran for their lives to take shelter in the school. They had no trouble getting in; luckily, the reddys had stinted on its construction and never attached gates or doors to the entrances.

The three families were stranded there for three days and three nights with no food, no dry clothes, no bedding. The two infants cried and cried for milk until they could no longer cry or even move. Their mothers stared down at the infants' limp limbs helplessly.

All the families could do was wait and hope. The storm was international news. With the heavy rains, the great Godavari River had swollen until it burst its banks and swallowed up hundreds of villages. Hundreds died in the swirling waters.

On the fourth day, when the sun came out, the villagers of Telaprolu discovered the Christian families huddled inside the school. "This morning we have been looking for you," the villagers said. "There is no trace of your houses left. Where are you going to live?"

The Christians had no answer. The reddys came up with a plan. Sheltering the Christians in their own houses never entered the reddys' minds, though they were avowed Communists. But they generously offered to let the Christians move into an old grain storehouse attached to a rice mill owned by one of their caste fellows.

When the Christian families emerged from the school, they were astounded by the destruction. All over the delta you could see human and animal carcasses lying about wherever they had floated into a shrub or fallen branch. Many children had been carried away. Most villages in India had no electricity, but in the nearby towns that did, many people were electrocuted when they stepped on high-voltage wires brought down by the wind.

For three months the three Christian families lived together in the old storehouse. They never quarreled over the limited resources they shared. There were no separate rooms, no kitchen, no toilet. They all lived in one dark, sprawling, musty, rat-infested space half filled with rotting, flood-damaged grain and the tiny insects that lived in it. They set up brick hearths to cook on and spread out old clothes to sleep on.

They lived in a peculiar harmony arising out of their common deprivation, their isolation from the rest of the village. They were all quite helpless, but at least they were all together. Papa played with the babies of the other families. The grown-ups helped each other with cooking and other chores. They shared rice, lentils, sugar, salt, and milk.

While the Kambhams were still living in the storehouse, Papa, then thirteen, became a "big person"—that is to say, she got her first period, an event that is celebrated as a mark of a girl's reaching maturity. Papa's family didn't miss the chance to celebrate. Prasanna Rao was determined to observe the occasion as grandly as possible. He took every measure to ensure that his daughter would not feel her mother's absence at this time.

Relatives on both sides—members of the Kambham and Medapati families—set out from their respective villages to converge in Telaprolu. They brought sweetmeats, green lentils, turmeric, sesame oil, new clothes, and bangles.

The Christian families living with the Kambhams helped with all the preparations. The teachers built a tent outside the storehouse. Carey gathered bright green coconut leaves.

For ten days and nights, Papa stayed on a bed of bright green coconut fronds under the frond-covered tent. For those ten days she drank a mixture of sesame oil and raw eggs; she ate rice and green lentils cooked with ghee. Every day she bathed in warm water and applied turmeric paste to her feet.

On the tenth day, Prasanna Rao threw a great feast of goat-meat curry and *pulauv* (pilaf) for all his relatives, colleagues, and friends (untouchables only, of course). They presented Papa with the gifts they'd brought. She delighted in the attention. The change she had lately felt in herself was being announced with great fanfare.

On the eleventh day of the rite of her entering womanhood, Papa returned to school to find all eyes on her. No one needed to say anything. Everyone knew what had happened. The boys and the teachers all knew why a girl would spend ten days absent from school and come back in new clothes with gobs of turmeric smeared on her feet.

After three months Prasanna Rao's family left the storehouse and moved into a new house a reddy man had built for them. He charged Prasanna Rao rent to stay there. On top of that, Prasanna Rao had to agree to educate the man's son and make sure he scored well on all his exams. But now the family lived in a *pukka* (solid) house made of bricks—not a mud hut with a thatched roof—with three separate rooms, one behind the other like cars on a train.

◎

ONLY ONE OTHER GIRL WAS in Papa's class, a rich brahmin whose father owned a cinema hall. She was intelligent and beautiful, but Papa never thought to compare herself to this girl. Her own father was the most popular teacher in the school, and she was also proud of her talented brother. Papa was the tallest girl in the school and stood first or nearly first in her class in every subject. Including the one that had always given her the most trouble, maths.

Ever since schools had closed in respect after Gandhi was assassinated, Papa had prayed before every maths exam for Nehru's death. One time

Marthamma was pleased to see her granddaughter kneeling in prayer and asked her what she wanted from Lord Jesus Christ. When Marthamma heard what it was, she said to her granddaughter sternly, "It is not done to pray for such things."

But Papa had finally overcome her fear of maths through hard work—she committed the whole textbook to memory. That's all it takes in India to do well in school, just memorize everything. And Papa had a great memory. She could recite page after page from her English and Telugu textbooks word for word.

Papa wanted to take the advanced class, composite maths. Only by studying composite maths could one become a doctor, an engineer, a physicist, or a chemist. It would have been an unconventional and audacious choice for a girl to take composite maths. But Papa was an excellent student, and the most famous maths teacher in the area was her own father. With his help she could have gone far indeed.

Yet Prasanna Rao's greatest concern was his daughter's chastity. He believed that girls are born to debauchery. And boys, he thought, are naturally predatory. When he taught private classes in composite maths at home, the front room of the new family house was full of boys. Papa was never under any circumstances allowed to enter that front room while a class was going on. So she sat alone in the second room and studied general maths, which did not require special tutoring. Once every two weeks or so her father would sit down with her and clear her doubts about square roots or the Pythagorean theorem.

Papa hardly talked to the only other girl in her class, the brahmin girl. But Papa did find a friend, an eighth-class student named Bharati. Bharati was a madiga, the martyr Noble's daughter.

Bharati was a quiet, tragic girl who studied hard and kept to herself. She was dark but extremely beautiful. Once when she and Papa were walking together, Papa felt thirsty. Since they were walking close to where Bharati lived, Papa asked if they could go to her house and have a glass of water.

Bharati became agitated and said no. When Papa tried to argue with her, the girl flew into a fury. Her reaction was entirely out of character and seemed to make no sense. Only many years later did Papa come to understand.

Bharati lived in the madiga goodem. The madigas are forced to eke out a living by trading in dead animals. When an animal falls dead in the village of disease or old age, a madiga comes to haul it away. The carrion flesh is sold to untouchables as meat, and the hide is tanned and made into leather goods. Not all madiga families engage in this occupation, but even if only four or five of them do, the whole madiga goodem is polluted by the festering piles of guts on the ground and dripping pieces of flesh hanging in the sun. The smell of the blood is everywhere.

When Papa asked to come over, Bharati was caught in a situation she had never before encountered. Never had she expected that an outsider would want to come to where she lived. She had to refuse, but she couldn't say why. When she was forced to defend this refusal, her shame changed into anger.

A few weeks later, Papa went to school only to be told it was closed for the day. It was the day of a maths exam. Had someone died? Yes, but not Nehru.

The night before, Bharati had been sitting at the entrance of her hut studying for the exam with a small kerosene lamp for light. Her mother was asleep on the ground outside. They were so poor they couldn't afford a lamp with a glass cover over the flame. Bharati dozed off. The lamp fell over. Kerosene spilled. The hut caught fire. Thirteen-year-old Bharati, the daughter of the martyr Noble, was consumed in the blaze.

◎

THE FIRST GENERAL ELECTIONS IN independent India were to be held at the end of 1951. Nehru himself was coming south to Andhra to drum up support for Congress Party candidates. Satyam, Sulaiman, Rama Rao, and Subba Rao made plans to take the bus to Guntur, where the man who'd ordered the massacre of the people's army in Telangana would be speaking.

The Congress Party had reason to be concerned about its fate in the elections, especially in Andhra. All across India, Nehru's government was facing demands for a redivision of the old provincial boundaries drawn up by the British. At least thirty major languages are spoken in India, and several of these linguistic groups were asking for states of their own.

When the British ruled the subcontinent, they divided it up for their own convenience into units called provinces or presidencies. The whole of south India was contained in the Madras Presidency. Within this province lived speakers of four mutually unintelligible languages: Tamils, who spoke Tamil; Andhras, who spoke Telugu; Kannadigas, who spoke Kannada; and Malayalis, who spoke Malayalam.

When independence came, Nehru and the Congress not only kept these very different peoples lumped together in one province but also imposed the north-Indian language of Hindi on them and everyone else as the national language.

The Telugus were at the forefront of agitation for a separate state. The rich peasantry—kammas, reddys, and *kapus*—who now had profits from agriculture were looking to invest it somewhere. But Andhra had little industry, and that was dominated by the north-Indian baniyas and marwaris (moneylender, merchant, and trader castes) represented by Congress. The Telugu elite needed to drive out competition from non-Telugus and carve out a territory for themselves.

The demand for an Andhra state had grown so popular that, as elections approached, Nehru was forced to concede to it in principle. But he clearly wasn't happy with the idea, and still less with the precedent it set for other parts of the country.

So when Nehru came south, protest was in the air. He faced angry crowds in Vizag after admitting that he was personally against linguistic provinces. He claimed to be willing to make an exception in the case of Andhra, but few took comfort in this assurance.

At Guntur, Nehru attracted the largest crowd of the whole tour. He was pleased because he planned to give his most important speech of the southern campaign there, to be delivered in both English and Hindi— the language of the former colonial rulers and the language that the northern native rulers were trying to force on the South.

But when he stood up to speak, he faced a sea of ominous black flags. Among the hundreds of thousands forming the tightly packed mass were Satyam and his friends—who, since they didn't have any flags to bring, came equipped instead with black umbrellas.

Nehru looked out uneasily at the vast, unruly throng. They were chanting something he couldn't make out, but it didn't have a friendly ring.

He started to speak, confident that his oratory would win over and silence any hostile voices. But his microphone failed. He looked about helplessly. No one seemed to know what the problem was. In desperation, he tried doing without the sound system, but his voice was hoarse from the strain of the tour, and the crowd kept growing louder.

Enraged, Nehru turned to the local Congress leaders seated behind him and took them to task for not having arranged a working public address system, not to mention a more disciplined audience. As he yelled, the microphone mysteriously started working, picking up his bitter, contemptuous tirade and transmitting it through the loudspeakers for all to hear.

When Nehru realized what had happened, he tried to resume his speech. But after a minute, his microphone failed again.

So he went on without it, addressing the crowd in Hindi and English, trying to make himself heard as best he could. But his frail, aristocratic cadences were drowned out by the thunderous slogan echoing from every corner like a war cry:

"We want Andhra State! We want Andhra State!"

Nehru walked off. He had been scheduled to speak for an hour but lasted only twenty minutes. On his way out, he called the disturbances an insult to the many people gathered to hear his words. But everyone knew he'd been shouted down.

Police officials escorted him from the scene. It was dangerous for him to be in town at all. He was whisked to the train station in a jeep.

But the waving black flags of the multitude followed Nehru like death, swarming around the special train waiting to take him away. Satyam and his friends found a spot right along the tracks.

As the train pulled out, Nehru made a show of waving goodbye to his supporters from an open door. Waiting at the side of the track as the prime minister's car was passing, Satyam saw his chance. He darted forward to grab Nehru's arm and pull him down. The old man withdrew his hands with a look of utter terror and disappeared into the car.

At Guntur that day, Satyam met more Communists than he had ever before seen in one place. He learned that it was the Communists who had brought in the angry anti-Nehru throngs. And a Communist, working as an audio technician, had sabotaged the public address system.

Satyam received a Communist booklet explaining how the Telugus had been hindered from blossoming culturally and economically. How their growth was stunted, their resources stolen. The waters of the Kaveri River, which flows through Telugu country into Kannada country, were called *sisuvu ku dakkani stanyam*, "mother's breast milk denied to the infant," in a poem by Sri Sri that concluded the booklet.

No slogans like "Out with the Indian army!," "Down with the doras' rule!," or "Land to the tiller!" were raised at Guntur that day. The protesters had been mustered around the watchword Visalandhra (Greater Andhra), a call to carve out a Telugu state from Madras and merge it with Telangana. It wasn't a new slogan for the Andhra Communists, but it had turned into their principal one. Visalandhra had meant little to the impoverished rural masses who rallied to the Communist banner in the days of the armed struggle—it did not touch their concerns. But the Communists were now appealing to different sections of society. They launched a new party newspaper and called it *Visalandhra*.

Satyam asked the Communists he met at Guntur how he could work for the party. They gave him two tasks. One was to organize the landless madiga laborers in Telaprolu into an agricultural union. The other was to spread propaganda throughout the surrounding area in a folk style called *burra katha*, which combines singing, dancing, storytelling, and social commentary. Party youth were going from village to village in burra katha troupes to agitate for socialism and a "separate Andhra." Sri Sri even set up a workshop in the village of Pedapudi to train these performers. Satyam quickly picked up the style on his own and formed a troupe with the thief Subba Rao as the main singer.

◎

IN SATYAM'S MIND HIS WORK among the laborers in the madiga goodem and in the villages with his burra katha troupe was all in preparation for a renewal of the armed struggle throughout the region. He was excited when, one afternoon, Senagala Viswanatha Reddy came to see him at the tea stall. The leading Communist of Telaprolu, Reddy had gone underground when the Nehru government started hunting party members, only to be tracked down and jailed. He had recently been released and had returned to live with his family in Telaprolu.

Senagala Viswanatha Reddy took Satyam aside to tell him the party would be holding a secret meeting in the village. It was the first time Satyam had ever been invited to a party meeting. When he inquired about its agenda, he was told, "Ahh, that is top secret."

Some forty members from twenty or thirty villages, among them the most important comrades from the whole Gannavaram area, were invited to the secret meeting. It was held in the place police would least expect to find a gathering of Communists, the Rama Temple.

On the day of the meeting, those invited arrived at the temple one by one. They were led into a spacious, gloomy room in back. Everyone sat on straw mats laid out on the floor except for the speaker, who took a seat at a little table in front. Another chair beside him was for the chairman of the meeting.

But there was no consensus as to who should act as chairman. Senagala Viswanatha Reddy was nominated, but others objected on the grounds that he had some internal charges pending against him. Another senior comrade, Pulla Reddy, was proposed. But Pulla Reddy also had some charges pending. Everyone whose name came up seemed to have some charge or other pending.

At last it was decided that Satyam, though only twenty and not nearly as senior a cadre as many of those present, was the most fit to act as chairman. No charges of any kind were pending against him, and he'd been the sole party activist in Telaprolu for the past couple of years.

So the meeting was called to order and the speaker, Anjaneya Shastri, began his report. Satyam observed that Shastri had typical brahmin looks and mannerisms. His teeth protruded a little beyond the bounds of his lips, and when he spoke, the words came out in such a rush that it was hard to catch them.

Shastri started by describing the origins of the people's movement in Telangana. Those assembled listened with interest. He wasn't saying anything they didn't already know, but they thought surely he must be leading up to some important news.

Shastri recounted the heroic course of the struggle, how many cadres fought, how many troops were raised, how many squads were organized, how many rifles they carried, and so on. His audience kept waiting to hear the purpose of the meeting. As the speaker came to the end of his allotted two hours, he turned from the greatness of the struggle to the difficulties faced by the people's army, the vicious repression it had endured. His audience was by now exhausted from the effort of following this long speech.

Surveying the puzzled group before him with satisfaction, Shastri sped on to his conclusion. Nehru's army was strong and well equipped. The people's army had only this many rifles left, it had lost this many troops. "And so it has been necessary to withdraw the armed struggle," he said in closing.

The words "withdraw" and "armed struggle" jolted everyone out of their stupor. But they were all too stunned to speak.

The first to find his voice was Subba Rao. He was not a literate man, but he had been Satyam's friend for two years now, and everything Satyam read or heard about he explained to Subba Rao.

Satyam had heard from this mouth and that mouth that the leaders of the party had split over whether to continue the armed struggle. The two factions were so deadlocked they finally resolved to ask Stalin himself to settle the question. Posing as crew members on a Soviet ship leaving from Calcutta, four of the top leaders of the Communist Party of India sailed to Moscow. They returned with a report of their discussions with Comrade Kishen (their code name for Stalin) and his top deputies. No one Satyam knew had ever laid eyes on this legendary Kishen Report, but its conclusions were well known: the people's army must make a tactical retreat, regroup, and then march on Krishna, Guntur, and the other coastal districts. Satyam and his friends had been waiting to take up guns and join this struggle. They knew it was coming, the only question was when.

But what Shastri had just told them didn't seem to allow for this scenario. So Subba Rao stood up and asked, "Okay, sir, we will retreat, but only to march forward, is it not?"

Shastri answered, "Don't entertain any hopes! If you do, we take no responsibility for it."

Satyam felt sorry for his friend. Subba Rao must have used the wrong tone. His question had been misunderstood. As chairman of the meeting, Satyam interceded, entreating, "Oh, Mr. Shastri, please don't be angry. We know Comrade Stalin said to retreat only to regroup, but you only spoke of retreating. Can you please explain, for our sake, what comes after this retreat?"

Shastri rapped on the table. "There is nothing to explain!"

That made it clear. He wasn't there to discuss the decision he was handing down. After that, no one had anything else to say, and the meeting soon concluded.

Shortly after the temple meeting, Satyam met Thuppeta Subba Rao, an untouchable schoolteacher from Krishna district who had gone to fight in Telangana.

When the party announced that the armed struggle was being withdrawn at the advice of Stalin, Thuppeta Subba Rao was furious. He could not believe Stalin would say such a thing. He insisted on seeing the Kishen Report with his own eyes. The leaders had to show him a copy. He showed it to Satyam.

Satyam read the report and saw the party had not been lying. Stalin wanted the peasants to put down their guns.

With this report from Stalin the party leadership was able to silence the many cadres who bitterly opposed ending the armed struggle. The leadership gave in to Nehru without even demanding amnesty for the ten thousand party members who were rotting in detention camps. The leaders were eager to campaign in the upcoming elections.

Thuppeta Subba Rao had a lot to tell Satyam. To members such as him who had risked their lives and sacrificed their livelihoods, the party had nothing to offer. They were forced to live by hard labor—pulling rickshaws, carrying loads of bricks on their heads, and laying roads—while still on the run from the police.

Yet the party did make arrangements to protect the top leaders who remained in hiding. Cunning arrangements. They realized that everyone would expect to find them hiding out in poor neighborhoods among their untouchable followers. That's the first place police would go looking for Communists.

So the party leaders did the opposite, hiding out in the most luxurious circumstances imaginable. They installed themselves in fabulous mansions that had until recently belonged to Muslim aristocrats who had been ousted along with the Nizam, now converted into hotels. To fit into these surroundings convincingly, they went so far as to outfit themselves in expensive clothes and sunglasses.

These things that Satyam heard from Thuppeta Subba Rao made him think. He thought about what he'd seen with his own eyes since coming to Telaprolu.

The reddys of Telaprolu were all Communists. And every one of them owned sixty or seventy acres of land. Papa's classmates wore silk and gold and lived on butter and curds.

He heard these things, saw these things, but what did they mean? According to the laws of dialectics as Hanumayya had explained them back at A.C. College, all things contain contradictions. That is because they are always in motion, either arising and developing or disintegrating and dying away.

Both rich peasants and landless laborers were in the party. Was it necessary for the laborers to ally with the rich peasants to defeat the big landlords? Which was the horse and which was the rider?

Elections were coming. The Communist candidates filed their nominations while still hiding out in the jungles. This was the first election in India with no property requirement to participate. The poor people were eager to vote for the heroes who'd led an armed struggle under the

slogan of "land to the tiller." And the rich peasants who supported the uprising against the Nizam now rallied to the slogan closest to their hearts:
"Separate Andhra." By banning Communist candidates, Nehru would
only undermine the legitimacy of the whole system. He decided to let
them run.

The Communists held an election rally in Telaprolu. They led a procession through the village to draw in support. Satyam marched in front
with a red flag. One of the landlords whose estates they were passing ran
up and stopped the march, demanding to speak to the leaders. One of the
landlord's *palerus* (bonded laborers) had left his work to join the rally, and
the landlord wanted his slave sent back. The Communists asked the paleru
why he had joined without the landlord's permission. The man replied he
had asked permission that morning but the landlord had refused. When
the laborer saw the people marching past with their flags and banners,
shouting slogans, he was inspired to join them. The Communists took the
paleru by his arms, returned him to his master, and marched on.

Satyam was stunned. He lowered his red flag. "What is this?"

He was told that the servant belonged to his master. When the paleru
became a paleru, he must have entered an agreement. An agreement between two people cannot be dissolved by a third party.

"But the purpose of a Communist party is to break those agreements,"
Satyam pointed out.

The leaders had nothing to say to that.

Satyam saw the contradictions. But he led the rally onward. What was
more important in the end, that the paleru be allowed to join the rally? Or
that there was a party whose rally this paleru and millions like him longed
to join in defiance of their masters? Who was it for, this red flag Satyam
waved?

Poor peasants, rich peasants, they all came out to support the Communist candidates. They came out in the hundreds of thousands in their
bullock carts adorned with mango leaves, turmeric, and vermilion. To
cheer them on, troupes of young people sang and danced with their costumes and their cardboard props. A beautiful and talented seventeen-
year-old madiga girl in Satyam's troupe by the name of Akhilabai drew all

eyes to their performances. They started early, at five in the morning, going around to the different caste colonies with four drums. They sang to wake up the public, to welcome the sun:

> Go, brother, go!
> Go and see
> How the world goes on.

> Go, brother, go!
> This so-called Rama's kingdom
> Is a kingdom of demons only.
> Go fire up your fury
> Until this very government
> Lies dead.

On the day before elections, Communist supporters from all the surrounding villages gathered in one huge rally in Telaprolu. At the end of the day Satyam was the speaker at a public meeting. He began by saluting the martyrs of the armed struggle and explained the need for a separate state. The crowd broke out in cheers. Then, even though it had no place in the program the party was running on, Satyam called for a fight for a socialist society, "which alone can make bloom *Kalahari lo kalulavu*" (lotuses in the Kalahari). Papa teased him about that line: "Is this a speech or a poetry reading?"

For a party coming off a military defeat, with their candidates hurrying from jail cells to campaign platforms, the Communists polled spectacularly well. While they did not take power in the state, they entered the legislature as the main opposition party.

◎

ONCE THE ELECTIONS WERE OVER, Satyam had to find other outlets for his militant spirit.

During the months leading up to and following the elections, Andhra

faced severe food shortages. Food riots broke out in many places along the
coast, with hungry mobs pillaging grain banks.

According to the proponents of the Separate Andhra movement, the
lack of a Telugu state was to blame for the suffering. There were rumors
that food was being shipped out of Andhra to Tamil-speaking areas within
the Madras Presidency.

Whatever the truth, people were hungry and the central government
was doing nothing to help them. Conditions were especially desperate
among those who in ordinary times had the least. Satyam and his friends
were determined to do something.

Day and night, lorries ran along Trunk Road. Lorries full of rice.

And then one night, at one in the morning, a dog barked. A thin man
emerged from the dark and stepped into the headlights of a speeding lorry.

The lorry made a sharp turn and screeched to a stop, blocking the road
and stopping a caravan of lorries behind it. Satyam climbed into the back
of the first lorry he had stopped.

The dog barked again. An emaciated ghost sitting on its haunches
behind the bushes along the one-lane highway rose to his feet and ran silently toward the lorry. Then another ghost and another, tens of them,
moved out from the shadows.

As they gathered on the highway, Subba Rao, the onetime thief, dispatched the thirty young men who formed the vanguard to take control of
the fifteen lorries in teams of two. Their weapons were sticks.

The lorry drivers may or may not have been sympathetic to the plight
of the hungry looters. The madiga men bound their hands and led them
off to the roadside.

Sulaiman's first bark meant "Be ready." His second meant "Appropri-
ate the food." Having removed the drivers, the men quickly climbed inside
the lorries and handed down sacks of rice to the women waiting outside
in a line, who passed them from one to the other to a low-lying spot that
could not be seen from the road. Long ditches had been dug in advance to
conceal the plunder.

At 4:30 a.m. at an emergency meeting of the goodem labor union, the
action was declared a success, but retaliation was expected. As it had been

Satyam's plan, he was the first one the police would be looking for. He had to leave immediately.

Satyam looked around at the wretched men and women he had been working among for the past two years. He would not see them again.

In Telaprolu, Satyam had transformed himself from a dreamer in a library into an organizer. "My friend Telaprolu," he later wrote. "You were my study center. My comrade Telaprolu, you were the first chapter in my lifelong struggle. Red salute!"

THREE

⊚ ⊚ ⊚

FLEEING TELAPROLU ON THE REAR rack of a bicycle pedaled by Subba Rao, Satyam made his way to Gudivada. The old family house in Slatter Peta was still there, and still belonged to his grandmother. The widow Bodemma was still living across the street. Mr. Guntur Bapanayya and his family were still there, too.

Guntur Bapanayya had been a Communist member of the legislative assembly (MLA) since 1952. Back when Satyam was a teenage Congress supporter, he'd disapproved of Mr. Bapanayya and used to smile when Carey taunted him on the street. Today Satyam was filled with admiration for this man whose fame had spread far.

Though Bapanayya's name means "brahmin man," he was an untouchable. In his manner and his way of life, Bapanayya personified the simplicity that people associate with communism. MLA though he was, he was so kind and unassuming that you would never have known it. He wore the humblest clothes, thongs on his feet, and combed his hair forward over his brow. His whole family lived in a single room rented out by a poor widow. When Bapanayya first moved to Slatter Peta and met Papa, who was still living there at the time, his heart went out to the poor motherless child. He would call her over and carefully remove the lice from her hair, crushing them between his nails.

Some said he wasn't very militant, and there was truth in the charge. During the repression of the armed struggle, he was jailed along with other leaders in the town of Kaikalur and languished there without trial in filthy and unlivable conditions. But when guerrillas attacked the prison to give their comrades a chance to escape, Bapanayya alone remained in his cell. He spent years there until the Communist political prisoners were finally let out.

Bapanayya's desire to serve the poor and downtrodden was sincere, and for this reason his popularity among untouchables was unmatched. He easily won every election until his death, after which it was hard to get a Communist elected in that constituency.

Satyam met Bapanayya's teenage brother-in-law, Nancharayya, who had recently quit college and was living with his mother in an untouchable shantytown on the outskirts of town called Chinavani Goodem. Nancharayya's face was black as coal, with bulging yellow eyes and a knobby nose. The moment you looked at him, you could see he was an untouchable and the son of illiterate coolies. He was proud of this and looked down on untouchables who saw themselves as better than their brethren for being educated or having converted to Christianity. Despite his devotion to his Communist brother-in-law, during his brief stint in college Nancharayya became an Ambedkarite, an admirer of the untouchable leader Ambedkar, who tried to organize untouchables in a separate party to demand legal and social reforms.

As soon as Nancharayya laid eyes on Satyam, he fell in love with him.

It was the purest love, pure as crystal. Satyam's intelligence, his charisma, simply amazed Nancharayya. While he didn't have a sophisticated grasp of Satyam's politics, Nancharayya admired him as a fighter on behalf of the poor. He became devoted to him, taking over for Satyam's brother and sister in doing those things Satyam wouldn't do for himself: shaving his chin, clipping his nails, handing him tooth powder, bringing him food when he was hungry.

Nancharayya was a great joker. Every occasion in his life—whether the birth of a baby or the death of his mother—was a source of jokes for him. "Kadedi kavithaku anarham" (Name one thing that isn't fit for poetry), wrote Sri Sri. Nancharayya might have said, "Kadedi hasyamu-naku anarham" (Name one thing that isn't fit to be made fun of). He finally brought Satyam out of the gloom in which he'd been living since Flora refused him. Nancharayya made him laugh again.

Not long after they met, in the spring of 1952, Nancharayya proposed an idea over tea at the Taj Mahal hotel. He told Satyam they should form a branch of the Communist Party's People's Theater in Gudivada. Though not himself a Communist, Nancharayya had played in a Communist the-ater troupe in college. A gifted performer, he also knew how to direct and choreograph. A propaganda street-theater troupe like the ones the party sponsored in other places would be an excellent forum for his talents. Satyam, meanwhile, could put his own skills to use and give vent to his militancy in these quieter days.

They took the idea to the party leaders and were told there was no money for such a thing. During the armed struggle, even the Gudivada party unit had found the money to sponsor propaganda troupes. Now no one would think of it. "Have you lost your minds?" they asked. "We can hardly afford to keep up our whole-timers. Do you know how much it costs for even simple sets and lighting? And actors and dancers would need to be paid on top of that."

But Satyam and Nancharayya were determined to find a way. They went off to think the problem over. Satyam followed his friend home to Chinavani Goodem. After Nancharayya's mother fed them, they went out into the chilly winter night wrapped in an old blanket. Nancharayya showed

Satyam the canal flowing beside the shantytown. They came upon a *ballakattu*, a kind of raft, moored along the bank. Nancharayya knew the man who plied the ballakattu and his wife well. The two friends sat down on the side of the vessel. Wrapped in their blanket, smoking cigarettes and drinking tea supplied by the ballakattu man's wife, they talked and laughed into the early hours. Every now and then a passenger came by and they would go back and forth across the canal. There, under the bright moonlight, they came up with a plan.

◎

THE CASTE WHOSE OCCUPATION IS the most degrading, the most indecent, the most inhuman of all, is known in coastal Andhra as *pakis*. In print, they are called manual scavengers or, more euphemistically still, porters of night soil. In plain language, they carry away human shit. They empty the "dry" latrines still widely used throughout India, and they do it by hand. Their tools are nothing but a small broom and a tin plate. With these, they fill their palm-leaf baskets with excrement and carry it off on their heads five, six miles to some place on the outskirts of town where they're allowed to dispose of it. Some modernized areas have replaced these baskets with pushcarts (this being what's thought of as progress in India), but even today the traditional "head-loading" method prevails across the country.

Nearly all of these workers are women. They don't know what gloves are, let alone have them. As their brooms wear down, they have to bend their backs lower and lower to sweep. When their baskets start to leak, the shit drips down their faces. In the rainy season, the filth runs all over these people, onto their hair, into their eyes, their noses, their mouths. Tuberculosis and other infectious diseases are endemic among them.

When India developed into a modern society with public buildings, schools, offices, railways, cinema halls, and sewage systems, these paki men and women were hired as janitors and sanitation workers. Since the pakis' work is a caste occupation, their wages are not true compensation but charity that may be given or withheld. Because of the resulting fluctuations in their income, most pakis are forced to borrow at high rates and become mired in debt. Even their hours of work are irregular. Those who work for the railway are told a day's work stops when the trains stop coming. The trains never stop coming.

The pakis of Gudivada lived in a separate *peta* of their own, located behind the Gowri Sankar Cinema Hall. Cinema halls were typically built in poor neighborhoods because better-off people wouldn't live within range of the noise. But the Gudivada pakis loved having a noisy cinema hall right beside their homes. From outside its walls they could enjoy the music and dialogue all day and all night. And they befriended the ushers, who when the hall was not full would let them in to sit for free in the floor class (that is, on the bare floor—the cheapest class of seating in Indian theaters). By the first or second week of a movie's run, every paki in Gudivada could recite all its dialogue word for word, with every nuance in tone, and sing all the songs. At night, they would get in for the late show that otherwise only unrespectable types, and the prostitutes they brought with them, attended and learn the dances that went with the songs. Every man, woman, and child in the paki colony loved to perform. Even the elderly pakis loved to dance, although they preferred their traditional *koya* dances to the cinema choreography their children and grandchildren were learning.

Satyam's idea was to recruit volunteer performers from the paki colony in place of paid professionals. Nancharayya predicted just how the party leaders would react. He described the scene acting out the reactions of the party leaders, mimicking their voices and gestures. Yelling, seething, his nostrils quivering, his face turning red, he showed Satyam what he should expect.

And that was just the reaction Satyam received. What will it do to the party's reputation, the district leaders demanded, to associate publicly with such dirty people?

In the 1940s, when the Communist Party first came to Gudivada, the pakis were spontaneously drawn to it. But after setting up a paki union and a municipal union for the paki sanitation workers, the party did little organizing among this community. The only member who had anything to do with them was the town secretary, an impoverished kamma man named Atloori Seetharamayya, who was also secretary of the paki union. On this account the other kammas in the party used to mockingly refer to him as "Paki Seetharamayya." They never considered him and his wife as their own because they subsisted on food donated by the pakis.

After the district leaders went off shaking their heads, Satyam got Atloori Seetharamayya to call a meeting of the town committee. At the meeting Satyam explained at length how absurd it was for a party of the oppressed to be ashamed of being represented by the oppressed. A chasm had opened within the party between the haves and have-nots. It had to be returned to its proletarian tradition.

Atloori Seetharamayya, while sympathetic, was not a deep political thinker and, in any case, had no funds at his disposal. But he told Satyam if he wanted to go out and recruit a troupe that expected no payment and performed at its own expense—well, he was welcome to try.

That was all Satyam needed to hear. He and Nancharayya walked right over to the paki peta behind the cinema hall. Satyam had never seen houses and alleys cleaner than the ones he found there.

They met Adinarayana, the secretary of the all-paki municipal workers' union, who was delighted with their plan. The residents of the colony were no less keen. The only problem was, they were all busy. One good thing for pakis in Gudivada was that enough shit was produced in the town every day to give every able-bodied man, woman, and child among them paying work. Only after they got back home in the evening, scrubbed themselves clean, and put on fresh clothes were they ready to perform.

Satyam recruited ten residents of the colony to sing, dance, and play instruments for the troupe. Many children, both boys and girls, offered to join. Two paki sisters known as Pedda Parvathi (Big Parvathi) and Chinna Parvathi (Small Parvathi)—one thirteen, the other eight—were excellent dancers, the little one especially. Eighteen-year-old Venkatesu could really play *doluk* (a type of drum). To these Satyam added mala laborers recruited from Mandapadu, including one Maddali Venkateswara Rao, the greatest singer in the whole area.

Satyam decided to give his troupe a name that would set it apart from the People's Theater groups sponsored by the party in other places. He no longer believed that all of the "people" were on the same side. As he saw it, two lines operated within the party, a feudal line and a proletarian line. He called his performers the Toilers Cultural Forum.

Once assembled, the Toilers had little time to prepare. In the second week of January, on the eve of the harvest festival, the Communist youth organization was holding a districtwide dance and drama competition in the village of Guraja, twenty-five kilometers away. The Gudivada town committee refused to give the Toilers bus fare to get there. But Satyam would not be discouraged. "The Chinese, they walked thousands of miles," he said. "What is twenty-five kilometers?" So, taking inspiration from Mao's Long March, the fifteen troupe members loaded their props, costumes, and instruments on their backs and set off on foot.

The Toilers had prepared two plays to present for the competition. In the first, a landlord finds out some of his harvest is missing. He blames the paleru and punishes him brutally. Unfortunately, by the time the troupe reached Guraja, the man who played the paleru was shaking violently. He had come down with a high fever from walking in the sun and was unable to perform. The second play, called *Rickshaw Puller*, about the inhumanity of using a man as a beast of burden, proved impossible to stage for lack of a key prop. The troupe couldn't find a single pulling rickshaw in Guraja to use for the performance—they'd all been replaced by rickshaw cycles.

Greatly disappointed not to be able to take part in the drama competition, they decided to enter for singing and dancing. They had formidable rivals in the troupes from Guraja and Mudinepalli, another big center of Communist theater. Those troupes had elaborate sets and props and paid performers, many of whom would soon move on to Madras, the cine capital of south India. They were lavishly funded by rich kamma supporters, landowners who intended to turn their agricultural profits into capital by investing in the rising film industry. Accordingly, the People's Theater troupes served to train aspiring kamma stars, directors, screenwriters, and lyricists.

The competition at Guraja went on for days. At the end of the week they announced the prizes. Chinna Parvathi, the eight-year-old girl, won first prize for dance, and Satyam first prize for singing. The audience's verdict gave Satyam the courage to approach the party leaders gathered there and ask them to invite the Toilers to perform in their home villages. They all refused this offer with a comradely smile. The paki dancers were too wild, they explained, and spoke funny Telugu. "No, mister," they said, "your shows are too much like *mala bhagothams*" (Indian minstrel shows performed by untouchables).

But then a big, burly man came up to Satyam. He smiled and offered many encouraging words to the Toilers. When the man introduced himself, Satyam recognized his name immediately. Back in Telaprolu, the librarian used to tell him, "You are like Kondapalli Seetharamayya. He used to cycle from Jonnapadu to read in this library."

Kondapalli Seetharami Reddy was the son of a landowning reddy family. Like the great Sundarayya, the main organizer of the Telangana revolt, he dropped the caste name Reddy to signal his rejection of caste feeling. He and his wife had joined the party in their youth, at the time of the armed struggle. While she toured the countryside in the People's Theater, he took training in firearms and went off to fight in Telangana. He had a reputation for being good at wielding a stick and training others in hand-to-hand combat. This last part, inevitably, was what impressed Satyam most. He admired this man, twenty years his senior, who was distrusted by the party leadership but had a following among the militant youth. Seetharamayya likewise saw something special in Satyam. Their meeting at Guraja would be the beginning of a long, eventful association.

After the competition, the Toilers were exhausted. Nancharayya put Chinna Parvathi and another little girl on a bus, while the rest of the troupe, including the poor man with a fever, set off on the long march back home.

From then on the Toilers put on shows in one or another of the low-caste colonies in Gudivada every evening except for Sundays, when the municipal workers had a day off and the troupe could travel to neighboring villages. They had to do their own publicity on the way to the venue, so instead of taking the shortest route, they would walk through four or five nearby villages to advertise the show, chanting slogans and singing revolutionary songs as they went. They crossed rice fields and mango groves, carrying their drums, their harmonium box, and their gaslights on their heads and their costumes and makeup in sacks. They would always raise a pair of red flags, one in front and one in back of their procession. Children would follow them from village to village to see the show.

When they arrived at the malapalli or madiga goodem where they were performing, they announced their show by circling the colony two or three times, beating their madiga drums, and clapping their hands. They performed outside on the ground. For lighting, they tied a stick up crosswise and hung two gas lanterns from it. In place of curtains, they borrowed straw mats from the villagers.

Before each performance, Satyam would make a brief political speech. Then the troupe would sing and dance. Before the drama started, Satyam would announce that the actors had to leave as soon as it ended so they could get up early for their jobs, but that he and "Mr. Director" (Nancharayya) would be spending the night. "In the morning we will be coming from door to door," he told the crowd. "Please, we ask you to give us a fistful of rice." On their way back to Gudivada they would sell the rice they'd collected. It might fetch fifteen rupees. Five rupees went to rent the gaslights for another week. Another five rupees went to the family of their lead singer, who was the most desperately impoverished member of the troupe. The remainder they put into a fund for other expenses that came up. The local people would arrange meals for the troupe.

Fond of that *Rickshaw Puller* play, Satyam and Nancharayya kept a lookout for a pulling rickshaw. Finally, they spotted one in front of the house of a government doctor. They went to see the doctor-amma, hoping to borrow it for a single night's performance. But she was glad to get rid of it. So the Toilers were able at last to stage a production of the play, which turned out to be a great success, and from then on they carried all their equipment in that rickshaw, which could easily be pulled by one man.

◎

BACK IN TELAPROLU, PRASANNA RAO'S other two children were getting ready for their final exams. Prasanna Rao had no worries about his daughter, but Carey was a constant concern.

Carey, at sixteen, was a wild kid, always getting into fights. Twice he had been expelled from high school.

The first time was in Gudivada, after a battle with the Kathari brothers. The Katharis were a golla family who through gangsterism, it was said, had acquired a monopoly over the bus routes out of Gudivada. The three Kathari brothers were older classmates of Carey's. These sons of the bus baron ruled the school, intimidating students and teachers alike. They wouldn't let Carey and his untouchable friends use the playground. One day the conflict broke into a scuffle when Carey punched one of the brothers in the mouth. That was just the beginning. The Katharis' gang and Carey's gang clashed throughout the day, chasing each other through school corridors and finally into the streets to fight it out in the main bazaar.

The next day the headmaster expelled Carey, and Carey alone. He had to go live with his father in Telaprolu and enroll in his father's school.

In Telaprolu, Carey again got himself expelled. A classmate of his threw a paper rocket at his teacher. Carey knew who did this but wouldn't say. The teacher sent him to the headmaster, who prepared to cane him. Carey was indignant. Why should he be punished for refusing to snitch? He grabbed the headmaster's wrist and held it tightly—so tightly that the headmaster not only dropped the cane but fell to the floor and broke into tears.

Prasanna Rao asked Carey's best friend, Pulla Reddy, to keep an eye on Carey for him. Pulla Reddy obligingly asked his friend if anything was troubling him. Carey confided that he was plagued by urges that he knew were morally wrong but could not control: he longed to touch and fondle girls. Carey could never think of one code for himself and another for other people. That females of all sorts were always chasing after him only deepened his predicament. Pulla Reddy felt for his friend's anguish even while being privately amused by it.

Carey's unwelcome impulses finally got him into trouble during the annual *mela*, a weeklong village festival. He spotted a reddy girl who had just emerged from the temple where she'd gone to pray. She stood on the veranda with one arm raised over her head, resting her hand against a pillar, watching the setting sun. Carey saw her breast silhouetted by the evening light. He couldn't help sneaking up behind her to feel it, startling her.

A hullabaloo broke out when the caste men saw this. An untouchable kid cupping a caste girl's breast, and in a temple no less. They ran up the temple stairs and surrounded him. Carey wasn't scared, only ashamed. Just at that moment his caste friend Jagga Reddy rushed up, shouting, "Hettt! Toottt!"—flinging his arms and legs every which way to distract the men and give Carey a chance to escape.

Carey could have gotten his whole family killed over such an episode. He knew he couldn't let a thing like that ever happen again.

He fell two years behind in school due to the expulsions, then further still by failing English. He had fallen so far behind, he'd become his younger sister's classmate. The headmaster told him, "You will come to nothing." Carey was deeply hurt, but never showed it.

The next year when Carey and Papa got their hall tickets for the final exams, they couldn't believe their eyes. Not only were they assigned the same exam center, but by sheer chance their seats were right next to each other.

Carey's weak point was English. Papa knew Carey might fail again and worried how that would affect him. When the English exam was passed out, she lifted her paper to let her brother cheat. But Carey stared down at his own paper without flinching.

"Lord Jesus, praise be unto you," intoned Prasanna Rao a month later when the newspapers published the exam numbers. Carey had passed.

But neither of his sons could ever make Prasanna Rao as proud as his daughter did. Papa won gold medals for maths, science, and English, and silver medals for Telugu and social studies. Wearing his best pants and shirt, Prasanna Rao attended the honors ceremony and received the awards on her behalf.

By then Papa was already in Gudivada. She and Carey were so eager to join their brother there that they left the very evening they finished their last exam. They were going to Gudivada College for Intermediate. Their grandmother soon followed to keep house for the three of them.

◎

LIKE SATYAM BEFORE THEM, CAREY and Manjula (as Papa began to be known) were going off to college without the means to do so. Despite what their father was earning from private tutoring, he still had many commitments to poorer relatives. He didn't have enough to support two children in their studies.

Satyam sought advice from Mr. Bapanayya, who suggested they apply for scholarships available to untouchables.

To apply, they needed a municipal councilman to sign a form attesting that Manjula and Carey were Adi-Andhra (untouchable) Christians. Mr. Jalari Immanuel, the council member from Slatter Peta, flatly refused. Immanuel was one of those untouchable Christians who like to delude themselves that conversion from Hinduism has freed them from the caste system. "There are no touchables and untouchables in the eyes of our Lord Jesus," he scolded Satyam. "You should be ashamed to think of yourselves in those terms." Immanuel wrote in their caste as simply "Andhra Christian," then signed, stamped, and handed back the forms.

For Satyam it was a minute's work to add *Adi-* in front of the words *Andhra Christian* in a careful imitation of the councilman's handwriting. As promised, Mr. Bapanayya saw to it that the applications were approved right away.

The scholarships would pay for books and tuition. Their father would send rice and lentils for meals. The three siblings planned to lead a beautiful, disciplined life together, to live according to their ideals. Reuniting in Gudivada, the three were so inseparable that people came to refer to them as a single entity: Satyam-Carey-Manjula.

Six hundred and fifty boys were in Manjula's college to only fifty girls. Even though it was a coed school, the sexes were so segregated that they never even entered a classroom together. The boys went in freely while the girls had to wait in the ladies' waiting room until informed that the lecturer was passing by. The girls then lowered their eyes to the ground and fell into step behind the lecturer. As he led them into the classroom, the boys all stood up. To an outsider it might have looked as though the boys were being chivalrous to the girls, but in fact they were showing respect to the master. The girls took their seats together on one side of the room in a row close to the dais, while the boys all sat on the other side.

At Gudivada College, 90 percent of the lecturers and students were of the kamma caste. In Manjula's batch of only thirteen girls were seven kammas, one was kapu, and five were malas. Unlike in Guntur, with its well-off, educated population of "traditional Christians," the boys in Gudivada College didn't care for mala girls. At the end of the first week, someone mischievously posted in the ladies' waiting room a list of the nicknames assigned by the boys to the girls they saw in class. Anasooya, who walked in with her eyes glued to the floor, was Blushing Bride. Vidyadhari was Maya Sasirekha, a mythological Hindu princess. The kamma girls were given fond nicknames, while the mala girls received insulting ones such as Fat Calf (Sampoorna) and Wan Sheep (Manjula).

Although the girls all stuck together and even walked to and from school as a group, the caste girls looked straight past the mala girls and never bothered to learn their names. The mala girls, used to such treatment in their home villages, didn't think anything of it.

But there was one mala girl whom all the caste girls were fond of and wanted to be friends with: Manjula. The caste girls thought of her as "advanced," as "fast," as hardworking, as friendly, as soft-spoken and well-spoken. The reasons had everything to do with her upbringing.

The other mala girls in her class had lived all their lives segregated in malapallis. They came from impoverished, illiterate backgrounds and were the first in their families to be educated. Among caste people they felt inferior and out of place. Manjula, on the other hand, had spent years living in a village proper, where the rich reddys treated her family with respect. Whenever Manjula went out, they would say, "There goes the master's daughter."

Manjula's most singular advantage, what set her ahead even of the caste girls in her class, was her connection to her elder brother. It was highly uncommon for college students to read literature, and this was especially true for girls. Manjula had read Sarat novels in high school, and the summer before college she had read the short stories of India's Nobel laureate Rabindranath Tagore *in English*. She read the poetry of Sri Sri, the height of cultural fashion among young people. Her own brother, who was fast becoming as distinguished as Sri Sri, showed his poems to *her* for approval. Under his influence, she could even talk about world politics.

When Manjula returned home, she would tell Satyam every single thing that had happened to her that day from the time she went off to school. She left nothing out, reciting every little incident in the order it occurred as though she were picking up beads and stringing them one by one on a long thread. He listened as she talked on and on about the events of her life like the *vasa pitta*, a bird that chirps nonstop. In turn he told her about politics, philosophy, poetry, whatever he was reading or thinking. They used to stay up until two, three in the morning, going to bed only reluctantly.

She told him about her English lecturer, Goparaju Sambasiva Rao. "Oh, really!" Satyam said. "Do you know who he is?" Satyam explained he was the brother of Goparaju Ramachandra Rao, the famous founder of the rational-atheist movement in Andhra.

Influenced by his progressive brother, this lecturer of Manjula's had married a widow and even encouraged his wife, who had little formal education, to write poetry. He was devoted to the uplifting of untouchables as well as women, and when his eye fell on Manjula, he devoted himself to uplifting her. As it was Mr. Sambasiva Rao's habit to take a walk in the evenings, he began to make a point of passing through Slatter Peta so he could stop by the shack where Manjula lived. Sometimes he would even take a cup of tea with her, a remarkable thing for a brahmin to do.

Sambasiva Rao advised her not to limit herself to textbooks. He pushed her to take part in extracurricular activities, starting with a debating competition.

"Yes, why not?" Satyam said when he heard. He trained her thoroughly for each debate, which had topics like "Is education good for females?" and "Pen or gun? Which is superior?" Satyam taught his sister how to stand, where to put her hands, where to pause, where to raise her voice. "Shoulders square. Remember to look at the audience." He wrote out entire speeches for her to memorize, then watched her as she practiced them.

The debate took place in an auditorium with a speaking platform, a sound system, special lighting. But with all that *hungama* (fanfare), only four students turned up to participate. In those days even boys rarely dared to attempt public speaking. For a girl to do it was unheard of. Manjula didn't speak perfectly. In fact she talked like a little girl, *vonkara-tinkara* (haltingly), and she wasn't even expressing her own ideas. The whole performance was her brother's handiwork. But none of that diminished her achievement. After that debate, Manjula became a star in her class.

Encouraged by Sambasiva Rao and her brother, she went on to participate in a mock legislature and even a radio quiz show. For the latter, Satyam coached her for weeks on every subject, from politics and history to Telugu literature and current events. He took her by train to the All-India Radio station in the big city of Vijayawada and waited nervously outside the studio. After all the distance they'd traveled, she couldn't answer any of the questions. Finally, she got one right, as if she'd thrown ten stones and one happened to hit the mark. Her brother and Sambavisa Rao both assured her it was all right, that she would learn.

Manjula's classmates wondered why she didn't major in science. "You could have become a doctor," everyone told her. But with no composite maths in high school, science was not an option for Manjula. Satyam had dissuaded her from taking Telugu, and she was scared of English, leaving her to choose between political science and history. She took history.

Carey opted for maths and economics, to Manjula's great relief. As it was, her younger brother slapped her twice a day to warn her to behave like a proper lady. "Why do you sit on the veranda?" he would say. "Don't talk with that girl in a short-sleeved blouse." "You were seen laughing in the street." If she'd had to sit in the same classroom with him, she would have been scared to breathe.

It was only for lack of choice that her family had allowed Manjula to attend a coed school. There was no ladies' college within a hundred miles. Since she had to sit in classrooms with boys, her family made sure she looked as unattractive as possible. One weekend when Prasanna Rao came to visit, he and his sons and mother-in-law sat together and decided that Manjula ought no longer to wear half saris, which looked too youthful. All her old clothes disappeared overnight. To replace them, her father bought a bolt of coarse white cloth without a spot of color and cut it into four pieces. Even brahmin widows dressed better than sixteen-year-old Manjula. They wore white, too, but proper saris, not lengths of fabric with no borders. In Slatter Peta, Manjula was given a new nickname: Musali Papa (Geriatric Baby). The decision about Manjula's dress had been made right in front of her, but no one asked her what she thought of it.

While Carey told her outright what to do and slapped her when he thought she was straying, Satyam never treated her that way. Instead, he and Nancharayya would make fun of bad girls in her presence so she would be led to think, "Oh, I should never do that thing."

Only bad girls wear two braids.

Only bad girls part their hair on the side.

Only bad girls learn to ride a bicycle.

And so on.

Manjula would do anything to avoid being talked of in this way.

◎

A FEW MONTHS AFTER HE formed the Toilers, Satyam was drawn into a historic political struggle in his state.

Language groups across India were demanding states of their own. But the Telugus' cry for a separate Andhra was the shrillest, and it was led by Communists. To Nehru it seemed as if the rear end of the country had caught fire.

On October 19, 1952, a former disciple of Gandhi's named Potti Sreeramulu announced that he would fast until a separate Andhra state was granted.

Forty-five days later, Nehru wrote to a Congress leader in Madras, "Some kind of fast is going on for the Andhra Province and I get frantic telegrams. I am totally unmoved by this and I propose to ignore it completely."

On December 15, on the fifty-eighth day of his fast, Potti Sreeramulu died. Within hours the news of his death had, as one newspaper reported at the time, "engulfed entire Andhra in chaos."

When the news reached Satyam and Nancharayya, they rushed to the Gowri Sankar Cinema Hall, where hundreds of people were pouring into town from neighboring villages. They had no leader, no direction.

Satyam sent word to his troupe members to come at once. They brought their drums and a megaphone. Satyam addressed the crowds: "Come, let's flood the streets like a tidal wave!"

Along the way, more people joined, leaving their homes, their businesses, their schools. They roared:

Nehru, Nehru,
Andhra rashtram—
istava,
chastava!

(Nehru, Nehru,
Andhra state—
you will yield
or you will die!)

The impromptu procession grew bigger and bigger. When it reached the municipal office, Satyam went upstairs to address the crowd from the rooftop:

"Dear friends! We are thousands upon thousands! We are an army! An army that will liberate three million Telugus!"

He announced he would lead them to the *tehsildar*'s office—the main government office in town—where they would hang a black flag as a symbol of mourning for Potti Sreeramulu.

As the crowd prepared to move on, the police stirred. Satyam picked up his megaphone to say, "O police! This battle is not with you. Our fight is with the Nehru government. You and us, we are *bhai-bhai!*" (brother-brother).

But as the marchers approached the tehsildar's office, they came face-to-face with a line of fifty policemen standing with rifles drawn. This prompted a three-way split in the crowd. Some turned their backs and fled. Some stood still—they didn't run away, but neither did they advance. And in the front, led by Satyam and Nancharayya, a group of some fifty people kept moving forward.

"Step back!" ordered the police commander. "Or you will be shot!"

"We dare you!" Satyam replied.

"Young man," came the response, "why do you want to die unnecessarily?"

"I am ready to die!"

Satyam felt no fear. His dream was coming true, his dream of dying for the people. The whole town was in a state of high melodrama. He could hear women sobbing in the street.

Just then, police clerk Surya Narayana emerged from the tehsildar's office and made his way through the line of police. "Oh, mister," he told Satyam, "the deputy superintendent wants to speak with you. Follow me!"

Satyam didn't know what was going to happen. He told Nancharayya to remain where he was, but Nancharayya replied, "If you go, I go."

The clerk escorted the two young men into a huge office, where they were greeted by the deputy superintendent, looking grave. Unexpectedly, he shook their hands and politely asked them to sit down.

"Look, mister," he said to Satyam, "do you think I am opposed to separate Andhra? I merely ask you to conduct your protest in a peaceful manner. If there is violence, then, as a police officer, I must do my duty. Our hero Potti Sreeramulu has become a martyr. I do not wish you to become one, too." The deputy superintendent then ordered tea to be brought in and, in a gesture of respect, served it to the leaders of the protest with his own hands.

Minutes later, Satyam and Nancharayya unfurled a black flag from the terrace of the tehsildar's office. Returning to the head of the crowd, they led another march through town. The marchers stopped to hang black flags from every government building along the way.

Finally, they reached the railway station. From the rice mill on the other side of the railway tracks, a huge procession of workers under the leadership of the Communist organizer Brahmam joined the one Satyam was leading. Brahmam gave Satyam a warm embrace.

A freight train was ready to pull out of the station. They decided to halt it. Satyam sent instructions to the railway guard and the boiler-room workers. As Brahmam unfurled a black flag from the top of the railway station, Satyam climbed atop the engine and gave an impassioned speech. As agreed, the police stood by.

"We must fight till the end," Satyam told the crowd. "We must fight until we achieve a separate Andhra state."

The disorder in Gudivada was mild compared to the rioting that broke out in other towns and cities across Andhra, where attacks on government offices caused millions of rupees' worth of damage. Many were shot dead by police. After two days of this, Nehru officially conceded the demand for a separate Telugu state, setting a precedent for the revision of state borders along linguistic lines that would be carried out across the country in the coming years.

◎

AFTER THE SEPARATE-ANDHRA AGITATION, the party leaders made Satyam a town committee member. However much he annoyed them, it would be hard to do without him. At the age of twenty-one he was already a powerful leader in Gudivada. He commanded solid support among the students, the rice-mill workers, and the residents of all the untouchable colonies in town.

He was important enough that when other Communists came to town, they made a point of paying him a visit. And whenever a cadre from Guntur would come to see him, Satyam would ask after his old friend and comrade from A.C. College the untouchable mathematics lecturer Manikya Rao. That's how Satyam learned the shocking news that Manikya Rao was on the run. How had he gotten into this trouble? Simply by falling in love.

Manikya Rao had been hired to tutor a girl named Niranjanamma from a wealthy kapu family. Nineteen-year-old Niranjanamma confided in her handsome twenty-four-year-old private master. She was terribly un-happy. Both her parents had died when she was little, and her life was in the hands of her grandmother Rangamma, an old widow who controlled the family property.

When Rangamma's husband died, she could not, as a woman, inherit the property, which went to her son. But since he was too young at the time to take charge of it, Rangamma was made legal guardian. The siz-able plot was in the center of town. On this land Rangamma built a large compound and took in forty or fifty unfortunate women who made their living by prostitution. She charged these women protection money, main-taining a retinue of goondas to make sure they paid up. The family for-tune grew larger and larger.

Yet, as a woman, Rangamma had an insecure hold on this wealth. It depended on her influence over her son, who continued to bow to her authority even after he came of age and married. But when his first wife died without bearing him a child, he needed to remarry. His bringing another woman into the family might pose a threat to Rangamma's position. How could she tell what kind of girl she was? So Rangamma arranged to marry her widower son to one of her granddaughters, Niranjanamma, who was then only fourteen years old.

Niranjanamma told Manikya Rao all about her tragic marriage to her much-older uncle. A man whose body was home to all sorts of ailments. An ignorant, incapable man who had studied only up to third class, whereas Niranjanamma was about to earn her bachelor of science.

Late one night, Niranjanamma sneaked out of the family house, hired a rickshaw, and presented herself at Manikya Rao's doorstep. She was pregnant. The child was his. "Here I am. I put my life in your hands. It is yours to do what you like with it. I'm never going back."

Manikya Rao tried his best to console her. Before they could decide on what to do, the discussion was cut short. Rangamma's rowdies, armed with rods and cycle chains, were breaking down the door.

Manikya Rao and Niranjanamma didn't even have time to find san-dals. They rushed out the back door, scrambled over the compound wall, and ran for their lives through the darkened streets.

Manikya Rao told his beloved not to worry. He was a Communist in good standing. The party would get them out of this trouble. At an ungodly hour, they knocked on the door of a town committee leader, who took them in.

The next morning an emergency meeting of the Guntur party committee was called with Manikya Rao present. The leaders were all kammas.

One of them rubbed his chin and said, "Now, this man is one individual. Suppose we help him. One man is helped. But how many kapus in this city will stop supporting us? That will be bad for the whole party when we run in municipal elections." Another admonished Manikya Rao. "A lecturer should behave like a lecturer," he lectured. "What is all this?"

Manikya Rao did his best to defend himself. "Mister, it is not like that. This matter . . . it's a very complicated matter. Anyway, you can see what a bad situation I am in."

"*Array*, we see it. Your case is moving. But what are we to do? Why bring your personal problem and rub it on the party's head?"

That was their attitude. They didn't deliver him to the enemy's doorstep. They were even willing to give him help personally, "as individuals." But as a party, they refused to take up his cause.

Satyam could not sit on his hands while his friend's life was in danger. Manikya Rao and Niranjanamma were in hiding, no one knew where. Satyam made inquiries. A student in Gudivada College named Rama Rao (who was to become Satyam's closest friend) had the information he needed. Manikya Rao was staying in a remote village with a relative of Rama Rao's.

When Satyam saw his old friend, his heart turned to water. The man was in poor physical condition. Someone had given him a couple of shirts, besides which he had only the clothes he'd escaped in. Without sandals, he had to walk ten kilometers a day into a neighboring town to work as a private tutor. The first thing Satyam said to him was "Masteroo, we are here. Come with us to Gudivada."

But Manikya Rao had been hiding out safely in that small village for some months. "Why should I go?"

"Look," Satyam said. "Today I found you here. Tomorrow Rangamma's thugs may come."

"They can come to your place, too," Manikya Rao pointed out.

"Let them come," Satyam told him. "We will hack them to pieces just as they come. Here there is no one capable of protecting you."

With this assurance, Satyam brought Manikya Rao and Niranjanamma to live with his family. How he was going to feed them he didn't consider. The household survived on what Prasanna Rao sent. Every grain of rice counted.

But no one at home said a word against this plan. Manjula and Carey were happy to do anything they could to assist their adored brother in his courageous scheme to defend an intercaste couple. They stopped going to classes and devoted themselves to the cause full-time. Carey and his friends took turns protecting Manikya Rao, with Carey sleeping at night on the floor at the foot of Manikya Rao's bed. Manjula looked after Niranjanamma's needs and kept watch over her. Even Marthamma was glad to do her part. They conspired to keep the matter from Prasanna Rao, who only visited every now and then.

When Manikya Rao had run away with Niranjanamma, a delegation of kapus had gone to the principal of A.C. College and complained, "Manikya Rao kidnapped one of our girls." The principal assured them that Manikya Rao would never teach there again.

Manikya Rao planned to seek a position in Vizag. Satyam appealed to sympathizers to scrape up the money for Manikya Rao's train ticket and a decent set of clothes. Niranjanamma would stay behind until Manikya Rao found a place for them.

A letter from Vizag to Gudivada took about a week, sometimes longer. But weeks and weeks passed with no word from Manikya Rao. Carey and Manjula couldn't return to their studies and leave Niranjanamma without protection. Satyam worried that Manikya Rao was having difficulty finding a position. Satyam collected more money, but he didn't know where to send it. No one knew anything. They didn't know if Manikya Rao was alive or dead.

In the meantime, the untouchable communities of the town had adopted the couple's cause as their own. Well-wishers poured in at all hours of the day. Malas from Slatter Peta and Mandapadu, madigas from Noble Peta and Goodman Peta, pakis from Paki Peta, Nancharayya and his mother and all their relatives and neighbors from the shantytown of Chinavani Goodem—all devoted time to show their sympathy and lend a hand. Some cooked, some helped with daily chores, some ran errands, some stood guard. As word spread, untouchables from surrounding villages, near and far, would come. Forty, fifty visitors filed in day after day. Marthamma cooked for them, made tea. The provisions Prasanna Rao was sending for a household of three were soon exhausted.

Niranjanamma, distraught over Manikya Rao's disappearance, made increasing demands. She needed a new sari. She wanted to go out. To keep her spirits up, Satyam came up with some extra money for her to spend. Manjula would have to accompany her to the bazaar, the cinema, wherever she wanted to go. While Niranjanamma never behaved as if she had anything to fear, Manjula always kept an eye on their surroundings and looked searchingly into the faces of everyone they encountered. This was a dangerous thing for a teenage girl in India to do, and in time it developed into an embarrassing lifelong habit.

At last, Satyam decided Niranjanamma could stay with the family no longer. He'd learned that Rangamma's thugs had visited Manikya Rao's old hideout. That showed they were still on the couple's trail. In time they would track Niranjanamma down in her new location. If they got wind she was hiding in Gudivada, the malapallis were the obvious place to look, Manikya Rao being a mala. And who would be more likely to take him in than Satyam?

Also, the untouchables who thronged to offer help and encouragement could see Niranjanamma's belly getting bigger and bigger. Despite their sympathy, an undercurrent of rumors started to circulate among them: "What is this girl really doing here?" "Did Satyam have anything to do with her condition?" "What has happened to her husband?" "Why is he not coming back for her?" Satyam could see how it looked. As a public figure, a mass leader, he couldn't afford to let himself be tarnished by scandal.

Where, Satyam asked himself, was the *last* place in town that anyone would expect a sympathizer to put up a respectable, uppercaste girl such as Niranjanamma? In the prostitute-caste colony. So Satyam moved her to a hut he rented there. Naturally Manjula, whose duty it was to follow Niranjanamma like a shadow, had to go and stay there with her.

This was all too much for Marthamma. The family finances were already in ruins. Her grandchildren had abandoned their studies, and now Manjula was going to live in the prostitute colony! Who would ever marry her knowing she'd done that?

When Niranjanamma gave birth, Manjula was asked to look after the child. She began to have misgivings about giving up her education, everything, to become another woman's babysitter. The cause was just. No question about that. But then shouldn't the party take it up? Was her brother correct to substitute his own family for the party? Could he win this struggle on his own? Were they really helping to bring a revolution?

News finally reached Satyam of what had happened to Manikya Rao in Vizag. Manikya Rao had secured a lecturer post at the famous AVN College of Andhra University. The first day he walked into a classroom, police were waiting there for him. They wrestled him to the floor in front of his students, shackled his hands and feet, and dragged him away.

Rangamma also had a close relative named C. Ammanna Raja, a powerful woman in the Andhra Congress Party. Through her the interests of kapu landowners were represented within the party, and through her the party garnered their support. She was also a member of the academic senate of Andhra University. When Rangamma appealed to her for help, she launched a statewide manhunt for the runaway couple. Every police station in every district of Andhra was under orders to cooperate with Rangamma's men.

Manikya Rao was taken back to Guntur, where he was held in jail. The charge? Beguiling and eloping with a minor girl. The charge was obviously false. Its purpose was to force Niranjanamma to appear in court, giving her family an opportunity to abduct her.

When his parents posted bail, he jumped it and disappeared. He was afraid to let Niranjanamma know what had happened for fear of putting her in danger.

He tried to find work elsewhere. But Ammanna Raja had his master's degree, his bachelor's degree, and his high school diploma revoked. Even his birth certificate was nullified. After sixteen years of schooling, he had no official proof that he could read and write, that he even existed. At last, he was hired in the small town of Kavali by a private tutorial college (prep school) that did not check up on his degrees. That's where he was hiding when Satyam finally traced him.

Protecting the couple would require all the support Satyam was able to muster. He spoke with his friends and family. He marshaled whole families, whole neighborhoods, to the task. "We talk of ideals. We say caste should go. People should be free to marry across caste lines. Is it enough to say these things? This struggle we are faced with now is not a matter of words. It is real life."

Satyam sent a small band, including Carey and his friend Nelson, to Kavali with knives tucked under their belts. Four men would stay by Manikya Rao's side at all times. Once Manikya Rao was under protection, Satyam set up a meeting between Niranjanamma and Ammanna Raja's brother, who had recently married Niranjanamma's sister and taken over the hunt for the eloping couple on behalf of the family.

This was a risky move. But Satyam was emboldened by a shift in the balance of political forces in the state.

A bitter caste feud had divided the ruling Andhra Congress Party. When the government collapsed in 1955, new elections were declared. With Congress forces split, the Communists seemed poised for victory.

Millions of supporters who had previously hidden their sympathies came out to join the campaign. Satyam saw tens of thousands of rice-mill workers and agricultural laborers turning out to hold mass rallies. Fearless, wielding sticks and sickles, they paraded through villages and towns. The prospect of a Communist government coming to power in the state through the ballot—becoming the first-ever elected Communist government in the world—was as electrifying for sympathizers as it was alarming for their enemies.

This was the moment that Satyam seized when he offered Niranjanamma's brother-in-law, the leader of the family forces, the chance to meet with Niranjanamma at the neutral location of Vijayawada.

He told Niranjanamma, "He will ask you to come home with him. What will you say to him?"

"I will say, 'Look, Brother, how can I go with you? There is a baby now. How can he grow up without a father?'"

Satyam was pleased. "When you say that, the enemy will weaken."

When the meeting took place, Niranjanamma stayed strong. "I am not coming back," she told her brother-in-law. "I have a baby and I am breast-feeding him. If you try to take me away, he will starve to death."

Her brother-in-law refused to believe there was a baby. He sent word that he wouldn't return Niranjanamma unless they brought this baby to show him. Satyam sent a message back: "If you want to see the baby, you must come to Gudivada."

Satyam decided to attend this meeting personally. The place was to be the college guesthouse at the railway station, which Rama Rao had arranged through the student union to use for the evening. Carey and Nelson stood guarding the door from outside. Inside, Satyam waited with two other friends who never left his side. Rama Rao was hiding behind a screen, holding the baby in his arms.

When the kapus arrived, Satyam addressed Niranjanamma's brother-in-law: "You can't do anything to us here. If anything happens to our sister or her baby, we will take your heads. Don't try to force us or frighten us. We'll pay you back with interest." Satyam spoke these words and left.

The kapus asked to see the baby. Rama Rao came out from behind his screen to show it to them. One of the kapus made a move toward the child. Rama Rao ran out with it, as planned.

The kapus left Niranjanamma there and went away, disappointed. With a baby in the picture, they had to recognize the situation had changed. Rangamma was reluctant to yield, but Ammanna Raja had a more practical view. "Why, the story is finished," she told her. So Rangamma finally sent word to her granddaughter that she could live with Manikya Rao in peace as long as she kept quiet about this affair.

For Satyam and all his friends and followers, it was a great victory.

For Manikya Rao and Niranjanamma, it was the beginning of a new life together. They settled down in Vijayawada, where Manikya Rao got a teaching job in a private tutorial college.

◎

NIRANJANAMMA'S DEPARTURE COULD NOT HAVE come soon enough
for Manjula. In the last days of the affair, she had begun to worry more
and more about the effects of the campaign on the family's finances and
her own prospects in college. Besides, Niranjanamma's self-centeredness
had rubbed her the wrong way.

When it was time to take her final exams, Manjula was ill prepared.
She entertained no hope of passing. When the marks were posted on campus, she saw how lucky she was. In English and British history she'd earned
a score of 35—the lowest passing mark. Even that seemed like a miracle.

On her way home, Manjula passed a young man named Aseervadam,
whose family had recently moved into the house opposite hers. Despite
their being neighbors, Manjula had never spoken to him. She greeted him
with a politely tentative half smile (as always, she was self-conscious about
her slightly protruding teeth). But Aseervadam—poor Aseervadam, it was
not his fault—thought that Manjula had her eye on him. That was a natural enough conclusion in Slatter Peta.

God had given Manjula another chance. She made a solemn vow not
to squander it. Even before classes resumed, she took out a book to study
in advance. She sat up in the front room long after her grandmother had
gone to bed to read in the flickering light of a small kerosene lamp.

No one else was home. Her brothers seldom returned before three in
the morning, if they came home at all. It was June and the heat at night felt
like a thick towel dipped in steaming water and wrapped around one's face.
Most people slept on the street in front of their houses. Those who slept
inside left their doors wide-open.

Around eleven o'clock, Manjula heard a faint noise. When she looked
up, Aseervadam was right beside her like an apparition. Startled, she
shouted, "What is this? Why have you come?"

Instantly, Aseervadam realized his misunderstanding. This girl had
meant nothing romantic or sexual when she smiled at him in the street.
He fled the house as quickly and quietly as he'd come in.

That would have been the end of it if not for what Manjula did next.

She could have kept quiet about what had happened. But in the morning she couldn't resist telling her grandmother, proudly describing how sternly she'd chased that young man away.

And that would have been the end of it if not for what Marthamma did next. She, too, could have kept quiet. But she was aggrieved by the incident and had to tell her grandson.

Satyam understood it was not his sister's fault. He also knew nothing serious had happened. And it was clear to him that Aseervadam realized his mistake.

But Satyam couldn't let the matter end there. He and Carey often stayed out late. If others came to know what had happened between Aseervadam and his sister, they might get the idea that it was all right to enter the house and approach her at night. He had to do something to make sure such a thing would never happen again.

One morning soon after, as Aseervadam was turning a corner on his bicycle, he spotted Satyam and Nancharayya standing together in front of a tea shop. Satyam opened his umbrella. The sky was perfectly clear, and Aseervadam barely had time to wonder what was happening before ten to fifteen young men descended on him. They pushed him off his bicycle and beat him. When he had only a few breaths left in him, they all stopped as though by secret agreement and left him in the dirt.

Satyam and Nancharayya now ran to his side. They hailed a rickshaw and rushed him to the general hospital. Satyam had followers among the staff there. He urged them to take good care of Aseervadam. After the doctors had tended to him, Satyam and Nancharayya drew up chairs to his bedside. "You know why this happened, right?" Satyam asked. "Be sure to tell your brothers and your friends. But when your mother and your father ask you, we want you to keep your mouth shut." Aseervadam then understood everything.

After thanking the doctors and nurses, Satyam and Nancharayya loaded Aseervadam into a rickshaw and took him home. His family was just sitting down to lunch. His brothers got up from their plates and stood by the inner door with food stuck to their hands while their mother quickly washed up and came out of the house, wiping her hands on her sari. When she laid eyes on her son, she started weeping. "What happened, my son?" Satyam and Nancharayya explained that they had found him lying in the street, assaulted by some gang, and taken him to a hospital. Aseervadam's father thanked them for their kindness as his son turned his head away in shame.

One Sunday afternoon a few weeks later, a mob of fifty men in their teens and twenties, armed with sticks and bicycle chains and iron rods, showed up outside the Kambham house. They said they were looking for Satyam and Carey. The two brothers were off in the other untouchable ghetto campaigning for the Communist ticket in the upcoming elections. But Prasanna Rao, who was visiting for the weekend, was at home. He sent Marthamma and Manjula out the back door and asked a neighbor to take them to stay with another Communist family living in Slatter Peta. Then he went back inside, looking for something to defend himself with. He picked up a thick piece of firewood from the hearth and, wielding it as menacingly as he could, came out roaring, "Evadrrrra akkada!" (Whoooo's there!)

The audacity of this middle-aged man thinking he could scare them off with a piece of firewood only enraged the mob. They soon had him laid out on the ground, where they kicked him around like a soccer ball. They pulled him to his feet by his hair and threw him against a wall. Then they pushed him to the ground and whipped his body with their chains until he lost consciousness. Finally, they stormed into the family house and destroyed everything inside while the neighbors stood watching. When Prasanna Rao came to, he remembered the men telling him they were there to avenge Aseervadam.

Satyam went into hiding while Carey, Nelson, and some other friends lay in wait. When the time was right, they forced their way into Aseervadam's house, vandalizing it and thrashing the whole family, including the parents. They forced them to reveal who the gang was that had assaulted Prasanna Rao.

Surya Samajam (Sun Society) was a youth club for kamma landlords' sons who had all failed out of school. Having nothing better to do, they spent their time in sports, in championing the merits of various kamma cine stars, and in hooliganism. They supported Congress and hated Communists such as Satyam and Carey.

But they also had special reasons for detesting Carey. Besides being a better sportsman than any of them, he was also keen on enforcing the rules of the games. He was constantly getting into violent disputes with Surya Samajam over their cheating and hogging of local playing fields. And Carey had another cause that got him into trouble with that gang. He led a group of his friends—all fearless mala sons of bitches like himself—in protecting the honor of untouchable girls in town from caste boys who saw them as cheap and easy.

Satyam understood how a poor untouchable fellow such as Aseervadam had been able to organize an attack against Satyam's family. Aseervadam and his brothers had brought the matter to Surya Samajam, which had taken up their grievance as a pretext to strike out at Carey.

So Satyam considered the matter settled. He'd had Aseervadam beaten up because he tried to touch Manjula. Then his family was attacked, so he ordered an attack on Aseervadam's family. He saw no reason to perpetuate a bloody feud with Surya Samajam.

But then he heard something that changed his mind. The town secretary of the Communist Party was passing by a Congress election rally when he was spotted by a mob of Surya Samajamists in the crowd. They went after him with sticks and chains. The terrified man ran for his life, finding safety only when he reached the party office.

Similar incidents were taking place all across Andhra. The election battle had turned violent. The Congress Party, still ruling at the national level, was shaken by the prospect of a Communist electoral victory in Andhra state and had dispatched one S. K. Patil, a well-known Congress strongman, from Bombay with sacks of cash and scores of men under his command. Their mission was to hire and train local hooligans such as Surya Samajam to terrorize Communist activists and threaten voters.

Satyam understood the party could not ignore an attempted attack on one of its leaders. It wouldn't look good if it came to be known that the town secretary had been made to flee and hide. Supporters would be intimidated and demoralized.

So the next day he organized a counterattack. A hundred members of the Student Federation of India (SFI), the student wing of the Communist Party, waylaid both Surya Samajam and the Youth Congress and beat them with sticks and chains and rods.

As election day approached, an escalating series of attacks and counterattacks between the Communist youth led by Satyam and the Surya Samajam spread throughout town, turning bloodier and bloodier. In the end, the town authorities invoked emergency powers and imposed Section 144 (a curfew) on the town. It was forbidden to gather or move about in groups of more than three. No one was allowed out on the streets after 8:00 p.m.

After the elections, Congress incited Aseervadam's family to file assault charges against Manjula's family. Satyam's lawyer friends advised him to file countercharges. The case went to trial.

This case, as do many in India, went on and on for years until well after the concerned parties had lost all interest. Aseervadam and Manjula would go on to sit in the same classroom for three years with no conflict. After earning his B.A., Aseervadam got a job in the Cooperative Department and became a colleague of Nancharayya's, one of the organizers of the attack on him. They both became active in their union and got along well. Aseervadam even became an admirer of Satyam's and invited him to his house for tea. He told Satyam that his hunch was right—Surya Samajam was recruited by the local Congress branch with the money brought in by S. K. Patil.

This episode had a far-reaching effect on Manjula. The men in her family had risked their lives for her honor. The bruises on Prasanna Rao's body left permanent scars that she would notice when he lay dead. Grateful to her father and brothers for what she saw as their sacrifice on her behalf, she vowed never to disappoint them, especially in relation to boys and marriage.

Satyam's aim had been to protect his sister's honor. But in the end Manjula was known by one and all as the girl who'd caused all the violence in town.

When Manjula returned to college, the family worried what she would have to face there. They were afraid she would find obscene things scrawled on walls or desks linking her and Aseervadam, that the boys would heckle and the girls would shun her.

Contrary to these fears, no one in the college uttered a word about the whole affair. Because of her brothers, they didn't dare. Only later would she come to know that her classmates had given her a new nickname and used it behind her back: Narahari—Slayer of Men.

◎

WHILE SATYAM WAS FENDING OFF the Congress hooligans, he was also throwing himself into election work on behalf of the Communists.

With the Toilers he performed street-theater dramas that he and Nancharayya had composed specially for the campaign. In one, Satyam played N. G. Ranga—the kamma leader who had defected from Congress— dancing crookedly with his walking stick.

Satyam was also in charge of campaigning in all the untouchable colonies in and around Gudivada. He visited these constituencies daily. The poor people were solidly behind the Communists. Rallies were called on huge tracts of farmland. The dried paddies left fallow for the season would be filled with supporters. Bonded laborers left their fields and walked great distances to attend.

Satyam saw all this and thought, "All these people, these thousands of people, they support us, they will vote for us. And why not? We will give them land. That's why we are sure to win."

But the anti-Communist panic spread by Nehru and S. K. Patil was having its intended effect. Many middle-class intellectuals—teachers, lawyers, writers—turned away from the party. Even the Progressive Writers Association split, with the majority going over to Congress. The leading Telugu newspaper, *Andhra Prahbah,* fired its chief editor, a liberal who had come out in support of a strike by the newspaper staff. The new editor introduced a daily front-page feature: a cartoon captioned "If Communism Wins . . ." One day it showed old people lining up to be hanged, the next day women drawing plows in the field like oxen with yokes around their necks. S. K. Patil printed up pamphlets denouncing the Communists as traitors to the Indian nation. He covered walls with lurid posters illustrating the horrors of Communist society in China and the Soviet Union.

In the end, Nehru and S. K. Patil, using bribes and threats, succeeded in reuniting the warring factions of the state Congress Party into an anti-Communist bloc. The landless masses turned out for the Communists in even greater numbers than before. But the party lost support among rich peasants and smallholders, including within its kamma base. The Communists won only a handful of seats in the new legislature.

The consequences of the defeat were immediately felt. Right after the elections, a wave of mass evictions began. Untouchable laborers and their families were pushed out by landowners intent on increasing their holdings by force.

Satyam and his friends took up their defense. When Satyam got word a settlement was being threatened, he would lead a group of militant youth to occupy the land. They would stand guard for weeks on end over the poor families living there, warding off the landlord's family members or hired thugs. As Satyam was frail, incapable of delivering a punch even to a willing and stationary target, Carey led the fighting when it came to physical confrontations. In the meantime, Ganji Rama Rao, who was skilled at petitioning the government, and a group of lawyers sympathetic to the party would file a complaint and take the landlord to court. Sometimes they won, sometimes they didn't.

Few in the party leadership approved of these actions except for Krishna district secretary, Kondapalli Seetharamayya, the hard-bitten Telangana veteran Satyam had met at the street-theater competition in Guraja. He encouraged Satyam and his friends with fatherly pride.

Satyam was asked by the party to become a whole-timer, but he said no. He had seen how whole-timers in the party were treated. Even though it was the Communist Party, the leaders behaved as though the cadres were workers and they were the bosses. They doled out allowances as infrequently as possible and as grudgingly as could be imagined. It was too degrading for Satyam.

His father would support him only if he went back to school. So Satyam finally passed his Intermediate exams and enrolled in Gudivada

College with his brother and sister. But Satyam took little interest in classes. Every day he made the rounds of his wards—Mandapadu, Goodman Peta, Paki Peta, Billapadu, Erikepadu. Then he had his drama troupe to run, political classes to teach, anti-eviction battles to organize. He was out all day, returning home at three in the morning. Marthamma would leave some rice and curry on a covered plate for his supper.

Once in a while he showed up in class to maintain a minimum attendance record. One morning on his way to campus he saw a pitiful sight. A colony of poor migrant lepers from Tamil Nadu were gathered outside their huts, wailing and beating their chests. A bulldozer was knocking down their homes, sent by a landlord who wanted to take over the land. Satyam flung his books aside and ran in front of the bulldozer. His friends Nancharayya, Rama Rao, and Vishnu joined him, and together they halted the destruction. A few months later a court awarded the land to the lepers, who renamed their colony Satyamurthy Nagar out of gratitude.

FOUR

⊚ ⊚ ⊚

AFTER SPENDING ALMOST A WEEK away from home fighting an eviction, Carey returned at six in the morning, exhausted. He was hot with fever and cold with chills.

He was also worried. In a skirmish the night before, a kamma thug came at him with an ax. Carey dodged the blow and stuck a knife in his attacker's arm. The man would surely complain, and then it would get back to the party. Once again Satyam would face criticism for Carey's "violent methods."

As he turned the corner onto the street where he lived, Carey spotted a young nurse and remembered his promise to confront her supervisor, who, she'd told Carey, was sexually harassing her. It was one more thing on his mind.

Carey walked in the door and fell into bed. Just as sleep was coming, Marthamma demanded, "Get up! Help me carry the water bucket."

Of the three siblings, Carey was the only one who ever helped with hard chores. Satyam was a prince and couldn't be asked to button his own shirt. And Carey didn't like the idea of Manjula's doing hard work before she got married. Soon enough she would have to do all the housework for her husband, and Carey wanted to spare her the drudgery until then.

So Carey got up to help Marthamma carry her bucket. Marthamma, old and frail and shorter than him, lagged behind. It irritated him. He just wanted to get back to bed. "Come on!" he said, and shoved her. Marthamma fell over and let out a heartrending cry. The fall had shattered her hip.

"It wasn't me. She just fell," Carey kept telling his brother and sister. He knew he had pushed her, but still he defended himself. Satyam and Manjula were there and had witnessed everything. They said not a word.

Carey lifted Marthamma in his arms and carried her to her bed. She would never again get up on her own.

With their grandmother bedridden, the siblings had two concerns: Who was going to take care of her, and who was going to take care of them? They summoned Uncle Nathaniel to take Marthamma away to Parnasa. That solved the first problem. But who was going to cook and clean for the three of them?

It was time for Satyam to get married.

◎

AFTER FLORA'S REJECTION, SATYAM SWORE he would never again fall in love. "The first girl who asks me, I will marry her," he told himself.

Then a girl did, and he didn't. During the election campaign a kamma girl in the Student Federation hinted she would consider him a good match. But he didn't want to marry a caste girl. She might like him, but what if she looked down on his family, on their house, on their neighborhood?

147 ANTS AMONG ELEPHANTS

Mr. Bapanayya, the untouchable Communist MLA, had recently put forward his niece Karuna. Karuna was beautiful, educated, and worked as a teacher.

But Karuna expected the man she would marry to get a good job and provide for his family. Satyam could see it wouldn't work.

The towns of Gudivada and Gerikapadu are next to each other, with Gudivada's malapalli of Slatter Peta adjoining Gerikapadu's malapalli of Erikepadu. Separating the two was only a shallow stream that was easy to wade across. In summers, Satyam loved to go over after supper to his comrade Goodapati Nagabhooshanam's house in Erikepadu.

One warm night when Satyam arrived at Nagabhooshanam's, all Satyam's friends were already there—ten, fifteen of them—laughing and smoking and chatting loudly. In one corner, three chaps were playing drums. Others were singing and dancing. Satyam jumped in. His comrades shook their heads. "Now where did he learn to dance like that?" They cheered him on: "Hey!" "Hoy!" "All right!" "Go on, brother! That's it!"

The drummers and Satyam goaded each other into an escalating frenzy. The shack shook into the night. The men, women, and children of Erikepadu who were all just getting ready to go to bed left their houses and gathered at the open door to watch this handsome young man dance. Satyam went outside to dance under the full moon, encircled by the admiring crowd.

Comrade Nagabhooshanam couldn't contain his pride and delight. He said, "Look at our young Communist."

Pleased with all the cheer, Satyam lay down smiling on Nagabhooshanam's floor, folded his hands across his chest, and closed his eyes.

When he opened them, he saw what he took at first to be a beautiful bright painting set up before his eyes. A painting of a lovely red-complexioned girl in a red sari filling her shiny brass pitcher at a well.

Satyam propped himself up on his elbows and rubbed his eyes. The frame of that painting was in fact the doorframe of Nagabooshanam's shack. There was a well outside and a reddish sun in the sky. Struck by the beauty of the red-complexioned girl, Satyam walked up to her.

She was Maniamma, Satyam's second cousin. Her parents lived in

Sankarapadu, the tiny village settled by the family's ancestral clan, but she spent most of her time with her aunt and uncle in Erikepadu.

Satyam stopped at the well and asked her to pour him water to wash his face and rinse his mouth.

"What, Maniamma, how have you been doing?"

She acted coy. "Ah, I'm fine. Heard you were dancing away until dawn." Her uncle had been in the crowd cheering him on the night before.

Satyam came to the point directly. Would she marry him? She needn't answer right away, but could she come by his house and let him know by three o'clock?

Three o'clock on the dot, Maniamma came to Slatter Peta and told Satyam yes. "Now it is your turn to go to Sankarapadu and ask my father for my hand," she added.

Sankarapadu is only sixteen kilometers from Gudivada. Satyam caught a bus for part of the journey, and the rest of the way he had to walk, as there were no roads into Sankarapadu.

Sankarapadu is like an encampment in a wilderness. But for a cluster of seventy huts and one pukka house, there is nothing there. Even to buy a matchbook, you have to walk five kilometers to the next village.

When Kutumba Rao heard Satyam ask for his daughter's hand, he was delighted. An impoverished man such as him wouldn't have dared to dream of getting an educated, talented man such as Satyam for a son-in-law.

Prasanna Rao, too, was overjoyed at the news. For some time Prasanna Rao had been dropping hints to his son about Maniamma. He would talk about how much he had done for his children, how nice it would be to have a daughter-in-law who would mingle with the family as if she had always known them, who would be glad to look after him in his old age.

That night, Satyam and Maniamma sat together in back of her house. After holding each other and kissing for some time, Satyam gave his fiancée a speech about their future life together. He told her how the party was in bad shape after the defeat it had suffered, how he needed to devote all his time outside of studying to political work. Maniamma said she understood. Then Satyam listed his demands. He had five.

First, after marriage, Maniamma would have to take care of him in every way and see that he sat home and studied and passed his exams.

Second, Maniamma must tend to all his sister's needs, cook her meals and wash her clothes, while she studied so she could pass her B.A. exams with a first class. That was important.

Third, after exams, he and Maniamma would go to Parnasa and bring Marthamma back. "My grandmother served us all her life," he told Maniamma. "She should die in our house. It will be your responsibility to look after her."

Fourth, when Prasanna Rao grew old, Maniamma would have to take care of him as well.

And, finally, Satyam explained, Carey was a wild man. If Maniamma was going to be part of the family, she would have to put up with his temperament.

Maniamma gladly agreed to everything. Satyam was a hero in her eyes and in the eyes of the entire village for marrying her, a girl who couldn't even graduate from high school, without asking for a dowry.

He made one further demand, though, which Maniamma didn't accept. She couldn't. She wouldn't accept it, she told him, even if the king of England offered to marry her without a dowry.

But Satyam refused to drop it. He said he would not marry in a church.

When Prasanna Rao heard this, he got up and walked out of the village in tears. Satyam refused to budge. The engagement was off.

Satyam waited. He figured Maniamma would come around. Yet when he saw her again in Erikepadu, poor, bewildered Maniamma told him that she couldn't even see what the problem was. It wasn't something that a Sankarapadu girl such as Maniamma could understand.

Satyam thought it over, and as he did, he began to think like this: He was already twenty-four years old. Maniamma had agreed to every one of his stipulations but this one. Her beauty—it was something else. But how could he compromise his principles as a Communist and an atheist?

He called to mind the Marxist distinction between form and content. The content here was Maniamma. Whether they had a church wedding or a party wedding where the bride and groom simply exchanged garlands in the presence of party leaders—that was after all merely a matter of form.

When Manjula was told of her brother's engagement, the news struck her like a hammer blow. Without a word she went inside, lay down, and stared up at the ceiling with tears running down her cheeks.

Satyam had replaced her dead mother and, for many years, her absent father. Even now, he was more of a father to her than Prasanna Rao could ever be. Though only six years older than her, Satyam had always addressed her as *amma*, the way members of an older generation—fathers, uncles, grandfathers—address a girl to show their fondness.

Now she felt betrayed. He was going to share his life with another woman. "So it was all an illusion. He is a liar. My family, they all conspired and kept me in this state of delusion all these years."

And to be replaced by Maniamma? Maniamma had been Manjula's schoolmate in high school, and Manjula had always been scared of her. She was high-spirited and her friends were all wild. She often quarreled with other girls. No one dared cross her.

"My brother is a gentle and soft-spoken man," thought Manjula. She couldn't imagine a worse match for him. She cried nonstop for days.

Everyone warned Prasanna Rao. Maniamma was a black widow. But he wouldn't listen to any such talk. Growing up, he had always looked up to her grandfather (Prasanna Rao's uncle), who was better off than anyone else in the village. He owned the single pukka house standing among the huts. Before meeting Maryamma, Prasanna Rao had always hoped to marry into that family. But Maniamma's beautiful aunts were all given to suitors who, though they lacked his education, owned some land. Now, through his son, Prasanna Rao had a chance to vicariously fulfill this dream. He enthusiastically started making preparations for the wedding, to be held in Sankarapadu, which was the couple's common ancestral village. The first order of business was procuring provisions for the wedding feast.

ON THE MORNING OF the wedding, Manjula was woken by loud cries from the alley next to her uncle Gollayya's house in Sankarapadu. She sat up in fright and started praying: "O Deva! Jesus Lord, save us!"

A cousin of hers sitting nearby put her sari end to her mouth to hide her smile. "What, Papa, no need to be scared. They're chasing the pig."

When Prasanna Rao announced his son's wedding to the village, everyone started drooling at the thought of the pig. A wedding in an untouchable colony is a festival, and at the center of the festival is the feast, and at the center of the feast is the pig. As soon as a match is fixed, both the bride's house and the groom's house get hold of a piglet, either buying one in an untouchable market or catching a stray. For weeks the families raise their pig with great care.

A wedding pig is no ordinary pig. It must be treated with respect. No one is allowed to talk harshly to it, even if it should get in the way: "Hey, watch your mouth! That's the wedding pig!" The families feed it as well as they can, giving it starch water left after rice is cooked to drink, or sometimes even cattle fodder. Most untouchable families don't have that kind of food to spare, and the best thing about a pig is that it can feed itself. The staple for pigs in India is what's delicately called *malinam*—filth. They eat human shit. If the wedding family is too poor to feed their pig, it's not a big deal. The pig simply goes around the village eating shit and gets just as fat. Untouchables will often marvel, "Shit it may eat, but a pig's meat is the sweetest meat of all!"

But the announcement of Satyam's wedding meant more than just the prospect of a pig. Prasanna Rao had risen above the condition of all those he'd left behind in Sankarapadu. He was a teacher, not a farmhand. He had lived in cities and towns. He interacted with caste people, with other educated people, people with jobs. In the eyes of the villagers he was wealthy—he owned four and a half acres of land. His son was the first ever college-going man from that village. And now that eldest and favorite son was getting married! There would be a lot of pork at his feast. Prasanna Rao, it was said, might even get a pig of that exotic new breed.

Only a year or two earlier, a new breed of pig had arrived in the country. They are known as *seema pandulu*—European pigs (they came from

Russia). Some call them red pigs because their skin is pink and hairless and smooth. They're raised on farms, in pens, not let loose in the streets. They're fed a calibrated diet and grow many times fatter and larger than Indian pigs. In fact, they seem to have nothing in common with the black, hairy, filthy native pigs. But whenever anyone tries to raise one of these foreign pigs on his own, pretty soon it loses its caste and turns into an ordinary Indian pig, its pink turning to black, its fat shrinking away, as it runs through the streets, wallowing in sewers and swallowing the effluvium.

Everyone in Sankarapadu looked forward to tasting a European pig at Prasanna Rao's son's wedding. But Prasanna Rao's son had other ideas.

When the matter of the pig came up, it pained Satyam to realize that his relatives were so different from his caste friends. He had attended many of his friends' weddings while living in Gudivada, and except for Nancharayya none of them had served meat. Meat is believed by Hindus to be impure. Brahmins, the purest caste, eat no meat at all, not even fish or eggs. Untouchables, being impure themselves, eat even carrion beef—the flesh of cows that drop dead by the roadside of age or disease, which, since cows are sacred and cannot be slaughtered, is the only kind of beef that falls to human consumption under Hindu law. Middle castes, except for merchant castes, eat meat but never beef, and it is inauspicious to serve any meat at all at births, funerals, or weddings.

Satyam considered it uncultured and even barbaric to eat the flesh of a pig on any occasion. A pig, to caste Hindus, is a symbol of filth. Untouchables are commonly associated with two creatures: the crow for its blackness and the pig for its foulness. When people assembled under the banyan tree to plan the feast, Satyam told them there would be no pig.

The elders took the cigars out of their mouths. "What, what! A wedding feast with no pig?"

Satyam replied, "There won't be any meat."

They couldn't believe their ears. The most fabulous wedding they would ever attend was turning out to be the worst one they had ever heard of. They wanted nothing to do with it. Men, women, and children turned and went home disappointed. But Satyam was unmoved.

Discussion in the village went on for several days. In the end, the elders came to Prasanna Rao with a proposal: How about a pig for the village and hens for the "having-read people" (the educated ones)? Satyam said, "Never!" Prasanna Rao took his son's side. He had stopped eating beef in Vizag when he had to hide his caste for the sake of being allowed to rent a room in the house of a caste-Hindu family, and now the very thought of beef was revolting to him. He didn't mind pork himself, but he could understand how his son felt. Instead of a pig, he had bought sacks of vegetables and—from some kammas whose children he taught in Telaprolu—some strange, uppercaste flour-based foods: *appadams* and *laddoos*. The villagers decided to boycott the wedding feast.

One thing saved the day. Neither Prasanna Rao nor Satyam had a say in what the bride's family could or could not serve at *their* feast on the night of the wedding. Everyone knew Kutumba Rao had already been raising a pig for the last few weeks.

Whether Kutumba Rao had bought his pig or caught it himself was not clear, but it was a black Indian pig. That was the pig the young men of the village were chasing on the morning of the wedding when they woke Manjula with their cries.

Manjula went out to watch the agile young men, armed with long thick sticks and clenching cigars between their molars, running through the village, loincloths pulled tight over their crotches and between their buttocks, their bodies shiny with sweat. One carried a special net. The children of the village, twenty, thirty of them, naked, dust coated, wild haired, runny nosed—the girls among them also all naked but for their snail-shell anklets and the little silver or copper disks strung around their waists to preserve their modesty—ran alongside the hunters. Everyone was screaming as loud as he or she could, and the pig was screeching even louder. Wild with fear, it whizzed past the huts like a cannonball, desperate to escape the murderous youths. A cloud of dust rose from beneath its hooves and the feet of the men right behind it.

The pig is chased, instead of just being tied down and butchered, to save its blood. The blood is what makes it tasty. The idea is to scare the pig with screams and cries and make it run for its life until it collapses from exhaustion.

In Sankarapadu that morning, young women and girls admired the muscles rippling beneath the men's glistening brown skin as they wielded their sticks. The women's eyes ran all over the hunters' bodies, taking in the smalls of their backs, their thighs, their chests, their narrow waists, the lips that held their cigars. Each thought fondly how her own man ran faster than the rest, how he tackled the pig expertly to the ground. The men were aware the women were watching, and they tried their hardest to impress them.

The pig ran and ran for half an hour until it could run no more and finally dropped to the ground. One hunter threw his special net over it, and the others raised their sticks and beat the animal half-unconscious. They carried it to the center of the village and tied its snout shut with a rope. They tied its front legs to a pole and stood it up on its hind legs. The dazed pig looked up at the sky.

As a piglet grows in size, its neck soon gets so fat that as long as it lives it is never able to lift its head and look at the sky. But a wedding pig, in the last moments of its life, gazes skyward at last. Untouchables will say of an unfortunate man who has lived in poverty all his life, never having had a moment of happiness but for a small respite at the end when his son gets a job and is finally able to take care of his parents, "Veedu pandi lanti vadandi. Chacchipoyye mundu akasanni choosedu" (This fellow is like a pig. He saw the sky for the first time at the end of his life).

On that wedding morning, the men responsible for preparing the pig gently roasted the still-living pig and carried it to the bride's house. For lack of a cutting board, they unhinged the front door and laid the pig on it. Two elders, Uncle Nallayya and cousin Abednego, were invited to do the honors and carve the pig.

A few years before, a brahmin in Gudivada who worshipped Gandhi had spread the principles of nonviolence among all and sundry, especially the cruel and crude untouchables. One day, he found himself in an untouchable colony where a wedding feast was taking place. Before the men could lay the pig on the door, the brahmin pushed his way forward and laid himself down in the pig's place. He wept. "How can anyone with a heart hurt this voiceless animal? Are you not human? Haven't you heard the teachings of our Great Spirit Gandhi?" He pleaded with the untouchables to cut him up before they took a knife to that creation of God's. The youth in that colony, full drunk, pinned the brahmin down and held a knife to his throat before their elders intervened. The brahmin scurried off and never tried that again.

Good thing he didn't stay to watch what they did next. If he had, he might have fainted. Manjula herself couldn't bear to watch as the wedding cooks separated out the intestines, which would make a tasty sauté. Other special parts were carefully removed: the heart, the brain, and the liver. A curry made out of these is not meant for everyone. A portion is given to the pastor who performs the wedding, and the rest goes to the wedding families.

For days, the pig would feed the whole colony. They'd make soup with its bones and curries out of its hooves and testicles. People would swear how divine it is to eat pork fry while drinking. "Chicken is nothing," they'd say.

But the affair of the pig is more than its taste. It's the circus of hunting it, the feats of the men. It's heroic, it's romantic, it's erotic. It's a metaphor, it's rhetoric. It is deeply philosophical. But these are all mere superstructures. At the base, it's economic.

"The cheapest meat for the cheapest man on earth."

◎

THE MORNING OF THE WEDDING, everyone in Sankarapadu, from the ancient to the just-born, congregated in the church by the lotus pond. Except for the pastor in a rusty chair, everyone was seated on the mud-dung floor. The pastor kept switching unpredictably between the roles of officiant and reveler, one moment speaking of the sanctity of marriage and the next cracking obscene jokes at the expense of the groom or crooning a cinema tune.

Few of Satyam's friends were invited. Rama Rao, a high kamma and close friend and follower of Satyam's, was asked not to come. Satyam told him, like a good Communist, "The cost of the feast will go up if you come."

Not: "There will be pork, there will be tribal dancing. I wouldn't want you to see how my folks live."

But Satyam's untouchable friend Nancharayya was there. Manikya Rao came, too. He consoled Manjula, trying to assure her she was not losing her brother.

Manjula looked through her tear-filled eyes, dazzled by the sight of the bride and groom. It was, she thought, as if God had gathered all the beauty in the world and poured it in front of the pastor in two glowing heaps.

Satyam was wearing a white shirt; a fine cotton cloth (called a *kanduva*) over his left shoulder with a *zari* border (patterns woven with silver thread); a long beige zari-bordered *panche* (a traditional men's garment) wrapped to fall in delicate pleats from around his waist down to his calves; and a pair of leather thongs on his feet. His soft curls, washed with herbs, shone in the morning sun.

Maniamma was wearing a beige silk sari with a red zari border. The women of the village had rubbed her skin with cream and turmeric before they bathed her. They decorated her eyes with *katuka* (eyeliner), hung twelve red glass bangles on each arm, and wove jasmine blossoms into her long, silky hair.

The pastor finished his ritual with a song:

Pelli kante mundu, mana peddalu
Pandi pelli chestarayyo
Panditlo. . . .

(Even before the wedding, our elders
Perform the pig's wedding
In the tent. . . .)

The guests were impatient to get out of the church and on with the revelries. Men wearing just loincloths would wave handkerchiefs and dance. They would climb up on one another's shoulders and get thrown off when they least expected. The pinnacle would come when they chased the main reveler and pulled off his loincloth. People would laugh when he ran off covering his crotch with his hands.

But it was not to be. Satyam imposed a ban on drinking. Without "getting poured," the men in charge of the wedding revelries weren't in the mood.

The afternoon feast, courtesy of the groom's family, was the most insipid in the history of Sankarapadu. Prasanna Rao served vegetables and lentils. The villagers made faces as if they were throwing up. Laddoos, appadams—such stuff was too dainty for their taste.

With each disappointment the groom doled out, they muttered, "This man's system itself is separate": Satyam's ways were incomprehensible to them. Their consolation would be the feast at night, courtesy of Kutumba Rao. Until then they went home and sulked.

Then all at once they heard cinema music echoing through the tiny village. They came out of their houses, crying with joy, "Or-oray, they brought stupor for Satthi-fellow's wedding, they brought stupor!" They substituted for the English word *mic* the Telugu word closest to it in sound—*micum* (stupor). Satyam had a Communist friend who owned a sound-system rental shop in Gudivada. Many of the villagers had never seen a single electrical appliance in their lives. At the day's end, the cinema songs, blasted earsplittingly through a loudspeaker, more than made up for all of Satyam's follies.

⊙

AFTER THE WEDDING, THE VILLAGE celebrated the couple's first night together, after which Satyam returned to Gudivada by himself. On a convenient date soon after agreed to between the families, Maniamma's family brought her to Slatter Peta and left her there.

The day Maniamma came to live with him, Satyam said to her, "Let's go get our grandmother back." By tradition, the responsibility of looking after Marthamma fell on her eldest son, Nathaniel. But she had spent half her life raising the Kambham children.

Accompanied by a group of his friends and their wives, Satyam and

Maniamma went off to Parnasa. On their way they bought a string cot to carry Marthamma back home.

When Nathaniel's family got word of Satyam's arrival in Parnasa, they hastily propped Marthamma up in her cot and tried to arrange things to look as if they had been taking good care of her. But Satyam could see she had been reduced to a mere skeleton. She stared at her beloved grandson with eyes of glass.

Right away, Maniamma tucked in her sari and plunged into her duties. Working as a team, she and the wives of Satyam's friends set about bathing the old woman and combing her hair. The men laid her on the cot and bore it on their shoulders to the railway station. At the end of the train journey, they had to carry the cot on foot across two villages to reach Slatter Peta.

Satyam had a mattress made for his grandmother. Since she couldn't get up, they cut holes in the mattress and cot and placed a pan underneath. Carey cleaned her bedpan every day—a fact he would insist on ever after, perhaps to assuage his conscience.

Maniamma took care of feeding and washing Marthamma. To please her, Satyam would read her the Bible and pray. Then they would all drink tea together.

Satyam, the only one of the siblings old enough to remember their mother's death, could see by the way his grandmother rolled her eyes and gasped for air that her death was near. When it came, the three of them together with Maniamma gathered around her bed.

Not a single paisa was in the house for Marthamma's burial. Everything had been spent on the wedding. Satyam had to go to the Communist bookstore in town to borrow five rupees. The necessary flowers were sent by his supporters among the untouchables he'd saved from eviction, the pakis from among whom he'd recruited his troupe, and the rice-mill workers he'd organized in defense of Manikya Rao. They all came out en masse for the funeral.

Who could have imagined that the body of this diminutive black-skinned untouchable woman, a gleaner of fields, a singer of songs of toil, a pounder of rice, a Bible woman, the widow of a railway coolie, the mother of a plantation slave, a woman who'd never spent a single moment of her life on herself, would be carried to her grave in a procession of hundreds of men and women carrying red flags and singing "The Internationale"?

Aunt Nagarathnamma came late, after everything was over. The moment she walked in, Satyam, who had not shown his grief till then, burst into tears. Nagarathnamma's daughter snapped at him, "If you'd cared about her when she was alive, there would have been no need to cry so much."

Satyam was in no state to respond.

Nagarathnamma took him aside and inquired, "Did she admit her sins to Lord Jesus?"

Satyam told her he was not aware that she had committed any.

"If I were with her at her deathbed, I would have prayed and made her confess."

While they were discussing Marthamma's sins, Nathaniel's family was eager to get a look at what possessions she had left behind. The only thing she owned was a small iron trunk eaten through with rust that she had never let anyone touch. No one knew what she kept in it.

Nathaniel's wife pried it open. Inside they found an old, chipped plate— the one her son David used to eat off of—and his high school graduation medal mounted on a small piece of silk. David, who was going to be the first in the family to go to college, died of TB at the age of sixteen. That was all except for a rickety wooden folding chair that she had acquired late in life. Nathaniel's son Sundara Rao called it first.

◎

THE 1955 ELECTIONS WERE THE funeral of the Communist Party in Andhra. Out of 169 seats they contested, they won just 15, while Congress won 119 out of 142 they contested. The rich peasants dealt the deathblow. They had supported the Communists in 1952 when the party was coming off the fight against the feudal elite in Telangana, but by 1955 that battle was over and won. The landed classes, by and large, united behind Congress.

Out of this unity arose new rivalries among the rich peasant castes. Now the kammas were vying with kapus for dominance.

The student-body elections reflected electoral politics in the state. The Communist student wing—the SFI—was weak and Congress strong, with a rift between kammas and kapus on campus. Some kamma boys were harassing nonkamma girls. Kusuma, a dazzlingly beautiful kapu girl, was a special target. The boys would challenge each other to cycle past her and snatch the jasmine blossoms from her hair. Satyam told his friends to be vigilant and try to defend the girls against these attacks. He also sought to take advantage of the underlying caste rivalry. Kammas dominated the Congress panel in the student elections, so Satyam recruited kapus for his SFI panel.

That was how he came to nominate Vithaleswara Rao for the post of general secretary. Vithaleswara Rao, the son of a wealthy kapu landlord and high town official, was tall, with high cheekbones and smooth, hairless dark skin that made him look like a sculpture in brass. While not especially studious, he was popular and always surrounded by a number of friends.

For her brother's sake, Manjula took an active part in the campaign. Not long after she joined, Vithaleswara Rao approached her and said, "I want you to be on my panel as ladies' secretary." Manjula blushed, smiled copiously, and modestly demurred. But Vithaleswara Rao insisted: "You will do it, and there will be no more discussion."

Against all odds, the SFI won and Vithaleswara Rao was elected general secretary. Manjula, quite unexpectedly, lost by one vote. But the girl who won wanted to be the ladies' secretary in name only and asked Manjula to carry out her duties.

The campaign marked the beginning of a friendship between Manjula, Vithaleswara Rao, and a friend of his, a kamma named Ashok. The two boys never missed walking Manjula home after classes. When they reached Manjula's house, they lingered in front of her door for hours. Each day when the two boys saw Manjula in class, their faces would light up. She would smile back.

As Ashok had a slight limp, whenever he and Vithaleswara Rao both

161 | ANTS AMONG ELEPHANTS

had something to say, Manjula would always pay more attention to Ashok. She was careful not to make him feel he was being treated as someone less on account of his handicap. But everyone in Vithaleswara Rao's wide circle of friends, knowing his feelings about her, thought of her as his girl. In those days a young man would commonly affectionately address his friends as *mama* (father-in-law) or *bammardi* (brother-in-law). When Vithaleswara Rao's friends spotted Manjula, they often joked, "Hey, son-in-law, look, there goes my daughter." His family knew how Vithaleswara Rao felt, too. They knew he loved watching her in the classroom, sitting there with lots of hair oil applied to suppress her irrepressible curls, running her palms over her head again and again in a vain effort to keep them down.

It wasn't Satyam's way to say anything about her friendship with these men to Manjula directly. Instead, he and Rama Rao would often talk about Vithaleswara Rao and Ashok in her presence. As that year they were studying *Paradise Lost*, Satyam would refer to Vithaleswara Rao as Satan and Ashok as Beelzebub. Rama Rao went further, telling Manjula that Vithaleswara Rao was a bad sort of chap and habitually saw prostitutes. "I know," Rama Rao said, "because I have seen him roaming the streets late at night." In fact, Vithaleswara Rao liked to go on patrol with a friend of his, a police inspector who was on night duty. In spite of this smear campaign, Manjula kept up her friendships with Ashok and Vithaleswara Rao.

Once, as the three approached her house, Manjula spotted Carey in the distance. She dropped her books, shaking like a blade of grass, and told her two friends, "You must leave now. Please go away."

"Why, what's the matter?"

"Carey might see us together."

"Why, what would he do?"

"What would he do? He would hack me to pieces and make little heaps of my flesh."

Vithaleswara Rao was taken aback. He could not imagine how this intelligent girl who showed so much poise and confidence in the classroom could be so scared of her brother. It puzzled him all the more because he knew Carey's reputation as a notorious skirt chaser. How could he be in a position to judge her?

Vithaleswara Rao didn't understand how Carey's mind worked. The more females who succumbed to his seduction, the more Carey was convinced that the entire female race was born loose, and the more tightly he sought to control his sister's movements.

Manjula feared another man: her history lecturer, Mr. Rama Prabhu. A dogmatic brahmin who despised untouchables, he flaunted his brahminism, wearing an old-fashioned panche (a traditional men's garment worn around the waist), a tonsure, and a forehead *bottu* (ritual mark). Every day, every single day, he made Manjula stand up and scolded her in front of the class. "Why are you here? If you want to giggle, giggle outside, not in my class." "Why are you looking there? If you cannot focus, why do you pursue education? Education is not suitable for the likes of you." All the students could see he was tormenting her for no reason. He always picked her to answer his questions. If she couldn't do it, he would disparage her intelligence, and if she did answer, he would say, "So you think you know everything? You know nothing!" When he did such things, Vithaleswara Rao and Ashok would send Manjula glances of sympathy from across the aisles. Rama Prabhu had the two men come to see him in the staff room and asked, "Why do you talk with that girl? Can't you see she's nothing?"

Then in January, Niranjanamma came to Gudivada to stay with Manjula's family in Slatter Peta for a week. During her visit, she noticed Vithaleswara Rao walking Manjula home and asked her, "What caste is he?" When Niranjanamma heard, she advised Manjula, "Forget about him. Intercaste marriage is not for you. Don't let it get into your head that you mean anything to him." This from Niranjanamma, of all people!

Manjula was hurt. She started to wonder, "Why does he always walk with me? There must be a reason."

Finally she asked him, "Are you befriending me because you want to get close to Kusuma?"

Vithaleswara Rao was bewildered. "No, I have no interest in Kusuma."

"Then who is it? Tara?"

Vithaleswara Rao was offended. "If I am interested in them, I can very well talk to them directly."

Then it dawned on Vithaleswara Rao. With her dark skin, tall and slender build, and high cheekbones, Manjula was considered ugly, considered herself ugly. But Vithaleswara Rao, an avid moviegoer, had picked up Western tastes in female beauty from Hollywood films. He liked tall, slender girls; he loved high cheekbones. As for skin, it wasn't dark or light that mattered to him. Manjula's skin was fabulously flawless, and that was what had caught his eye when they first met.

After Satyam's marriage, Maniamma was attentive to Manjula. In Telugu there is a saying, *Maradalu ardha mogudu*: "Husband's sister is half a husband." Maniamma, wanting to be a good bride, did everything for Manjula. To make her feel better about the marriage, Satyam and Prasanna Rao bought Manjula half a dozen saris—not plain white ones this time but real saris with floral prints and borders. Every day Maniamma washed those saris and starched and ironed them so Manjula could go to class in style. Her classmates began to look at her in a new light.

For all but the handful of women in Manjula's classes, including herself, who planned to go on to postgraduate studies, getting their B.A. was the end of their education and the end of an era of their lives. Now they would get married off and stop living for themselves. Marriage meant living for husbands, children, and in-laws.

On the last day of classes, the girls in Manjula's class were filled with strange feelings. They did not want to leave campus. They sat around chatting, saying nothing of substance. They laughed and laughed at the smallest things. In college, the girls had felt a kind of freedom they would never again have in life.

When finally it got too late to stay any longer, they started home together for the last time. First they reached the kamma neighborhood, tearing two girls away from the group. The rest went on to the kapu colony, where Kusuma said goodbye.

One by one, all the caste girls were dropped off. In the end only two remained, Manjula and Chandra Leela. The caste neighborhoods were behind them now—only the malapallis on the outskirts of town remained. Manjula lived in the better of the two, and Chandra Leela in the filthier and poorer one. The two of them walked on in silence.

Taking leave of Manjula, Chandra Leela lashed out at her with pent-up righteous fury. "You know, Manjula, I've always wanted to be your friend, but you only care to have caste friends, you don't care for your own kind! You really have mental problems. You hurt me and I wanted to let you know it." Leaving Manjula standing speechless at her doorstep, Chandra Leela went on alone to Mandapadu, the farthest and most isolated neighborhood of all.

"She's right," Manjula thought. "I do like kammas more. But I can't help it. I don't like poverty—I like kammas and I prefer their friendship." After that, she stopped thinking about it.

On the first day of preparation holidays (as they called the interval between the last class and the first exam), Vithaleswara Rao was filled with anxiety. At first he couldn't tell what was wrong. But after a couple of days, he realized that it was the prospect of not seeing Manjula. For three years, he had taken her company for granted, and now that time was over. It would be nearly impossible to see her. They lived in different parts of town, and a man cannot go out of his way to see a woman without a proper reason. From this moment on, he began making plans to ask for her hand. There was simply no other way he could continue to spend time with her.

Manjula knew this to be out of the question. Marrying for love was taboo for all castes and classes, and few respected this taboo more strictly than Manjula's family. It was the Christian way, or so the Western missionaries had taught them. And as untouchables striving to gain respectability in a caste society, families such as Prasanna Rao's had to be especially mindful of these traditional rules.

If there had ever been a chance of Manjula's going against her family in her choice of husband, the Aseervadam affair had foreclosed it. She'd vowed never to tarnish her honor. Manjula had warned Vithaleswara Rao never to approach her father for any reason.

But Vithaleswara Rao, taking this hint, nevertheless failed to understand how Prasanna Rao could object to a proposal from a popular, wealthy, politically powerful high-caste boy who also adored his daughter. "It should be the other way round," Vithaleswara Rao would say to his father.

Late one Sunday evening during the preparation holidays, Vithaleswara

Rao and Ashok came to the door of Manjula's house in Slatter Peta. Scared, she ran inside. They should know her father would be home on Sundays.

Vithaleswara Rao had come to ask Prasanna Rao to give his daughter permission to travel with the rest of the boys and the girls in her class to attend a classmate's wedding. Gentle and dignified Prasanna Rao exploded. Was this a new excuse for young people to freely parade around town together? Did the two boys think his daughter came from the kind of family that would allow her to go around in the company of boys?

Inside, crouching beside the hearth, Manjula trembled. She would have to convince her father that she had not put her friends up to this.

Vithaleswara Rao understood that as long as Prasanna Rao had breath in him, he would never let Vithaleswara Rao marry Manjula. And as long as she lived under her father's shadow, she would never disobey him.

But soon Manjula would be leaving home to pursue her master's. Hopefully he would get admission wherever she enrolled. Then they could be together for the next two years. That would be plenty of time to convince her to marry him, whether her family agreed or not.

FIVE

⊚ ⊚ ⊚

EXAM RESULTS CAME OUT. SATYAM, Manjula, and their father passed (he had enrolled in a B.A. program by correspondence). Carey failed. It was English again.

Many of Manjula's classmates passed, but only three of them were accepted by Andhra University: Manjula, Satyam, and their friend Ganga Raju.

On the day they were to leave for Vizag, Manjula made a special visit to her old history lecturer Mr. Rama Prabhu's home. He wouldn't let her into his house. Standing outside the gate, she thanked him: "Sir, without you pushing me hard the way you did, I never would have passed, let alone received a first class."

She meant it. She had the demented notion that this man had humili-ated and terrorized her with no other purpose than to make her study hard. As though Rama Prabhu were a stricter version of Sambasiva Rao, with the same ideals of uplifting untouchables but with different methods. Manjula wasn't aware of her tendency to prostrate herself before caste Hindus, especially brahmins. Throughout her life—in this and other ways—she coupled rebellion with obeisance.

On a sweaty summer evening, friends and family went to the railway station to see off Satyam, Manjula, and Ganga Raju. Manjula, beaming with excitement, sat at the window to wave goodbye. As the train pulled out, Carey ran alongside it and snarled at her, "Behave yourself." She shrank with hurt and shame.

The next morning they arrived at Waltair Station in Vizag. Vizag is a beautiful port city on the Bay of Bengal with pristine white beaches on one side and green hills on the other. Its endless streets slope up and down, lined with palm trees and street vendors. At nearly every corner you see a Hindu temple or a Christian church.

Vizag was also where Satyam and Manjula's mother was buried. Since fleeing the city during the Japanese bombing, they had never returned, except when Satyam, in the final year for his B.A., had visited Andhra University to represent his college in a statewide debating competition. The topic his team was given was "Capitalism or Communism?" Sat-yam's teammate, intent on accruing extracurricular credits, wanted to defend Communism because he thought it was easier. With a wave of his hand, Satyam let him have his choice. Arguing for capitalism with great passion, lyricism, and good sense, Satyam won his college the gold medal.

Returning to the AU campus as a student at the Arts College, Satyam settled into a hostel. In the mornings he liked to stand at his balcony look-ing out at the campus below. He soon noticed a pretty paki girl who came to clean out the latrines in the faculty quarters. She reminded him of his beautiful Maniamma, who was pregnant when he left home.

In his first week at AU, Satyam was called to a meeting for SFI mem-bers and a few Communist workers from the dockyards. They gathered late at night in an older student's room. A senior representative of the party had come to speak.

After Stalin died and Khrushchev took over as the Soviet leader, major changes occurred in international Communist policy. The purpose of the meeting was to inform those attending of the Indian Communist Party's new line.

Before the party man even started to explain, Satyam lost his temper. "If you want to follow Moscow's orders blindly, you do that!" he interrupted. "Don't expect us to do the same. We will study the documents ourselves and come to our own conclusions. Now you just go home."

Satyam could see what was going on in Russia. The Soviets were going the same way the Indian party had started to go under the leadership of Dange and Rajeswara Rao, who rejected any renewal of the armed struggle and relied solely on elections to bring the party to power. This unofficial faction proclaimed, just like Khrushchev, that socialism could be achieved peacefully through a gradual transformation of society. When Stalin was alive, everyone took his sayings as verses from the Vedas. But Stalin had been dead three years, and now Khrushchev was saying Stalin had committed crimes.

Not long after that meeting, Satyam learned that Sundarayya, the great organizer of the Telangana Armed Struggle, was visiting AU. Satyam was eager to approach him. After all, Sundarayya had opposed Dange and Rajeswara Rao on the question of withdrawing the armed struggle.

Satyam went to see him at the university guesthouse and asked, "This change in the party line, comrade, what are we to make of it? Where is the party going, and what are we students to do?"

Sundarayya, even Sundarayya, could only tell these young men— who were ready to sacrifice their lives—to pass their exams and find themselves jobs.

In the midsemester exams, Satyam stood first in political theory, economics, and history. While he was home in Gudivada for recess, Maniamma gave birth to a boy, whom he named Siddhartha. When the happy news came out, Satyam's supporters from the ghettos—pakis, field laborers, rickshaw pullers—flocked to the house bearing gifts. It made Manjula

gravely uneasy to see lepers from Satyamurthy Nagar take the infant in
their arms and kiss him, but Satyam made sure she didn't say a word.

Marriage and fatherhood had little effect on Satyam. All the passion
and poetry that was in him—little of it now went toward his wife and
son. His mind was still occupied with the problem of how to make an
Indian revolution.

He got his hands on some documents of the Chinese Communist Party
that put forward an alternative to the Soviet line. There Satyam at last found
a diagnosis of the ailment afflicting the Soviet Communist Party. The Chinese called it revisionism—a fundamental departure from Marxist doc-
trine. They attacked the Soviets for embracing the possibility of "peaceful
coexistence" between socialist states and imperialism and of a "peaceful
transition to socialism" in the capitalist countries.

Satyam saw that the Indian revolution had to take the Chinese path.
The toilers could never come to power by legal means such as elections.
His task was to assemble and train the cadres to build and lead an army of
peasant guerrillas. Its aim would be to liberate the countryside village by
village, driving off the landlords and gathering forces to ultimately encir-
cle the cities and capture state power. After years of questioning, Satyam
had found the way forward.

On returning to campus, he plunged into a serious study of the writings of Chairman Mao. Slowly a circle formed around him. Satyam earned
the sobriquet AU Mao.

This group of like-minded friends included Chalasani Prasad, a kamma
student a year ahead of Satyam with an impeccable Communist pedigree.
Chalasani's family—not just his immediate family, but the extended family
as well—had fought in Telangana. His own brother, his sister's husband,
and an uncle of his had been shot dead by police. Another uncle and several cousins had languished in prison for years. Chalasani admired his
dead brother dearly.

There was also Panchadi Krishnamurthy, a man of the *kalinga* caste,
from Srikakulam district. In Srikakulam, the kalingas, although officially a
backward caste, occupy the same social and economic status as do the
kammas in Krishna district. Panchadi, however, came from a poor kalinga

family. Satyam was struck by his handsome looks and the discipline he showed in his studies. He woke up early, bathed, dressed neatly, and combed his hair so as not to let a single hair stray. He sat and studied for an hour before class, and when he returned, he would have his tea and settle down again with his textbooks. He was studying economics.

Satyam reckoned that Panchadi would be a great asset to the coming Maoist movement. He tried to draw him into his circle. But Panchadi told him clearly, "Look, my family is very poor. They put all their resources into my education. I am going to get a first class and become a lecturer."

Yet he had a strong feeling for social justice. He could not hold out long. He was lured by Satyam's spontaneous disquisitions, the documents he would leave in Panchadi's room. His friend Chaudhari Tejeswara Rao, who often visited him at the hostel, also soon joined the Maoist circle.

Then there was Y. Koteswara Rao, a twenty-one-year-old from Nellore district. When he came to school, he was in the Youth Congress. Thin, uncouthly dressed, and obviously penniless, he was nonetheless brilliant and honest. Seeing that he came from a poor weaver-caste family, Satyam trained his sights on him and soon turned him into a Communist.

These and others gathered around Satyam. They all hated the Indian Communist Party. They all hated Khrushchev. They saw it as their task to prepare for guerrilla war.

Every morning at eight they met at the India Coffee House, where they read and discussed the day's news. At ten, they went to classes. At five, after class, they met again over tea to study the national and international situation.

Each of them chose a field of work to specialize in. Some wanted to become speakers, some theoreticians. Others, who wanted to become guerrillas, exercised furiously and learned to read maps.

Satyam would go to the pure white beach that Vizag was famous for to practice speaking. He faced the endless ocean, making believe he was addressing the masses. "You must rise to the hour," he exhorted the tide, and told the waves, "Yes, you are retreating, but you must retreat in an orderly way, with discipline, keeping in mind that this retreat is tactical only, that you will return to fight on when the time is right." This vision of the ocean as the masses and the waves as guerrillas would later inspire his famous poem "Alala paina nigha . . ." (Surveilling the waves).

At the start of his second year at the university, Satyam proposed capturing the student council in elections. His friends thought it would be impossible—the campus had a virulently anti-Communist atmosphere in the aftermath of the 1955 electoral defeat that made it dangerous to be known as a Communist sympathizer. But Satyam told his friends, "You wait and see," and set about his task.

He used the same strategy that had worked in the Gudivada College elections and allied with the enemies of his enemies, in this case with the Youth Congress. Congress students weren't perpetrating the anti-Communist intimidation on the AU campus; rather, the members of the Democratic Students Union (DSU), the student wing of the Socialist Party of India, were.

At first Satyam found it hard to understand how a group that called itself socialist could be so violently hostile to actual socialists like himself. The DSU was so far right that to them Congress was left-wing, and they menaced Congress students and SFI members alike. Satyam came to see that the ideology that stood directly opposed to Marxism was not capitalism but Gandhian socialism.

Gandhian socialists espoused the virtue of traditional ways and a traditional village economy. They stood for self-reliance, self-employment. Producing one's own food, weaving one's own cloth. They hated modern technology and heavy industry, which was why they hated Congress under Nehru, who did not share Gandhi's regressive fantasies.

The DSU students were mainly brahmins, and they were all rich. They wore what was coming to be the distinctive attire of the politically connected feudal elite: pure white cotton pants and shirts, starched and ironed.

Satyam joined hands with Congress. Together they put out the word that when Satyam was a student in Gudivada, he was implicated in no less than seven police investigations into anti-eviction struggles against powerful landlords. This gave the DSU members pause. "These sons of a bitches, they are violent sons of bitches," they said among themselves, and backed off their intimidation of Communist supporters, fearing for their personal safety. The SFI won.

Satyam and his friends wanted to assert their victory. Chalasani Prasad proposed that on behalf of the AU Literary Association they invite Sri Sri to speak on campus.

During the 1955 elections, when Telugu society split into Communists and anti-Communists, even the Progressive Writers Association split, with all its leading members going over to the anti-Communist side but for one man: Sri Sri.

For his loyalty to the party, Sri Sri paid a heavy price. Every day the newspapers printed an article or poem denouncing him. This man who had been a legend in his own time was painted in the press as a buffoon, a traitor, a terrorist. "Srirangam, nee rangam khalee, khalee" (Sri Sri, you are finished) was the jeering refrain.

In the 1955 campaign, as Sri Sri's performance troupe crisscrossed the state in support of the Communist ticket, troupe members noticed the great poet behaving strangely. He would latch onto certain names and words and utter them over and over nonsensically. His friends soon realized he had gone mad. Not wanting to give the anti-Communists the satisfaction of knowing they had driven Sri Sri out of his mind, they spirited him off to Madras and consigned him to a mental hospital, where he slowly recovered.

Satyam felt it was the duty of any Communist to show appreciation to Sri Sri for his unwavering refusal to desert his comrades. Chalasani being the keenest Sri Sri fan of all, Satyam appointed him to organize the event.

The day after it was announced, some DSU members came running to Satyam in a terrible state. "Tell us, Mr. Satyamurthy, is it true there is going to be a bloodbath?" Satyam asked them to explain. They told him how the evening before, as they were peacefully chatting in the India Coffee House, Chalasani had come up to them and said, "Boys, if you are thinking of making a scene when Sri Sri speaks, watch out! There will be a bloodbath!"

Unhappy as he was about Chalasani's acting on his own, Satyam told those who came to complain about it, "Just try and disrupt Sri Sri's speech and you will see for yourself what will happen."

While Chalasani busied himself booking rooms at the university guesthouse and arranging the audio system, Satyam organized a thirty-man security squad. The event took place in the open grounds in front of the India Coffee House. The security situation was more challenging than it would have been in an enclosed auditorium. Satyam and his men surrounded the crowd and kept a close watch.

Throngs of students attended. Many came because they admired Sri Sri, many others because they wanted to witness a bloodbath.

When Sri Sri went mad and for a time was unable to write, his friends in the Madras cine field set him up with dubbing jobs. Now he told the students, "I am currently doing dubbing. See, dub-bing. You know what I mean? *Dubbu*-ing." In Telugu, *dubbu* means "money." Sri Sri was pleased with this pun. Next to him sat his new young wife, Sarojini, to whom he turned and said, "I need to do dubbu-ing for my Sarojini." Then he fixated on her lips. "Lips lush. Lush lips. The movement of her lips."

He babbled on incoherently. The anti-Communists could have jeered, but under the eyes of Satyam's security team no one dared. The event was a failure, but at least Sri Sri left AU unscathed.

Later on, at Satyam's proposal, the students invited Kondapalli Seetharamayya to give a seminar on Marxism.

Kondapalli Seetharamayya, like Sri Sri, was in dire need of rehabilitation. The Communist Party was waiting for a chance to expel him. They didn't like his call for a renewal of armed struggle. But they hesitated because of the authority he had among younger cadres like Satyam, who admired him precisely for his militancy.

Looking for a reason to kick the man out, the party had fastened on rumors that he was having an illicit affair with the young widow of a Telangana martyr. Seetharamayya denied these accusations. "She is a widow with two children," he explained. "She has lost her husband. She is lonely. She is our comrade. I only want to comfort her. She is like a sister to me."

Unlike Sri Sri, Seetharamayya was a masterly speaker. He was so charismatic and compelling that if you left him with a consummate anti-

Communist for an hour, he would turn that man into a Communist guerrilla. The event was a great success. Seetharamayya left happy and encouraged.

In the last month of classes, a spectacular dinner was held for the graduating students. At the end of the feast, Satyam invited all the students to the back of the hall and asked them to look outside. Around the trash heap where the scraps from the dinner were thrown, tens of children and old men and women were fighting over these remains with stray dogs and pigs.

"This is the condition of the Indian people," Satyam said. "You are graduating. Think about what you will do with your lives, what you want to do for your country."

Only a week was left before exams. As he hadn't looked at his books the whole year, Satyam now needed to sit down and study without distractions.

But at this moment Carey appeared at Satyam's doorstep, tired and disheveled, with a young girl in tow. The girl looked scared. Carey said, "Brother, help us marry."

When Carey failed his B.A. exams, his father sent him to Bunder College in the town of Machilipatnam in a neighboring district. Carey shared a room with other students in the house of a goldsmith-caste man. He then promptly seduced the landlord's daughter. But this time he fell in love hard. Carey's roommates disapproved. They didn't like to see an untouchable boy fooling around with a caste girl, especially since they weren't getting such an opportunity. They ratted on him to the girl's father, who forbade her to see him.

He found a chance to elope with her and straightaway they went to Vijayawada to see Manikya Rao. Who better to help an intercaste couple on the run than a man who had gone through hell for his own caste wife?

But Manikya Rao turned Carey away. Now time was of the essence. The girl's family was hunting for her. Carey needed Satyam's help to marry her before they were caught.

"Okay," Satyam told him. "Let me talk to the girl." He promised to settle everything. In the meantime, he had his friend Rama Rao take Carey

to the beach to calm him down. As Carey anxiously paced the sand, Satyam
sent word to the girl's family. A few hours later, her brother showed up in
a car he had rented specially to track her down.

Satyam turned to the girl, who was hiding behind a chair, and asked,
"What would you like to do, amma?"

She took two small steps back, then one big hop forward, and went
running into her brother's arms.

When Carey returned, his girl was gone. He couldn't understand
why his brother, of all people, would break up an intercaste couple. He felt
betrayed.

He fell into Satyam's bed, covered himself with a sheet, and cried and
cried. For a whole week he went on crying pitifully, stopping only briefly
at mealtimes, when he would shuffle over to the mess and consume enormous quantities of food. Manjula, concerned for his welfare, came to watch
over him. She and Satyam had both waited until the final week before
exams to do all their studying for the year, and they both spent that cru-
cial week at Carey's side, trying to console him.

Satyam dropped his exams rather than fail or get bad marks. That way
he would have a chance to study on his own and attempt them later on.
Manjula took her exams and received a third class. The two siblings returned home shamefaced.

The two years Satyam spent at university were another two years devoted to politics. And his political efforts, too, had gone to waste. For all
their study and planning, the circle Satyam led never cohered into a
Maoist organization. When he and his friends graduated, each went his
own way.

Satyam was twenty-six years old. He had no M.A., no job, no money
of his own. And he had a second child now, a girl he named Anupama. It
was too much to ask his father, whose financial situation was dire, to go
on supporting him and his family. And poor Maniamma had been married for two years now and still didn't live with her husband. Instead she'd
been staying partly under her father's roof and partly under Prasanna
Rao's, where Satyam would pay her an occasional visit like a *sanyasi* (vaga-
bond). And every time he saw her, he gave her another child.

Now Satyam needed to find work. He learned of an opening for a subeditor at *Visalandhra*, the Telugu-language Communist daily based in Vijayawada. He was recommended for the job by a district committee member who had long been impressed by his intelligence.

Satyam was relieved. His plan was to spend one or two hours every day after work studying for his M.A. exams. Two months before exams he would take leave from the job to complete his preparation.

Since the job was in Vijayawada, Satyam planned to stay with Manikya Rao, who had been living in that city ever since he made peace with his wife's family.

Satyam's old friend was doing quite well, tutoring day and night and earning money with both hands. He and his fine wife received Satyam lovingly. When they sensed he had come to ask to stay a few days, Niranjanamma whispered something and she and Manikya Rao excused themselves to go into the kitchen. When they came back out, their attitude was very different. Manikya Rao dropped his air of hospitality and became mealymouthed. At last he mumbled something about having an appointment to go to. "You should come and visit us sometime," he told Satyam.

Satyam couldn't believe it. This was the man he had spent two years of his life fighting to defend. For whose sake Satyam had bankrupted his poor father and angered his grandmother. Whose wife Satyam's sister had watched over day and night, whose child she had cared for. Whom Satyam's brother had followed like a shadow day after day and guarded every night, sleeping at his feet at night, ready to kill. And now this man couldn't bring himself to let Satyam stay in his house for a couple of days. Manikya Rao and Niranjanamma turned him away just as he came, without even offering him a glass of water.

Satyam had never felt so much shame in his whole life. "They must think since I am poor, I have come back to get paid for the help I gave them," he said to himself. "Well, they have money, I don't. I don't want them to think that I am after some rupees. We helped because we wanted to. We want nothing from them."

Hurt, he went to see Kondapalli Seetharamayya, who had recently moved to Vijayawada. He had always been like a father to Satyam, and his wife, Koteswaramma, was fond of Satyam, too.

The Kondapallis' house, which they'd had built for themselves in

Mogalrajapuram, a new extension of Vijayawada, was not like other houses in the city. It was more of a cottage, a peaceful little cottage thatched with palm fronds. They had planted rosebushes all around it.

Seetharamayya and Koteswaramma were so happy to see Satyam. They made him sit on a cot and gave him coffee to drink. When they found out he was looking for a place to stay, they said, "Why stay two days only? Stay here with us as long as you are in Vijayawada. Bring your family here!"

It was a tempting offer. True, that cottage on the outskirts of Vijayawada was far from Satyam's office in the center of the city. But it was pleasant and comfortable, and he would be with friends. Satyam decided to rent from Seetharamayya and Koteswaramma.

Maniamma loved traveling to new places, especially towns and cities. Any place on earth was bigger than her village, Sankarapadu. Right away she got busy packing the family's things. When she saw Carey packing, too, she flew into a rage. "He mustn't come with us!" she demanded.

"What is this, Maniamma? Why are you saying this?"

Maniamma told Satyam of a fight she had had with Carey: "He called me names, he raised his foot to kick me." To her, Carey had crossed a clear line, raising his foot to his brother's wife.

Satyam was upset to hear this, but said, "Okay, you are right, that was unacceptable. But what can we do? Where is he going to go?"

Maniamma could not believe Satyam's response. Not only did he condone Carey's behavior, he wanted to invite him to live with them in Vijayawada.

She flung the packing at hand to the floor and went off to sulk on the doorstep.

In the end Maniamma prevailed and they moved to Vijayawada without Carey. The Kondapallis' cottage still smelled new and fresh, and the rosebushes all around it spread their own delicate fragrance. Satyam loved the place.

The cottage was divided into three portions. In one lived Seetharamayya with Koteswaramma, their two children, Karuna and Chandu, and Koteswaramma's widowed mother. Dashing Seetharamayya had rescued

Koteswaramma from a life of widowhood. In landed castes such as hers, the girls were married off when they were only months old. She was a child widow, and because it was taboo for widows to remarry, she thought she had nothing left in life. But Seetharamayya married her and brought her into the movement. They lived underground during the Telangana Armed Struggle, he as a guerrilla fighter and she as a courier. He was a big bear of a man, she a little bird of a woman. Though she was born into the reddy caste, everyone who saw the fastidious way she spoke and carried herself used to take her for a brahmin.

In another portion of the cottage lived Anasooyamma, the widow of a "martyr" killed in the Telangana Armed Struggle, and her two small children. She was the one the party accused Seetharamayya of having an affair with. He always denied these accusations, saying he was merely consoling her for her loss. They addressed one another as *annayya* (brother) and *chellemma* (sister).

Anasooyamma came from a wealthy kamma family. She was a healthy, full-figured woman who dressed in fine saris and had a lively tongue. While Koteswaramma cooked vegetables that her mother grew in the front yard, Anasooyamma prepared aromatic chicken curries.

In the middle portion of the cottage, between these two households, Satyam and his family set up their new home. It was nothing less than paradise for him to be living among these veterans of Telangana and listening to their stories. Maniamma was delighted to see all these high-caste kamma, reddy people treating her husband as one of them. They were nice to her, too, and the six children played together. The rose-bordered cottage was a little utopian world without caste.

But they had hardly settled there when trouble arose. The neighbors objected to a family of outcastes coming to stay among them. They pressed the Kondapallis to kick the family out. Even Koteswaramma's mother, Anjamma, openly threatened, "You tell them to go, or I go."

But the couple stood strong. They told everyone to go jump in the Ganga. Satyam was touched by their affection. Seetharamayya's teenage children, Karuna and Chandu, played with the little ones, his own and Anasooyamma's, who called them "big brother" and "big sister." The three families became that close. At night they would all set up their cots under the open sky and laugh together and sing revolutionary songs.

The *Visalandhra* office was located in Buckingham Peta, in the middle of the city. To get there Satyam needed to take a city bus, which stopped a couple of miles from where he lived. But he loved the cottage so much he was willing to make this trip every day.

Visalandhra was launched as a weekly during the last days of the armed struggle. For a time it had operated underground. When Nehru lifted the ban on the Communist Party and its publications, the paper came out of hiding as the organ of the Separate Andhra agitation. Now it had settled down as a daily and was run like any other capitalist newspaper while still touting itself as the Communist voice. The money was put up by a to-bacco baron sympathetic to the party who nevertheless expected it to turn a profit. The top editors and managers were party leaders, but they treated the staff, who were all members themselves, as mere employees.

The paper had twenty editors and subeditors. The chief editor and the members of the management committee were all kammas, while Satyam's direct supervisor, an assistant editor, was a brahmin.

Satyam's job was to take the national news that came out of the tele-printer, translate it from English to Telugu, give it a title, and format the text so it could be composed and sent off to the printer. Half the time he worked the night shift, but since the Kondapallis and Anasooyamma were living with his family, he did not have to worry about them.

One evening after Satyam had been staying at the Kondapallis' only a month and a half, he came home to funereal silence. Seetharamayya was standing at the window. Koteswaramma sat staring at the floor. Her children were holding Satyam's children and shushing them when they made a noise.

After years of hesitation, the party leaders had finally grown bold enough to expel Seetharamayya over his alleged affair with Anasooyamma. Seetharamayya explained that the two of them had sat together and de-cided, "They are accusing us of having an affair. Let us just go ahead and have one." They decided to go off to settle in Telangana, taking Anasoo-yamma's small children with them.

Satyam had no words. He held his comrade tightly and cried like a little boy whose father was leaving him. Whenever Satyam had acted against the party's approval—when he organized a rival theater troupe, when he fought the eviction of poor people in Gudivada, when he defended Manikya Rao's right to live in peace with the woman he loved— Seetharamayya along with Koteswaramma had always been there to encourage him, telling him that he was right. With the old man gone, Satyam would have to stand up to the degenerated party all alone. He hoped they would one day have another chance to fight together.

Koteswaramma felt sorry for Satyam. She called him over and consoled him like a mother. "Why do you cry so much? Do you think this man is worth it?"

It had become apparent to Satyam soon after he'd come to live there that the party's accusations were true. Seetharamayya preferred Anasooyamma's chicken curries to Koteswaramma's homegrown-vegetable fries. But Satyam did not hold this lapse against his idol.

Seetharamayya had nothing to say to Satyam. He took Anasooyamma and her children and went far away, leaving Koteswaramma and her children behind.

Koteswaramma bore the pain of this betrayal in silence. Though she'd known about the affair all along, she'd never imagined her husband would leave his family to go off with his mistress. He never bothered about how they were going to live. Koteswaramma had little education and had never held a job in her life.

⊚

TWO WEEKS LATER, SATYAM WAS summoned to his manager's office and sacked. He was humiliated. He couldn't say a word.

The manager, who wouldn't ordinarily have taken the trouble to explain himself to a mere employee, took pity on him and said, "You have no efficiency. You're too slow." Satyam did not always finish the galleys he was given and did not translate as fast as they would have liked him to. "You cannot take forever, polishing and polishing and chiseling and chiseling," the man told him.

Satyam understood what the manager was saying. The job was not like writing poetry. But Satyam had no experience in this kind of work. They knew that before they took him in. Where could he learn, where could he get the experience he needed? Someone had to give him an opportunity. This was not a capitalist paper, it was a Communist Party paper. He had moved his family here, relying on the job. He had no savings, nothing.

But the hardest part for him was walking out of the building in front of his coworkers.

In the evening all the subeditors came to Satyam's house to express their sympathy. Later Satyam heard that some of them had gone to the management and protested. Manikya Rao went to the office in person to speak out against how Satyam was treated.

It was whispered that he was fired because the management found out his caste. Others said management had learned he was the youth from AU who had told the party representative to go home, the firebrand student who had proposed a motion in the party to expel all the top leaders, including Sundarayya.

SIX

* * *

MANJULA ALONE AMONG ALL THE girls graduating from Gudivada College had got admission into a master's program that year. And of the boys, only Satyam and another classmate of theirs had been accepted to Andhra University as she was. Neither Ashok nor Vithaleswara Rao had gotten a seat. Manjula was convinced that whether she studied or not, God was on her side and she would always pass.

The ladies' hostel at Andhra University was located not on campus but in Maharani Peta, right on the beach, in the summer palace of an erstwhile raja. For the first time in her life but for a brief spell in Telaprolu, Manjula was living in a pukka residence. Not only that, it had a ceiling fan.

Two weeks after moving in, Manjula was informed by the watchman that she had a visitor. She was stunned to find Vithaleswara Rao waiting in the visitors' lounge. He was emaciated, disheveled, shivering as though with fever. His eyes were those of one who hasn't slept in ages.

He asked her how she liked the university, what she wanted to do after. No doubt he wanted to know if she would marry him, but neither of them referred to that. After a few hours talking to her, he left unhappier than ever, leaving a greeting card on which he had scrawled something vague like "Much water has passed under the bridge." Manjula would never see him again.

Every day the university bus picked up the girls and brought them to campus, where all the boys waited anxiously, sweating in the heat, making sure their hair was in place, jostling to get a glimpse of the girls as they got off the bus.

◎

MANJULA MADE A NEW SET of friends who considered themselves sophisticated. They read Telugu novels, talked about Sri Sri's poetry, and went out in the city to cinemas. They were smug and assumed they could pass without studying hard. They sat in the library or lounged on the verandas facing the beach, laughing and gossiping about everyone on campus.

They especially liked to laugh at the other Christian girls, the majority of whom went everywhere together, even to the bathroom. These other girls—Nessy, Sarada Kelly, Suseela, and the rest—went to church on Sundays and holidays and met in the evenings to read the Bible, sing hymns, and pray. They studied diligently and respected their elders and those in authority. They looked down in turn on Manjula, and especially disapproved of her going to the movies, which was considered a sin.

Another Christian girl in the hostel, Rajeswari, also did not belong to the Christian clique. She was the embodiment of a popular stereotype of untouchable Christian girls. As portrayed in Telugu movies and novels, the young woman of this type is named Lily or Rosie or Roja or Mary. Usually a nurse or a secretary, she is vulgar in her dress and behavior and constantly throws herself at men. Manjula and her friends called girls of this type moderns.

Rajeswari used eyeliner and lipstick, coated her dark face with talcum powder, and loosely braided her hair. She wore high heels, short-sleeved blouses, see-through saris whose ends were always slipping off her chest, and, most horrifying in Manjula's eyes, a brassiere! The other girls wore a smaller white blouse inside their blouses. To have straps visibly outlined against a girl's back was too shocking. When Rajeswari walked by, the boys made fun of her strong talcum-powder scent and loose braid, while at the same time tripping over each other to catch a glimpse of her bra strap through her blouse.

Rajeswari was friends with the only other modern in the hostel, who to everyone's shock was not an untouchable Christian but a brahmin. Manjula often wondered what was wrong with this girl. While many untouchable Christians liked to be stylish in this way, brahmins typically reveled in looking old-fashioned. But the boys would never harass a brahmin girl, however provocatively she dressed or behaved.

When exams came, every girl went mad with anxiety. The Christian girls spent their days in a frenzy of prayers and cramming. One night Nessy got on her knees to pray and fell asleep, waking up in the same position only five minutes before her exam started.

Manjula's friends, she accidentally discovered one night when she woke up to go to the bathroom, were hiding in closets and studying hard. The reason? It was all competition when it came time to apply for jobs. The higher your marks compared to the others', the better your chances would be. To dupe their classmates into complacency during exam preparation, the girls would pretend not to study at all.

When the exam results were issued, Manjula found out that God does not bless those who are lazy and go to cinemas. With the third-class degree she received, she would never get a college teaching position.

When she returned home with just a third class, she lost the respect of Maniamma, who now fought with everyone in the household. Maniamma would imply that Manjula had only been good at studies because she wasn't pretty, saying, "As soon as I was twelve years old, all the grooms

were chasing after me, making it impossible for me to focus on school-
work." Maniamma would denigrate Carey for trying to elope with a minor (knowing full well the girl had been of age) and constantly compared
the Kambhams unfavorably to her own family. Maniamma had never forgotten how Manjula had bitterly opposed her marriage, and now her resentment was rising to the surface. One day this conflict came to a head
when Manjula finally responded to Maniamma's attacks on Carey's character by asking, "What about your sister?" After Santhamma's husband
kicked her out, she had taken up with a kamma man as his mistress.

Maniamma was outraged. She dropped what she was doing, gathered
her children, and walked out, swearing that the Kambhams would never
see her again.

Prasanna Rao, coming home, learned what had happened and went
running after her to the bus station. Maniamma told him she could never
again live under the same roof with Manjula.

The menfolk discussed the problem and decided to send Manjula
away to get another master's and try, this time, to get at least a second
class. They needed peace in the house. They knew Manjula would not be
permitted to reapply to the regional university, AU. Her only chance to
pursue her studies was to seek entrance to one of the central universities,
of which the closest was Banaras Hindu University (BHU) in northern
India, a journey of two days by train. And it was now too late to file her
application by mail. She would simply take all that she needed and travel
to the campus to apply in person, with no assurance she would be accepted.

Prasanna Rao sold his house and the two hundred yards of land it
stood on for six hundred rupees. With three hundred of those rupees he
sent his daughter far, far away from home, to a place they had never been
to, where people spoke a different language, ate different food, wore different clothes, and even lived under a different climate.

For lack of money for an extra ticket, Manjula's brothers for once relaxed their policy of not allowing her to travel by herself. They just put her
on the train to Benares. She found her berth, tucked her luggage under it,
lay down, and promptly fell asleep.

Thussooook! The newly married marwari girl sitting on the opposite
side with her husband sneezed in her feminine way.

Manjula, startled, woke up agitated and began to mutter, "Naini? Naini?"—the name of the station where she'd been told the train stopped long enough for her to get out and refill her water bottle. The marwari groom replied kindly and knowledgeably in Hindi, "Naini, aayegee, duss, pundrah minit mein." Manjula made out only the "duss, pundrah minit" (ten, fifteen minutes) part. She lowered her feet into her pair of white Hawaii slippers and bent to look under her berth to make sure her green iron trunk was still there. From the small cloth bag in which Maniamma had packed food for the journey, Manjula pulled out a thin bottle whose label had long since been scrubbed off with Sunlight soap and water. Years ago Marthamma had bought it for ten paisa from a woman who sold empty tin cans and bottles and old newspapers. The train slowed and eased into Naini station, just as the marwari man had said, within duss, pundrah minit. Manjula got off and ran over to the railway tap on the platform. She splashed cold water on her sweaty, soot-encrusted face. Then she cupped her hands under the tap and drank to her heart's content. She filled the old bottle with water and carefully screwed the cap back on. Feeling refreshed, she looked up.

The train was pulling out of the station. Manjula's heart stopped. With one hand clutching the bottle and the other gathering the folds of her sari to lift it off the ground so she wouldn't trip over it, she sprinted frantically behind the moving train. The gigantic mountain of metal was slithering away like a dragon, spewing clouds of black smoke, as she, a speck of a girl, raced behind it, her braid lashing across her chest and the railway water sloshing in her belly.

She reached out her hand as far as she could until her fingers felt the steel bar on the door of an unknown compartment. With one last burst of effort, she caught hold of that bar and hoisted herself onto the second step leading up to the door. She was in. Tears did not stream down her cheeks because she was a brave girl, a strong girl. But her heart pounded and her temples throbbed from the enormous expenditure of energy and, not least, the thought of what would have happened had she not caught the train.

The green trunk was not just the only trunk in her family's possession; it contained the documents on her birth, the documents certifying that she had gone to school and passed, and the documents recording her caste, together with the three hundred rupees her father had given her.

Manjula arrived in Benares and hired a tonga, a horse-drawn buggy, to take her to the campus. The ladies' hostel was nearly empty, as it was still summer break. The warden of the hostel, a statuesque spinster, questioned Manjula and, finding she was so lost and clueless that she had traveled fifteen hundred kilometers without filing an application first, took pity on her. The warden let her stay in one of the rooms and asked her to write an application.

◎

IT WAS HELLISHLY HOT. NO fan. Unable to sleep, Manjula would lie in the open on the terrace as people did at home. People who saw her were horrified. "Don't you know in these parts people who sleep outside in summer are dead by morning!"

She submitted her application for the master's program in history, got accepted, and was given a piece of paper, which she carefully placed under her pillow.

The first day of class, the professor told Manjula her name was not on the list of registered students. She had neglected to read the piece of paper she was given and had literally slept on it. The writing on it was not some official gibberish, as she thought, but a warning that if she did not pay her fees by the required deadline, her admission would be rescinded. Manjula made an appointment to see the vice chancellor, but emerged from the meeting empty-handed and with tears in her eyes.

The sun was blazing and not a single leaf moved in the breezeless afternoon. As she walked back to the hostel, Manjula recalled her mother and her dying wish, her father and his fervor for education, her grandmother's hardships for the sake of Manjula and her brothers, her brothers who doted on her, the family house, her sister-in-law who had packed her meals, the disappointment she had caused them all, the hopes she had dashed—theirs and her own. As she thought of these things, tears burst out of her like water splashing out from under the lid of a boiling pot.

"Aapko koyee parayshawny hai kyaa?"

Manjula raised her head and saw a man of her own age standing in front of her. The man spoke no English and she spoke no Hindi. She kept saying things in a mixture of Telugu and English, appending *hai* to the end of each sentence in a pointless effort to make her speech at least approximate the sound of spoken Hindi. After a great while and many frantic hand motions, this patient man at last divined her trouble. He pointed toward a particular building and, with an encouraging wave of the hand, urged her to go in.

In the lobby, she saw a group of twenty-year-old men lounging around a table and chatting loudly. These were the student union men, and this building was the student union office. One of these young men, leaning back in his chair with his foot resting on the table, simply took her papers as he continued talking, and without even looking at her, scrawled something on them—*Admit her*, a simple order to V. S. Jha, the vice chancellor of the university—and handed them back.

That was how powerful the student union was. Universities such as BHU are training grounds for politicians. Today's student union officer is tomorrow's minister.

Summer was over, and the students returned to campus. The girls in the ladies' hostel were true ladies. The majority of them were fabulously wealthy—not the kamma type of wealthy that Manjula knew. Daughters of business tycoons, members of the aristocracy. One girl was even Nepalese royalty.

Her roommates were unfriendly. They blackmailed her for fun. Manjula had borrowed a Telugu novel from an Andhra girl who warned her not to lend it to anyone else. Manjula did, though, to a male classmate, who wouldn't return it. Manjula's roommates threatened to tell the Andhra girl. Another lesson for Manjula: never do anything that you have to keep secret. She finally went and admitted her misdeed to the Andhra girl.

Every girl in the hostel belonged to a clique. North Indians bullied south Indians and never mingled with them. There were separate messes for north and south. North Indians wouldn't go to the south-Indian mess while south Indians wouldn't dare set foot in the north-Indian one.

Within both north and south were subcliques based mainly on

language. BHU was a Tower of Babel. The students from Kerala were divided into two cliques, Christian and Hindu, while Andhra girls stuck together. They opted to live in a single room and did everything as a group. When a new Andhra girl came, the others looked after her and helped her get settled.

But no one helped Manjula, nor did anyone invite her to share a room. She was utterly isolated.

Desperate to find a group to belong to, Manjula looked for a church. Benares was the most quintessentially Hindu of cities, so it was hard to even find one. Also called Varanasi, it is an ancient city on the banks of the sacred river Ganga that has been a center of Hindu learning and piety for thousands of years.

The only church Manjula could find was the one established by migrants from Kerala. But when she went to see it, she found the Christians in that church were not like the Christians she knew. They all looked like elite, high-caste people. The service was ritualistic, with incense burning as in a Hindu temple. Manjula felt so out of place that she left in the middle of the service.

There was also the problem of English. Through the end of her B.A., all of Manjula's classes had been taught in Telugu. She had struggled at Andhra University to read and write in English, and at Benares she faced the same difficulty. Outside her classes, her lack of fluency was a source of shame on this cosmopolitan campus where English was the lingua franca. As Lohia, an independence leader second only to Gandhi in stature, once said, "The use of English is a progenitor of inferiority feelings."

Manjula had brought her father's military woolen rug with her, which was useless in Andhra because of high temperatures. Here, too, it was useless because it couldn't retain even the smallest amount of warmth. But she couldn't afford to buy something more suitable. She put on all her clothes and layered all her sheets and still couldn't stop shivering through the night, inevitably going to her classes drowsy.

One day a theft took place in the ladies' hostel. Some valuables were stolen. Immediately the authorities launched an investigation. Along with the campus police, two female professors came, equipped with a public address system. They ordered all the girls to come out of their rooms and gather in the quad. They announced rooms at random and ordered the girls of that room to go back in escorted by the professors. Manjula's room number was called.

"Vimala Saxena, Pushpa Aggarwal, Manjulabai. Please step forward and enter your room."

The professors searched the room thoroughly, looking even inside the soap dishes and books. They opened Manjula's green metal trunk. The two women peered into the trunk. When they saw what was in that trunk, their eyes opened wide. Slowly, in unison, they raised their heads and looked at each other in disbelief.

Manjula stood there with an embarrassed smile. No ill-gotten valuables were stashed inside that green trunk. Those two ladies were astonished at how little it did contain, and that of no value at all. They'd never known such poor people existed in this world. They said nothing; they were neither patronizing nor mean. But their shock was transparent.

Manjula understood why she was undergoing these torments. It was the wages of her sins—the sins of not having studied hard in AU, of having gone to the movies and had fun. This was her penance.

Papa prakshalana. Atonement for sins. She must not waste one moment on feeling sorry for herself. She must purify her soul. She must work hard now, with the aim of getting a first class. She studied all the time, spending long hours at the library. Except for meals and six hours of sleep, all she did was study.

At the end of first year, Manjula stood second, just two points below the first-rank student.

On her way to the library one morning, Manjula was accosted by the history department's peon. He told her the head of the department wanted to see her.

Professor R. S. Tripathi was old and doddering, but his renown as a historian was such that he was welcome to keep his position at the university as long he liked. Inside his office, Manjula saw her own instructor, Professor Pathak, sitting to one side with a broad smile on his face. He proudly introduced Manjula as the most brilliant student in his class.

As Professor Tripathi gazed at her, his face darkened; his eyes shrank into black slits. He was revolted by the sight of Manjula. One look at her and he knew she was poor and untouchable. The *Mary* in her name made it unmistakable.

"She is the one I told you of," Pathak explained. "You wanted to meet her." But Tripathi merely stared at her coldly and said nothing. Humiliated, Manjula excused herself.

She left the office feeling dizzy. As she walked to the library, she could feel the venom of this poisonous man spread through her veins, shutting down her heart, her brain. She was on the point of collapsing. She ran back to the hostel and fell on her bed. She stayed in for a week.

In the second year, Manjula's social life improved slightly. Her new roommates were an Andhra woman named Durga Kumari and a north-Indian girl named Asha.

By the rough hand of circumstance, the pure and the impure were thrown together. Durga Kumari was a brahmin doctoral student in mathematics. Despite her high caste, she, too, was ostracized by the Andhra clique because she was too old—thirty—and at that age sure to end up a spinster. And she was poor.

Asha, a *baniya* (as the merchant caste is known in north India), came from the richest family of any of the girls in the hostel. They sent her to the university with 150 sets of clothes so that she would never have to wash.

Even so, Asha was especially kind to Manjula. Asha went to the south-Indian mess with her. When Manjula met Asha's aunt, Professor Priyamvada Shah, Manjula learned it was not necessarily a curse to be a spinster, as she had always been taught. In elite circles, some women chose not to marry and didn't feel ashamed in the least. Miss Shah devoted herself to mathematics and saw family life as a distraction.

Manjula decided when she had a daughter, she would name her Asha.

◎

BENARES HAS BEEN A PILGRIMAGE center for over two thousand years. The pious come to the city to bathe in the Ganga and wash away their sins.

Though Manjula's roommate Durga Kumari was ostracized by her

Andhra classmates, as a brahmin she felt entirely at home in Benares. She loved going to the temples. Since she could not go alone, she asked Manjula to come along.

When they got to the temples along the river, Durga Kumari almost fainted from emotion. The force of the divine that infused every element there—the air, the water, the sand, the fire—consumed her brahmin soul. Manjula, on the other hand, almost fainted from disgust. The filth, the stink, the slime, the revolting activities going on all around them, overwhelmed her.

Surrounding the temples were thick masses of people in nothing but wet loincloths, displaying their potbellies, hairiness, hairlessness, diseased skin, running noses, coughing mouths, oily hair, hernias, sagging breasts, toothless gums, shaven heads, missing limbs, wrinkled arms, stiffened fingers, fungal toes. They were all bathing shamelessly, men and women together. The Hindu worship equipment, the dead flowers, the leftover food, were strewn all over. Manjula had seen many untouchable colonies, including those of madigas. But she had never seen, could never have imagined, a filthier place on earth.

On the Ganga, bodies burned on the ghats (steps leading down to the river) in ritual cremations, and the remains were pushed into the water, often only half consumed. The waters of the river were dark and dense. It was perhaps the most polluted water Manjula had ever seen. She watched in horror as the throngs of bathers took that water into their mouths, let it swirl into their throats, and swallowed it down.

Manjula and Durga Kumari faced an unspoken problem at the entrance to a temple. As an untouchable, Manjula was not supposed to enter. Should Durga Kumari pretend to be oblivious of her friend's uncleanness and walk in beside her? What should Manjula do? Should she pretend, out of politeness, that such a monstrous oppression did not exist and attempt to casually enter the temple with her friend?

Yet this dilemma resolved itself simply as soon as it arose. Manjula, of her own will, refused to enter even the holiest of temples, the Kashi Vishwanath. She knew if she took one whiff of that air into her lungs, she would drop dead on the spot.

But when the university girls planned a picnic to Sarnath, Manjula went along, thinking, "What kind of history student would I be if I am in Benares and do not visit Sarnath?"

Sarnath, just thirteen kilometers from Benares, at the confluence of the sacred rivers Ganga and Gomati, is where the Buddha first taught his dharma and attracted his first disciple. Sarnath was where, in the third century B.C., Emperor Ashoka built one of the many pillars bearing the inscription of his edicts. In utter contrast to the Hindu temples, it was a clean, peaceful place.

Except on that day. When the boys learned of the girls' picnic, they, too, planned one. They brought along a gramophone and a manservant who carried it on his head. The boys followed the girls, and the manservant and the music followed the boys. When the girls turned around to look, they made the servant kneel down and changed the record to "Mudh mudhke na dekh . . . ," from the hit Hindi movie *Shree 420*.

Don't look, turning, turning around
In the journey of life,
You are not alone
We are also there with you.

Manjula always loved the wealthier students' endearing mischief.

As their two-year program was coming to an end, Asha and her rich friends discussed the idea of giving farewell presents to Manjula. Asha knitted a sweater and told Manjula it was called a cardigan. Someone else gave her a sari; another, a handmade jewelry box. Manjula was overwhelmed by her roommates' kindness.

She packed her things, bought train tickets. Only one day was left. It had been two years, and the government had still not disbursed her scholarship (one of the many ways in which benefits owed to untouchables are undermined). If she left before the university took its cut, the rest of it would never reach her.

At nine in the evening before her departure, she took Durga Kumari and went to see Professor Narlekar about the money. The meeting couldn't have stood in sharper contrast to her earlier one with Professor Tripathi.

Although also a brahmin and renowned as a mathematician, Professor Narlekar was extremely courteous. His wife plucked jasmine blossoms, strung them on a thread, and gave each of the two women a piece of it to adorn their braids. She served coffee, and the couple chatted with the two women about their families. For Manjula's sake, the professor arranged for the clerk to arrive early at the office and went in early himself. Together they processed the scholarship, and Manjula was able to get her money before starting for home.

◎

AFTER TWO DAYS OF TRAVEL, Manjula reached her father's new home in Veeravalli, a village in Krishna district. She took a long, hot bath and washed the soot from her hair and skin. She was the only one living there with her father. Peace all around. For eighteen years studying had been her main occupation. With the end of her master's program, all that was over. She slept as much as she wanted. She felt calm.

A few days later, Manjula was cutting vegetables when an unexpected thought struck her: "What am I? What is the purpose of being? How can any human being ever be doing nothing?" From that moment on, her calm left her. She grew restless.

Then she noticed small plants sprouting in the yard. Every day she watched them in awe because by evening they would be one inch tall, and the next morning when she woke up they would be three inches.

The plants needed nothing from her. They grew by themselves on a patch in front of their house that needed no fertilizer, having at one time served as the floor of a cow shed. Manjula plucked the spinach, cleaned it, cooked it, sent some to neighbors.

After two months of doing little else, she received her marks list in the mail. She was shocked to find she did not get a first class. She barely got a second class. What could have happened? Had she deluded herself about her own ability? But everyone in the university had been amazed at how tenaciously she studied, and no one doubted she would do well. Could she have numbered her answers wrong? One number wrong, all the rest that followed would be wrong. Did she lose, or did they lose, some of her answer sheets? She stared and stared at her marks list. Then, like a photo developing, a picture formed in her mind. She had made top marks in all the papers except for those that were graded by Tripathi. With the poor marks from his papers, she barely averaged out to second class. His venom had a delayed effect, and Manjula's career would suffer.

She applied for jobs and got an interview for a position teaching political science at a Catholic college in Eluru. She dressed in a modest white sari and no ornaments, gathered her certificates in a loose pile, and caught a bus to Eluru. Just as she got off, the sky opened up. She was drenched to the bone; her certificates were a sopping mess. She was not going to get the job, she knew. Not only because one of her sandals had washed away in the rainwater, but also because she had not studied political science. History had been in demand when she started college eight years before, but by the time she graduated no history jobs were left.

But the Catholics loved her. They correctly assumed that her poverty, modesty, and plain white sari meant she would be docile. They told her to expect papers by mail.

Just as she returned home from Eluru, Manjula was asked to another interview, this time at A.C. College in Guntur. She went and was told to report for a three-month temporary job. It was hardly worth her going there for the sake of such a short-term position. But it didn't matter, she would be hearing from the Catholic college soon. Luckily O. Vijayalakshmi was in Guntur, working in another college and living on campus. Manjula came to stay with her, explaining, "I will be leaving in a couple of days, as soon as I get the papers from Eluru."

Days passed as Manjula waited for the envelope from Eluru to arrive. Her friend suggested that she buy her own comb and sheets and soap. "But just a couple of days," said Manjula.

Again and again her friend proposed, "Let us go to the bazaar and buy you a few things." Again Manjula demurred. Finally, summoning the necessary cruelty, OV told her, "Look, Manjula, you are not going to get the job in Eluru. You are going to stay here in Guntur."

OV finally told Manjula the whole story. Their classmate at AU, Sarada

Kelly, one of the Christian gang, was already working at Eluru. The Catholics had said to her, "We interviewed a girl, Manjula, whom we like very much. She said she was in your batch at AU." Sarada Kelly told them, "She does not go to church, she goes to movies," and the most damning of all: "Hers is a Communist family." Sarada did not say this out of spite, but because, as a Christian, it was her duty to tell the truth. Not to mention that her own sister interviewed for the same job.

Heartbroken, Manjula agreed to go to the bazaar.

◎

MANJULA MOVED INTO THE LADIES' hostel in A.C. College, where the faculty and students lived in the same quarters. Right away the women split into two camps: rich, fashionable, and religious Christians who were contemptuous of Manjula; and poor, rustic women who adored her. The latter hung around in her room and, seeing that she was even more of a bumpkin than they were, tried to teach her how to look fashionable, how to wear a sari properly, how to walk. "Madam, you just got your first job, you have to learn these things."

Susheela, another Christian from AU, was teaching at A.C. College. Susheela, who was fluent in English, and her friend Lilavathi took to mocking Manjula. On one pretext or another they would make her say English words with a z in them, and when she said j instead—a common mistake among Telugu speakers—they laughed at her. In A.C. College, they also disseminated Manjula's story: "That girl comes from a Communist family, that girl does not go to church." Twenty-four-year-old Manjula accepted this as her lot. Later, when she read Bernard Shaw, she realized others, too, had suffered the stigma of being irreligious: "Well, at least I am not alone."

On the first of the month, Manjula received her first-ever salary payment—a mere forty rupees because she had only worked a few days of that month. Like a good girl, without even counting it, she put it in an envelope, went home, and handed it to her father. She felt it was his money. The family owed money to one and all: the grocer, the milkman. With Manjula's income, they were able to pay off some of their bills.

But the A.C. College principal, Paulus, couldn't wait for Manjula's three-month assignment to be over. After hearing the rumors of her family's godlessness, he was impatient to banish Manjula from the college. Manjula was not keen to remain in such a hostile environment, but Paulus did not get another candidate and so was forced to ask Manjula to stay.

Satyam had just taken a job teaching at a private tutorial college in town. Manjula happily moved out of her hostel and found a rental place with him. Every day she cooked for the two of them and then walked miles to teach.

Since some women lecturers such as Manjula were not much older than the young women they taught, Paulus instituted a new rule to distinguish students from faculty: faculty women had to wear their hair in a bun. Every day from then on it was a struggle for Manjula to keep her unruly long thick, curly hair in a bun. She tried pins, clips, slides, bands, and hidden cords, but as soon as she managed to make up the bun, it would start to unravel. Balancing her bun gave her neck pain.

Nancharayya—Satyam's friend from Telaprolu, who was working in Guntur—once had occasion to walk Manjula to campus. On the way, he was half amused and half disturbed to see her doing a peculiar dance: balancing her bun while paying respectful *namaskarams* (greetings to elders) with her two hands full of books. Every ten seconds, silly smile and "Namaste, namaste, namaste, namaste, sir, namaste, madam."

"Papa, what is this? Do you know how silly you look with your endless namastes? You look like a clown doing funny tricks."

Manjula felt so embarrassed. But she'd been raised by a devout Christian grandmother who had beaten this humility into her. Once in her childhood she'd run into Marthamma's friend Pastor Israel in the bazaar where Manjula was playing with her friends. She dropped everything, folded her hands, and said, "Namaste." Then she went home and found Mr. Israel chatting with her grandmother. Once again, she folded her hands. "Namaste." Then she went back to the bazaar and yet again saw Mr. Israel and with folded hands said to him, "Namaste." The old man got nervous. Either she was crazy or she was up to some mischief. Shaking with fear, he fished out some coins, pressed them into her hands, and ran off.

After Nancharayya pointed out how it looked, she learned to be more sparing with her namaskarams.

Some people saw charm in Manjula despite her awkwardness. One of her students, a soccer star of some upper caste, asked to take her to a cinema. Manjula thought it was just a friendly gesture. As always, she asked Satyam's permission. Surprisingly he said, "Okay, if it's a matinee, you can go if you want to." So the two went to see a matinee.

A few minutes into the movie, the boy slowly slid his arm around her shoulders. Manjula got tense. Pretending as though nothing were happening, staring at the screen, without turning her eyes or getting agitated or excited, she picked up his hand at the wrist with two fingers, as if she were picking up a rotting fish, and placed it back in his lap, as though to say, "Here, this hand strayed onto my shoulder, take it back, it belongs to you." Again after a few minutes he slowly put his arm around her shoulders, and again, as casually as if she were merely wiping sweat off her neck, she retrieved his hand and returned it to him. It went on like this: the boy put his arm, the girl would return it. Then the movie was over. They both acted as if nothing special had happened between them, and he dropped her off at home. In class she was nice to him and he continued to adore her, but she never gave him another chance to see her personally.

Over the school holidays, Rama Rao came to visit. He took one look at Manjula and her bun and remarked, "Our Papa is growing old. We must marry her off."

Satyam said, "We have been looking but have not found anyone yet," although the parents of a desirable groom had in fact approached him. The boy, an untouchable though not a Christian, was a lawyer in Eluru. The parents were excited that Manjula was up for a job at the Catholic college nearby. "Even if she does not get that job, we have influence and can get her a job." For reasons he never explained, Satyam had rejected that match, leaving the whole family dumbfounded.

Then Rama Rao told Satyam about his roommate in Rajahmundry, where Rama Rao was the librarian at the college. "I adore that man. He's the same caste and a Christian as well. Teaches English literature."

Manjula had no part in this discussion. Rama Rao took Carey back with him so that his roommate could help him pass English. Carey returned and said how much he loved the man. Then Satyam went to meet him and returned with the same opinion. But, once again, for some reason, he let the match go by the wayside.

Manjula left it to her brothers to find her a husband. She continued to work over the summer and earned extra money by proctoring during examination season.

Proctoring can be either easy or hard, depending on your attitude. It is hard to do an earnest job, easy if you don't care. Owing to the twin influences of Christianity and Communism, Manjula believed that the task of removing all the immorality, injustice, and corruption from the nation rested upon the shoulders of people in positions of responsibility, however slight, and that everyone must do his or her part.

With this philosophy ingrained in her, she invigilated with utmost sincerity. Some of the students taking the exam were the sons of powerful men, violent thugs, but when she caught a student cheating, Manjula just yanked his cheat sheets out of his hands or pockets or underwear and flung them out the window. Then she would book the student, ruining his prospects. She struck terror in the hearts of students and lecturers alike. Some of her colleagues would request that she let their favorite candidates cheat. She told them no.

One student's father was a clerk in the A.C. College administrative office, and the student's brother was a lecturer in charge of examinations that year. Manjula watched the student closely and noticed he had a thick stack of answer sheets. "What is this, abba, it hasn't been half an hour since the exam started and I don't even remember him asking me for extra answer sheets. How come this bugger already has a two-inch-thick stack of answer sheets?" She investigated and found he had taken a stack of answer sheets the day before, written answers to all possible questions at home, and brought them to the exam hall. She booked him.

Word went out. The vice principal came running. First he held her hands, then he fell at her feet and pleaded, "Amma, please don't report him. If you do, his family will be on the street." The vice principal, the lecturer, the student's father, and the student begged her for an hour until finally she relented. But she confiscated and tore up all the fraudulent answer sheets.

Now that Manjula was making plenty of money, Maniamma wanted to come over to stay. Her sister Santhamma wanted to come, too. Santhamma had grown closer to her father-in-law, Prasanna Rao, and he asked Manjula to let her stay. Her pretext? She had contracted venereal diseases from her kamma lover and wanted to get treatment in the big hospitals of Guntur. Carey didn't want to be left out and said, "Why should I stay in the village? I also want to come." His excuse was, he could brush up his English, a subject he still hadn't managed to pass: "They have high-quality English in cities." They all came to stay.

Whatever she was paid, Manjula would promptly give it to Satyam. He gave her an allowance of fifteen rupees a month. Satyam enrolled himself in a bachelor of education program.

Exams signaled the end of the academic year. As her job was only temporary, Manjula had to reapply and interview for the next year. On the way to the office, she ran into the father of the boy whom she'd caught cheating. She namaskarammed him. The man told her, "Mr. Paulus is very angry with you. It seems that you don't namaskar him enough. He said that you are a disrespectful girl." The man advised her, "Just go inside his room and just tell him how sorry you are, ask for forgiveness."

Manjula sent word to Paulus asking to see him and waited on a bench outside his office. Her family's financial situation was quite bad. Her brother had three small children. Without her salary, they could not eat. She desperately needed the job.

Three hours passed; still no call from Paulus. He was purposely making her wait. Manjula decided, "I don't want to beg that nasty man! I don't care if I have a job or not." She went home.

Satyam never chided her for not thinking practically. He sent Maniamma and her sister and children back to live with Prasanna Rao. After some time, Manjula found work at the Government College for Women in Guntur.

Satyam and Manjula found a cheaper place to live, a meagerly furnished room in a prostitute colony near the college. Carey joined them.

Then Rama Rao got a librarian job in the same college. Nancharayya was already there. All the friends were back together.

And all of them leeched off Manjula for their expenses. Carey set up a credit line with a cigarette shop for him and his brother and Rama Rao to use, which Manjula had to pay. Rama Rao lived in Vijayawada with his wife, Vimala, and commuted to Guntur. Vimala gave him ticket money to get to work but not enough for the return fare. So Manjula would pay for his return ticket. It got so bad that Manjula's salary was not enough and she had to borrow money from colleagues. She felt she was losing respect in her college.

Manjula longed to get married. She had grown up for the most part without parents, raised by relatives who cared for her out of duty and by brothers whom she feared, always having to worry that she might inadvertently do something to displease them and lose their kindness. Her only hope of escape from this unending insecurity was to marry a man and form her own family.

With her education and her job, she should have made a desirable bride. But she was no such thing. She was dark, her family was poor, they didn't go to church, and worst of all, her brothers were violent Communist sons of bitches. Manjula was almost twenty-five years old. Her family was beginning to worry. Once she crossed twenty-five, it would be difficult to find a match. The fear of Manjula's spinsterhood spread like a dread disease through the family circle. Then Satyam received a letter from his old classmate at Andhra University, Ganga Raju.

Ganga Raju had become a lecturer in Anantapur, a southern district of Andhra. A young new tutor in his department was mala, also Christian. Ganga Raju rushed to the post office and sent a telegram to Satyam, following it with a letter: "If you let this man slip by, it would be the blunder of your life." The best thing about him was that he not only knew that they were Communists, he kind of fancied that they were.

Through Ganga Raju, Satyam invited the man to visit. He arrived in Guntur by train. Though Ganga Raju had dashed off a letter letting Satyam know which train he was coming by, Satyam impolitely forgot to meet him at the station. He had to find his own way to the prostitute slum where Satyam and Manjula were staying.

This tall, skinny, dark, handsome, painfully self-conscious and polite man wasn't dressed presentably, as a man seeking a bride should be. His pants and shirt were plain white, the front of the shirt covered with minute holes from cigarette ash. His skin was clear, his eyes smiling. He had a dimpled chin and a thin black mustache, and one of his two front teeth was coffee-stained. His middle finger was permanently discolored by nicotine.

Satyam recognized this man immediately. He was the prospective suitor he had gone to meet a few months before in Rajahmundry: Rama Rao's roommate.

Rama Rao, after he graduated, had got a job as a librarian in the government college in Rajahmundry. At the library, he noticed a man who always came in wearing white tennis shorts and carrying a tennis racquet. He would check out highbrow books in English, books no one else would dare to look at: philosophy, literary criticism, modern poetry.

Rama Rao had heard from someone that this man had earned his B.A. and M.A. from one of the oldest and most prestigious modern colleges in Asia—the Madras Christian College. No wonder he was so debonair. He'd studied under British and other European professors—civil servants, political leaders, and businessmen from around the world. Rama Rao found out the man even had an L.L.B., a law degree. However, since he did not get a second class in his M.A., he'd been hired at Rajahmundry only as a tutor, not as a lecturer.

Rama Rao was curious to get to know this man. As he needed a roommate, he proposed that they rent a house together and share the rent and cooking.

The man shared rent all right, but as for food, Rama Rao cooked and the man just sat at the table, cigarette in hand, with a book in front of him. Without taking his eyes off the book, this noble-looking man would sip the tea and eat the meals that Rama Rao put in front of him. That was how the sharing worked out. Rama Rao often wrote Satyam, "You would be interested in meeting my roommate."

When Satyam finally came to visit, he was impressed. The man talked about T. S. Eliot. Satyam's cheeks burned with admiration.

During his visit, the students at the college called a strike, demanding that their regular lecturer, a famous man and reputable teacher, be replaced by Rama Rao's roommate, Prabhakara Rao, a mere tutor. The famous lecturer had made the mistake of asking Prabhakara Rao to fill in for him and entertain his class one day when he was called away.

Prabhakara Rao decided to lecture this teacher's final-year B.A. students on *Macbeth*. No matter that the work was not on their syllabus. When he lectured, he was transformed. He went into another world and took the students with him. At the end of the hour, it was as if they had come out of a trance.

The principal responded to the striking students' demand, "But how do you expect me to appoint a tutor in the place of a lecturer? He doesn't have an M.A. These are not my rules. These are government rules." Yet the students stubbornly kept up the protest for a week.

Nonetheless, Satyam had not pursued Prabhakara Rao as a match for Manjula.

Carey, too, who had earlier visited Rama Rao in Rajahmundry, thought no less highly of the man. Carey was especially pleased to find out that Prabhakara Rao played tennis every day and was good at soccer, too. His English was so good and his voice so splendid the sports department used him as a commentator in cricket matches.

A few months after Carey's visit, both Rama Rao and Prabhakara Rao left Rajahmundry, Rama Rao becoming a librarian at the Government College for Women at Guntur, and Prabhakara Rao an English tutor in Anantapur College, where Ganga Raju met him.

Now here was Prabhakara Rao again, put forward a second time as a marriage prospect for Manjula. Two of Satyam's closest friends and well-wishers of his family had recommended this man as a suitable match for his sister. And finally he and Manjula had a chance to meet.

He took a seat on the only chair in the room. Manjula and Satyam sat on the cot. They didn't think to offer him tea or coffee or even water.

Few words were exchanged. Then Prabhakara Rao left.

After he went back to Anantapur, there was no word from him. And no other prospects for Manjula. Satyam asked Ganga Raju to find out what was going on with Prabhakara Rao, to see if he liked Manjula. Ganga Raju went looking for Prabhakara Rao and found him at the tennis courts.

"So have you made any decision regarding my friend's sister?"

"Yes, I like her." Prabhakara Rao blushed somewhat.

Ganga Raju immediately telegrammed Satyam the good news.

Even though Prasanna Rao had never seen the groom, he was satisfied since both his sons respected Prabhakara Rao for his scholarly qualities. But as the Kambhams began to think of wedding plans, no further communication came from Prabhakara Rao.

Three long months went by. Manjula had no other prospects. Then like a pleasant breeze in a suffocating summer came a letter from Prabhakara Rao: "My family will bring *nischitartham* to yours." Engagement ritual.

Prasanna Rao had earlier gone to Kakinada to see what Prabhakara Rao's family was like. He returned brimming with joy. They seemed like a respectable family.

When he returned home from that trip, a man was waiting for him. The man said he was looking for a bride for his son. Strange, no one had ever sought after Manjula, and now that she had a match, here came another one.

It was a good match. The boy was a forest ranger. Rangers make suitcases of money and regularly employed several peons and chauffeurs. And the proposal was very much according to the custom—the groom's family had come to seek the hand of the bride. Anyone would readily ditch Prabhakara Rao to go after this forest ranger.

But Prasanna Rao was a man of honor. "Forgive us, sir, we've already said yes to someone else." The forest ranger's father asked the Kambhams to at least meet his son. "Sorry, sir." The man went away much disappointed.

The Kambhams went into a frenzy preparing for the groom's party's visit. Prabhakara Rao's mother was naturally excluded, as she was a widow. Widows are held to be bad luck and barred from all auspicious events. His uncles Paul and Paulus and their wives came. The women wore elegant saris, and Mr. Paul wore Western-style clothes, while Mr. Paulus dressed in traditional attire. They were all finely dressed and smelled good, too, like cardamom.

Prasanna Rao and Satyam, all dressed up in their nicest and most respectable clothes, well-groomed and polite, stepped forward to receive them. "Please come in, please come in."

The two parties sat down to face each other. They exchanged a few words and laid out a plan. Manjula would come out to be presented to the groom's family. After she had their approval, they would give her the sari and jewels they had brought. She would go and put them on and come out again, and they would all pray and feast.

When Manjula came out for the first time, the groom's party made no effort to hide their disappointment. The bride's party was terrified. The groom's party did not present Manjula with the gifts.

Instead they said, "Let us pray." Then they dropped the bombshell: "You must give us five thousand rupees as a dowry."

The Kambhams were stunned. There had been no mention of dowry until now.

Aunt Nagarathnamma, who had come for the occasion, was outraged. "This man is a mere tutor! Our Manjula is a lecturer. How dare they reject her!"

Carey yelled at her, "You! You keep quiet. Tutor, lecturer, what does it matter if they like each other?"

"What is the problem, gentlemen?" Satyam asked.

Mr. Paulus said one of Manjula's legs was shorter than the other.

From inside the house, Manjula heard that. Just as she'd beat herself up when she got second class at Benares, trying to figure out what had gone wrong, she thought, "Maybe from sitting on the floor my foot might have become numb and I walked funny."

Prasanna Rao stood up. "We cannot afford a five-thousand-rupee dowry. Even if we could, we wouldn't pay." Not paying or receiving a dowry was a matter of principle for him. And to ask for it like this was an insult.

In all of this, Prabhakara Rao was silent. Then suddenly he got up and walked out quietly. Carey ran after him, baffled. Prabhakara Rao reached the train tracks and started walking on them. Carey was distressed, thinking Prabhakara Rao surely meant to kill himself. Carey ran up to him and, persuading him to turn back, took him home. Meanwhile, Prabhakara Rao's family had left without touching the feast. Then Prabhakara Rao left, too.

In the face of the other party's outrageous demands, the Kambham

207 | ANTS AMONG ELEPHANTS

men had stood firm. But as soon as they left, Prasanna Rao collapsed. Satyam wept. All three of them climbed into their beds and stayed there, sobbing. They would not eat, they would not sleep, they would not go out.

Now there would be rumors. Speculations as to what could be wrong with Manjula. After this engagement, Manjula was touched water. No one else would drink from the same glass. Where before she'd been hard-to-sell goods, she was now rejected merchandise. Not only were her prospects gone, but the honor of the whole family was spoiled. Prasanna Rao could not show his face in the street.

Prabhakara Rao wrote a letter apologizing for his folks' behavior and promising to convince his mother to accept the match despite the views of his uncles and aunts. But by now it was pure fantasy to continue to hope. In any case, Prabhakara Rao never wrote again.

Satyam approached Manjula with tears in his eyes. "I am sorry, amma. Again I ruined your life with my stupidity." He was referring to his handling of the Aseervadam affair.

Manjula determined to set things right for her brothers and her father. She was willing to do everything in her power to restore the family's honor.

"*Annayya* [big brother]," she said to Satyam, "I want to go to Anantapur and talk to Mr. Prabhakara Rao."

Satyam had to agree even though it was thoroughly ignominious behavior for a girl to travel hundreds of kilometers to approach a man. The two of them kept Manjula's journey a secret from the rest of the family. Ganga Raju was told to receive Manjula.

When Manjula arrived at Ganga Raju's house, she took a bath and ate. Then Prabhakara Rao was brought in.

When the two were alone, Manjula went off like a long string of firecrackers. Prabhakara Rao listened patiently as she blasted away: "Why, why have you behaved like this? Why can't you take a decision, one way or another? Why did you have to leave us in the lurch like this?"

He didn't reply.

"But why?"

He finally said, "I am like that. If I ever do what I should, it is by mistake. I only blunder into right. This is the weakness of my character."

He said all this in English. Manjula, despite her hurt and anger, was in awe of his command of English.

Ganga Raju took them both to see a movie. The next day Manjula took a train back. At college, O. Vijayalakshmi was eager to know what happened.

"He is an offensive man," Manjula said.

"Why?"

"He asked me an offensive question."

"What did he say?"

"He wanted to know if I know cooking."

"That's what you found offensive! Any man would ask that question. It is a compulsory question."

"But I very much take objection."

Manjula waited for his letter. Again there was no letter, and then they decided that no letter would ever come. Manjula would have to resign herself to a life of spinsterhood.

SEVEN

○ ○ ○

UNQUALIFIED TO TEACH IN GOVERNMENT colleges because of his third-class marks, Satyam had only been able to find work in temporary high school teaching jobs at private schools owned by kamma Communists. He went wherever he was offered a job, leaving Maniamma and the children with his father. By now he had fathered a third child, a daughter whom Maniamma had named Sri Devi.

After two years of teaching here and there, he received an offer from the party to move to Guntur and take up the editorship of a new youth magazine. Rama Rao couldn't believe that Satyam would be foolish enough to quit his job with three children to take care of, but he went ahead.

He agreed once he was sure that it was an unsalaried position. He had decided never to accept salaried employment from the party, having seen how the party treated their full-time activists, regularly withholding their allowances until they were forced to beg for a little to live on. One of the leaders said, "But you have to eat." He suggested that Satyam take up a second job, a paying position working for two Communist leaders in charge of the tobacco workers' union. "They need an office assistant. Your main job will be reading the newspapers every morning and giving them the gist. They are busy and don't have time to read papers. They also need someone who can make coffee and book train tickets when needed."

Satyam declined. Instead he got himself a job teaching history at Ravi College, a private school owned by a kamma Communist named Dhan. Dhan paid Satyam one rupee per day—barely enough to buy a meal.

Half starving, Satyam went to work for the magazine. He named it *Yuvajana* (Youth). Even though the magazine was entirely Satyam's work, the party made him answer to one of his batchmates from AU, a brahmin with an M.A. in Telugu literature. This man wrote nonsensical articles that read as if they were written by a five-year-old, and Satyam would have to rewrite them.

While working at *Yuvajana*, Satyam adopted a pen name: Sivudu. Meaning Shiva. The austere god with blue skin and three eyes, dressed in a loincloth of animal hide, adorned with ashes, garlanded with a cobra. The god who lives in the cemetery.

As Sivudu, he wrote an open letter to the president of India telling him to get out of Nehru's way. Nehru wanted to pass the Hindu Code Bill—a uniform set of rules to govern marriage, divorce, inheritance, adoption, and like matters among Hindus. It was a chance for oppressed Hindu women to finally get some rights, at least on paper.

The conservative elements of Congress egged on the president, Rajendra Prasad, in his fight with Nehru over this bill. They went so far as to campaign to change the form of government from a parliamentary model to a presidential one in order to transfer authority over legislation from the prime minister to the president.

Satyam's open letter was wildly popular. Readers of *Yuvajana* wondered who Sivudu was. One man, intent on finding out, traveled to Guntur to the office of *Yuvajana*. He was none other than Rachakonda Viswanatha Sastry—or Ra. Vi. Sastry, as he eccentrically styled himself—who would come to be known as the James Joyce of Telugu literature.

After heaping praise on Satyam, Sastry went back home and sent him a set of six stories to be published in *Yuvajana*. The series was titled "Six Liquor Stories." The moment he saw *liquor* in the title, Satyam tossed the manuscript in the trash bin. Owing to the Christian morality in which he'd been brought up, he strongly disapproved of alcohol. Because he never read the stories, he had no way of knowing they were tales of poor people, not stories advocating drinking.

Rejected by *Yuvajana*, Sastry sent his stories to another magazine. His "Six Liquor Stories" became classics of Telugu fiction. If Kafka had sent Satyam his "Metamorphosis," Satyam would surely have thrown it away, asking, "Who needs to read about a dirty cockroach?"

Within a couple of months, it became clear to Satyam that *Yuvajana* had been launched by the right-wing faction of the Communist Party to get the youth on their side in case of a split, after which it would survive as an organ of their new party. He quit.

He concluded it was time to forget about politics and find a proper job. And then there was Rama Rao nagging him. His adoring friend had for some time been openly critical of Satyam's attitude toward his family. Rama Rao had special sympathy for the long-suffering Maniamma. "Why does she have to live under other people's roofs? You are her husband. Her children are your children. Get yourself a job, take care of your family."

Shortly after, Carey came to see Satyam. Carey had passed his B.A., undergone a two-year training program in sports coaching, and was now teaching physical education as an assistant director in the sports department at the medical college in Warangal. He had come with a message from Seetharamayya, who was working as a teacher near where Carey was living, at St. Gabriel School in Khazipet. Seetharamayya had found a job for Satyam at the school and wanted him to join him there with his family. Satyam decided right away to accept.

On the train to Khazipet, Maniamma, pregnant with her fourth child, suffered from fever and chills brought on by severe anxiety. Satyam was bringing her to a strange country—Khazipet is in Telangana, the Nizam's old realm—where she knew no one. "Can he provide for us in that place, or will we simply starve and die?"

Indeed, to Satyam and his family, Khazipet was a foreign place. People spoke Telugu, but a dialect of Telugu they could hardly understand, and some people spoke a different language entirely. Men had beards and women wore black garments that covered them up from head to toe. The people had bloodred tongues from chewing pan (a mixture of fragrant and stimulating ingredients wrapped in betel leaves), and the streets and walls were splashed with red spit.

When they arrived, Maniamma still couldn't stop shivering. The children, too excited, flitted around the station like butterflies.

Carey came to receive them at the train station. He hired two rickshaws, which went trundling downhill so fast the children started screaming as if they were on an amusement-park ride. They stopped in front of the house that Seetharamayya had found for Satyam. Carey helped unload the family.

Seetharamayya, beaming, came over to welcome them. His own household was right next door and now included not just Anasooyamma and her children but his own children, Karuna and Chandu, who had come to live with him the previous year when their mother found a job as warden of a girls' hostel in Kakinada and couldn't take them with her.

"Now here we are!" Seetharamayya said to Satyam. "We must start planning our activity."

Satyam told him, "I just want rest."

A few months before, at the SFI state conference, Satyam had met his old classmate Panchadi, who asked him, "Why don't you move to Srikakulam? We are leading a movement there very soon." He told Panchadi the same thing he told Seetharamayya: "No, I want to find a job and live with my family."

Satyam had been occupied with political movements since he was eleven. At thirty-one, his mind and body needed repose. Now that he had a proper job, he only wanted to eat, sleep, lie down with his wife, look at his children.

In Telangana, the biggest city is the twin city of Hyderabad-Secunderabad, which was the capital of the erstwhile realm of the Nizam and later of the state of Andhra Pradesh. (As I write, the state is being redivided.) The second-largest city is Warangal, which consists of not twin but triple cities: Warangal, Hanamkonda, and Khazipet. After Hyderabad, Warangal is the greatest educational center in Telangana. People come from all over the region to go to school there.

The St. Gabriel School for Boys, in Khazipet, was the most prestigious boarding school in Warangal. All the students there were sons of rich landlords or Muslim aristocrats, men who had held titles of dora, nawab, or jagirdar under the Nizam.

At St. Gabriel, starting in the summer of 1962, Satyam taught English, Telugu, and social studies. A week after he started, the principal called him into his office. He asked him if he was settled, how he liked his house, whether he cared for the job. Then the principal told him he had walked past Satyam's classroom the other day. In a hushed and thoughtful voice, he said in English, "It was something like an ocean. It was silent, and then I heard roars of laughter like waves crashing onto the beach. And then silence again." He'd heard Satyam's class alternately paying attention to his lessons and laughing at his jokes. The principal was pleased to have Satyam at St. Gabriel.

Satyam, too, was pleased to be there. In the seven years they'd been married, Satyam had never provided Maniamma with either a home or his own company. Now that they were finally together, she realized how happy life could be. Though she had little education herself, her goal in life was to educate her children. When Siddhartha was six and they were living with Prasanna Rao, he couldn't go to school because he had no clothes to wear. Now she was able to buy him a school uniform and textbooks and pay the fees to send him to St. Gabriel. And Anupama was sent to the St. Gabriel's sister school, Fatima Girls' School, where she was first in her class.

The children thought their father owned St. Gabriel School. It amused him to see little Anupama walking the school premises. How proud her gait was! She walked like a little princess.

In no time Satyam grew close to his students. They liked to spend time with him at his house or under the mango trees. He directed the school play. The Catholics were delighted with his services.

But after only three months, his family's tranquillity was broken.

At 5:00 a.m. on October 20, 1962, the Chinese army fired heavy mortars and artillery on Indian troops at the border, decimating two brigades in a mere four hours. The strike was launched in retaliation for India's advances into Chinese territory after the Chinese government put down the 1959 uprising in Tibet. The Chinese went on to attack another Indian position, bombarding India's Seventh Brigade out of existence.

That same morning, Sundarayya, the leader of the dissident faction of the Indian Communist Party, issued a statement even more shocking than the news of the war itself: "We stand with China."

How can anyone support an enemy country? Sundarayya explained that in a war between a socialist state and a capitalist state, true Communists must take the side of the socialist state. So it was their duty to defend China.

This statement split the Communist Party in two. Within hours of its being issued, supporters of the dissident faction—thousands of Communists all over India—were rounded up and jailed without trial on charges of sedition.

These events shattered Maniamma's dream of a peaceful life.

◎

PARTY MEMBERS SUCH AS SATYAM had for a long time looked to Sundarayya to lead the Communist movement onto a revolutionary path. Just when Satyam had given up on him and settled down to live like anyone else, the war with China had forced Sundarayya to act.

Now a great historical task had fallen to Satyam. The leaders of the pro-China faction were all in jail. In Warangal also the dissident leaders had been locked up.

Satyam and Seetharamayya were both spared. They were not known to police in Telangana.

It was up to them to spread pro-China propaganda and try to win over the masses to the cause of revolution, to lay the groundwork for a new party that would be ready to take action as soon as its future leaders were released.

Satyam somehow got hold of a banned English-language pamphlet on the antecedents of the war and sat up through the night translating it into Telugu. He sent it to a sympathetic printer, who rushed the little booklet into press.

The pamphlet set out to show that not only should China be defended as a socialist state but it was also in the right in the border dispute. Both the United States and the U.S.S.R. had egged India on, even after the Chinese had repeatedly sought a diplomatic solution.

Equipped with that booklet, the two teachers entered the campuses of the Regional Engineering College (REC) in Khazipet and Kakatiya Medical College (KMC) in Warangal city. The majority of students in Warangal were from families who had taken part in the Telangana Armed Struggle and who still had Communist sympathies. It was easy to approach them.

Warangal also had many workers. The Azam Jahi textile mill was there, and Khazipet was a major railway junction. The mill workers and railway workers were made up largely of sons of Telangana peasants who had suffered under, and rebelled against, the dora system. They, too, were receptive to Satyam's propaganda.

There was no time for sleep. Every evening after it got dark, Satyam would set out for the textile workers' colony in Warangal. It was far, but because he wanted to keep his movements secret, he never took the bus. He walked the whole way through fields and scrubland. By the time he reached the colony and gathered the workers, it would already be midnight. He would get home at four or five in the morning, sleep until nine. By nine-thirty he had to be at school. Maniamma would heat the bathwater, get him to the well, scrub him clean with soap, feed him, and send him off to school with the word "Go!" as if she were calling the start of a race. He hardly saw his children's faces.

It was risky work. The government didn't take the appearance of seditious materials on college campuses lightly. The notorious Warangal police were hunting for those responsible. They questioned students suspected of pro-China sympathies, some of whom came to Satyam and Seetha-ramayya for help.

Meanwhile, a few students from St. Gabriel came to them with a mysterious complaint about the Catholic fathers. The two teachers took the leader of the unhappy boys, the fourteen-year-old son of a rich Muslim landlord, for a walk where they could be assured of privacy. They asked him to explain what it was all about. He told them the fathers were being disrespectful to the boys.

"Disrespect how?"

"I mean, they are ill-treating us."

"Ill-treating you how?"

Little by little, the boy was led by Satyam's questioning to say enough that the rest could be pieced together. The priests were entering the boys' rooms after dinner and falling upon them.

Seetharamayya failed to understand. Unlike Satyam, who had read of it in English novels, Seetharamayya did not know of this phenomenon whereby some men desired to fall upon other men instead of women. Satyam explained there was a term for it. "Hmm. Let me think. Ah, yes. It is called homosex." Seetharamayya was aghast. The two teachers promised to help the boys, but they wanted their role kept secret.

The following Monday, with the help of REC students organized by the two teachers, the St. Gabriel boys held a rally and marched into the principal's office. The Catholic management had never seen such disobedience. They expelled several twelfth-class pupils for their part in the protest. But when, encouraged by their supporters from the REC, the boys threatened to expose the "homosex," the administration decided to hush up the matter. They sent home some of the accused priests and took back the expelled students.

When it was all over, the principal, Father John, summoned the Muslim boy who had led the protest and congratulated him on the successful agitation. "Very good work, my son." The boy was pleased. Then Father John asked him how he had pulled off such an excellent thing. The boy—flattered beyond endurance—naively admitted that the new teachers had given him a lot of support. Now it was Father John who was pleased.

When Satyam learned that his role had been exposed, it didn't bother him too much. "What will happen?" he thought to himself. "What is forever? What is true and what is false? Only revolution is truth. Everything else may come or go." In those days he was in that sort of mood.

In the end, the management took no action against him. He was a popular teacher, valuable to the school, and besides, they didn't want to risk his causing any more trouble.

◎

AS IN MANY OTHER PARTS of the world, the 1960s were turbulent times for students in India. Inspired by the Chinese revolution, many educated youth were turning to Maoism. Satyam went out nightly to talk to students and hold classes for them. This new milieu was very different from that of Satyam's old comrades. These people were intellectuals. He was impressed by the high level of political discussion among them, by their eagerness to study Marxist theory. Their attitude seemed cultured, serious, free of pettiness. He tried to make them see that in the recent split, the correct line was Sundarayya's, and that when Sundarayya organized his new party, it would be the one to make a revolution in India. He encouraged the students to read and study Marxism, but the real task, he told them, was to prepare for the coming revolution.

As this activity was heating up, Seetharamayya announced he was leaving his job and moving away to Adilabad. "I must go and protect my parents. Their lives are in peril." His parents, like many rich kamma and reddy landlords from Andhra, had sold their five or ten acres of land and settled in Telangana, where they bought up twenty or thirty acres of land cheaply. They came under attack by Telangana landlords who resented this encroachment.

Seetharamayya assured Satyam, "Don't worry, I will visit every ten days. When I do, you can give me a report on the activity and we will plan everything together."

Seetharamayya did come back for a time to help campaign for the by-election that was about to be held to replace a minister who left office unexpectedly. Omkar, the Communist leader in town, was campaigning from his jail cell. While Seetharamayya ran the campaign office, Satyam went out on the road. The party hired a small car for him. The luxury of riding in a car was too much for someone from Satyam's background. He felt too embarrassed to ride in the backseat. Instead he sat beside the driver in a dirty khaki uniform and pretended to be a repairman. He claimed this was a ruse to evade police.

The pro-China Communists, having been released from prison after a cease-fire was declared in November 1962, formally broke with the old party in April 1964 by walking out of a national council meeting. This was the moment Satyam and Seetharamayya had been preparing for. The call to form a new party was expected any day.

Because of the organizing Satyam had done in Warangal, the pro-China leaders had solid support in the medical and engineering colleges, where students had split from the SFI to form a new student union loyal to the dissidents. The Azam Jahi mill workers backed them, as did the formidable railway workers' union in Khazipet. Field laborers and rural youth from Warangal, Jangaon, and the neighboring villages had formed village committees supporting the pro-China faction.

Upon his release from jail, Sundarayya had paid tribute to the young activists who had built up the new party in the leadership's absence. He told them, "We conceived the idea of a Marxist party. We gave birth to it and went away to prison, abandoning the infant on the streets. It was you who picked up that baby, you who cared for it and nourished it."

In July 1964, the dissident leaders and their ardent followers from the four corners of the country gathered in Tenali to hold the new party's founding conference. It was to be called the Communist Party of India (Marxist) or CPI(M), to distinguish it from the old, degenerated, revisionist CPI. Some 100,000 of the old party's 175,000 members quit to join the new, truly Marxist one.

When Satyam went to the conference, he was shocked to discover that the leaders had no program to show the members, not even in draft. He had expected to be told what the party stood for before being asked to join. The leaders' attitude was "First become members of the party, and then we will tell you its program." What were they hiding?

Sundarayya, having praised the hard work of younger activists such as Satyam, now brushed them aside in choosing leaders of the new party. Instead, he chose two old men. One was Jyoti Basu, the son of a wealthy Bengali brahmin family, who had studied in prestigious schools in England. The second was another brahmin, an ex-Congress man from Kerala, E.M.S. Namboodiripad.

The most glaring incongruity in Sundarayya's choices was that neither of these men agreed with the founding principle of the new party, defense of China. These old brahmins had opposed the split and were the last to quit the old revisionist party.

But Sundarayya wanted those men for their prestige. To accommodate their politics, he had to avoid producing a draft program.

Seetharamayya's request for membership was turned down. The new party didn't want him any more than the old one had. Sundarayya did not approve of Seetharamayya's extramarital affair.

Satyam joined the party despite his misgivings. It was useful to have a party affiliation to carry out his own activities.

But his hopes now turned to the movement his old AU classmate and comrade Panchadi had invited him to help build a few months before he'd moved to Khazipet. There was unrest in the tribal area of Srikakulam, not far from Vizag. The tribals were forbidden by the forest and revenue officials to live off the forest as they had always done. And when they went out onto the plains like Satyam's grandparents and tried to cultivate land, they, too, were cheated out of it by moneylenders and landholding castes. Deprived of any means of living, the tribals were ready to revolt.

Satyam planned to remain in Telangana with the aim of helping his friends from afar when the time came, and possibly starting something similar in the forests of Adilabad in the northern part of the region.

EIGHT

* * *

AFTER PRABHAKARA RAO'S FAMILY REJECTED Manjula at the engagement ceremony, she had no hope that anyone else would ever come forward to marry her. After all, engagement is practically marriage. Something had to be terribly wrong with a girl for her to be discarded at such a late stage.

Five months after she'd gone to have it out with Prabhakara Rao, she hadn't heard a word from him. Manjula was no longer just an unmarried woman. She was a spinster.

She was at home with her family for the summer when her father received a telegram:

"Wedding fixed. May 22."

It was from Prabhakara Rao's brother. No mention of a dowry.

Carey cried, "But today is the seventeenth!" They had no idea what had changed, and why the rush. But they did not pause to inquire. Shamelessly, they launched into a frenzy of preparation.

Tasks were divided up. Prasanna Rao had to find the money. Carey would do the heavy work, cutting wood and building the tent for a nischitartham ceremony that would take place at their home. Maniamma and her sister were in charge of the feast. Manjula had no money to buy wedding clothes, so she had to travel to Guntur, where the merchants would give her credit.

To get married in a church, Manjula had to first get baptized. As is the custom among the Andhra Baptists, the choice to do so had been left up to her, and she had never bothered until now. Sentimental Prasanna Rao wouldn't let her go to any church but the one in Sankarapadu.

For the nischitartham ceremony, in place of the terrible aunts and uncles they'd met earlier, some good-natured aunts and uncles of the groom were dispatched to the Kambham home. They brought the customary sari, the ring, and other gold jewelry for Manjula. She went inside and put on the sari and jewels. When she came out, Carey couldn't believe his eyes. He had always thought his sister to be the plainest girl on earth. In a nice sari and with a few ornaments, she was beautiful—albeit in an unconventional way. The ceremony concluded and the groom's party returned home to Kakinada, where the wedding was to be held.

There was neither time nor money to print invitations, or even to notify friends and relatives. Manjula wrote to O. Vijayalakshmi. O. Vijayalakshmi wasn't free to make the journey to Kakinada. But knowing Manjula had no womanly skills, and that her relatives were almost like bushmen, OV felt it was her duty to come and help Manjula prepare herself.

"Manjula, first, take all your wedding clothes out of the trunk." She did. "Now you put them on." Manjula put them on. "Now take them off." Manjula took them off. "This is loose." With a needle and thread OV restitched the blouse to fit better. She showed Manjula how to wear a sari properly.

"Now look at me. Listen to what I tell you. At the wedding, try not to look like a woman who has lost everything in life. Remember to smile once in a while."

The bride's party departed for Kakinada. It consisted of only two people, Prasanna Rao and Carey, for there was no more money for train tickets.

The moment Manjula stepped out of the house, Satyam broke down, fell to his knees, and wept. No one could console him. They all thought that he wept because he couldn't attend his sister's wedding. But it wasn't that. He was thinking of their common struggles, growing up motherless and abandoned by their father, their efforts to get educated, the shameful way in which her match had been arranged. What was to become of Satyam-Carey-Manjula?

The bride's party took a bus to Eluru, where they would catch the mail train. Manikya Rao and Niranjanamma joined them there.

In the untouchable slum of Elwin Peta, in the town of Kakinada, Prabhakara Rao's family, the Gidlas, were the most prominent family. Whenever their household held a celebration, everyone in the slum came to watch the spectacle, enjoying it vicariously. When Manjula's rickshaw arrived in Elwin Peta, the slum children ran alongside her, heralding her arrival: "The bride is here! The bride is here!"

When Manjula saw how Prabhakara Rao's family lived, it was as if she had been taken up in a spaceship and—*bhaiiiiiiii!*—she was instantly transported into a marvelous new world.

There were two two-storied houses, two separate buildings for two separate families who lived as one. They towered over the squalid huts all around them. To Manjula, used to living under a thatched roof, these large cement structures with two separate levels seemed magnificent dwellings.

In one house lived Prabhakara Rao and his brother Percy Lawrence, his half brother's wife, and their four children. In the other lived Prabhakara Rao's maternal aunt's family, with her eight children of various ages between thirteen and twenty-five. So many uncles, aunts, cousins, all living side by side. For Manjula, who had never had even one complete family, it seemed a dream come true.

And the way they dressed! The older ones looked dignified, the younger ones stylish, and all of them perfectly groomed. They were cultured in their manner and refined in their speech. Some of them even spoke English.

The women arranged a bath for Manjula. Wearing the sari she'd been given at the nischitartham, she came out to meet the fifty people who were there to see the bride. Among them was a petite woman of fifty—beautiful, well-groomed, with long dark silky hair—in a white sari with a fine border. Uncle Paulus jokingly introduced her to Manjula: "Amma, come here, this is our cook." It was, in fact, Manjula's future mother-in-law, Rathnamma, who, as a widow, could not come to see her before.

Rathnamma had been anxiously waiting to see her beloved son's bride. She took one look, and Manjula could see the thorough disappointment.

"What is this!" Rathnamma said, turning to her sisters and sisters-in-law. "This is what you found for my son?" When she had asked her son to describe Manjula, he had told her she resembled a pretty girl they knew, and Rathnamma was pleased. Now she felt deliberately misled. "Is this the marble figurine he dreamed of marrying?" When Prabhakara Rao was a little boy, he would point to a marble figurine and tell his mother, "I will marry a girl like this."

Paul's wife quickly took Rathnamma's elbow and steered her away, consoling her, "The girl is tired from the long journey."

◎

EVEN PRABHAKARA RAO HADN'T BEEN informed that his wedding was being fixed. He, too, received a telegram after it was set. This is how it came about:

Paul, Rathnamma, Satheemani, and David John were siblings, Paul being the eldest.

Rathnamma's husband had died, and so it was Paul's responsibility to marry off Prabhakara Rao.

Because he was the eldest living son, it was also Paul's responsibility to marry off his own brother, David John.

Satheemani and her husband, Paulus, took sadistic pleasure in interfering with the lives of Satheemani's widowed sister, Rathnamma, and her two naive sons, Prabhakara Rao and Percy Lawrence. For years they made sure the two boys never married and connived to condemn them to eternal bachelorhood.

Satheemani and Paulus had a daughter named Hemalatha, whom they wanted David John to marry. They were keen on this match because David John was a doctor. They went to Paul, who told them, "I cannot afford two wedding ceremonies. You have to wait until Prabhakara Rao also finds a girl."

Because of Paul's parsimonious stipulation, Paulus quickly settled for Manjula (she being considered, of the brides on offer, the least desirable in looks) and informed the parties by telegram.

The more Manjula learned of the circumstances surrounding her marriage, the greater her humiliation. It was a two-for-one deal for Paul: the two couples would be married in a single ceremony. And it had been arranged for the sake of David John and Hemalatha, with Manjula and Prabhakara Rao added on to save money.

Of all her new in-laws, she found David John the kindest. He addressed her as "amma," like Satyam, and advised her, "Eat well, amma, and avoid greasy food. Sleep well, nothing to worry about."

The morning of the wedding, Manjula felt sorry that she had no female relatives to fuss over her in front of the mirror. As she took out her sari, a girl her age came rushing in, Prabhakara Rao's cousin Sucharitha. Sucha, as she was called, was always darting here and there like a butterfly.

"*Vadina* [sister-in-law], wait, wait, what are you doing? You think you have no one? You are my vadina, and I am going to get you dressed." Sucha turned to her sisters, who were also gathered around Manjula. "Look how beautiful vadina's skin is. So smooth, so silky, soft like butter! Her hands and feet—so divinely beautiful, they should be displayed in a museum! They are not for anyone to touch!" Sucha helped Manjula with the sari, applied makeup to her face, then combed her hair ever so gently into an elegant wedding bun. The final piece of the ensemble was brought in, a white lace veil.

Manjula said firmly, almost harshly, "No. No veil."

When this news spread, women from both houses came running in. Holding their chins between their index fingers and thumbs, they gasped, "What, what, no veil?"

Manjula repeated, "No veil."

In the other room, Hemalatha was being fussed over by her sisters, mother, aunts. When she heard the news, she threw a tantrum. "Well! If she's not going to wear a veil, I am not either."

Knowing how much Hemalatha had dreamed all her life of wearing the veil, the women begged Manjula to change her mind. "If one bride veils and the other doesn't, where is the symmetry?"

Manjula gave in.

She went outside escorted by Prasanna Rao and Carey. They gaped at the sight of a car decked in roses, lilies, and chrysanthemums waiting to take them to the church. They had never ridden in a car before. Even the kammas they knew didn't use cars in their wedding processions.

As the two couples entered the church, the organist assumed his position, held his hands poised over the keys for a moment, and began to play his solemn music. The congregants fell silent and got to their feet.

Paul's wife, Graceamma, and Prasanna Rao walked Manjula to the altar, where the two couples were to stand before the pastor side by side. As Manjula passed by him, she spotted Rama Rao sitting among Prabhakara Rao's guests. She was pleasantly surprised to see her aunt Nagarathnamma and all Manjula's six cousins sitting in the front row. Her cousin Sarojini acted as Manjula's bridesmaid, but as Sarojini was a medical student, she was too dignified to perform a bridesmaid's subservient duties and merely stood beside Manjula. Sarojini didn't even lift the bride's veil when the time came for the groom to tie the three knots around her neck. With those three knots, Manjula was irrevocably married. The final prayers were said. "O Lord, guide this young woman and this young man to lead a moral life." Manjula clearly heard Aunt Nagarathnamma sniggering from the front row: "Oh, come off it! He's not so young a man!" Manjula realized she had never been told Prabhakara Rao's age.

David and Hemalatha got into one car. When the second car drove up, a man came up and asked Manjula and Prabhakara Rao to step in. The polite man, completely bald, was probably fifteen years older than Prabha-kara Rao, in Manjula's estimation. Prabhakara Rao introduced him to Manjula, telling her, "This is my younger brother Percy."

Manjula almost dropped her bouquet in panic. *"Baboy!"* she thought. *"Younger* brother? This old, bald man is a *younger* brother to my husband? This whole wedding is so shameful."

She couldn't get over the shabby way her family had gone about get-ting her married. All along, all they had wanted was to find some man and get rid of her fast. When the Prabhakara Rao match seemed to have fallen through, Rama Rao said right in front of her, "Let it go. Even if Prabha-kara Rao does not want Papa, he has a brother, we can offer her to him." And look at this brother Rama Rao had been talking about! He looked to be forty, forty-five years old.

Manjula stayed silent in the car. By the time they reached the photo studio, she had forgotten all about her grievances. Percy treated her with great respect, just like in the Sarat novels she read growing up. He was the younger brother-in-law character in those novels with whom the heroine would form a close bond. It was already revealing itself, the beautiful, loving family of her dreams.

On that day, Manjula acquired a new family that included not just her husband but her mother-in-law and brother-in-law: Prabhakara Rao (who was to lean on her in adversity), her mother-in-law (whom she was to re-spect and take care of), her brother-in-law (whom she was to love and find a wife for), and herself. In this new family of hers, there was no room for her father or brothers. They were all receding from her life, even Satyam.

In the photo studio, against the background of a false marble pillar, the four of them stood, the grooms in their suits and ties (no man in Manjula's family ever wore a suit) and the brides in their white silk saris and veils, with bouquets in one hand and the other in the hook of the groom's arm. Prabhakara Rao was smiling in his charming way, from ear to ear. They took a photo, a photo of their lives.

In the afternoon the feast was held under the colorful wedding tent. Many goats gave their lives for that meal. Those pukka houses of Prabha-kara Rao's family that Manjula was in awe of were nonetheless in the middle of a filthy slum and surrounded by hutments. Facing the tent was a large public lavatory equipped with ten holes in the floor. The area swarmed with millions of flies, and every now and then the smell of shit wafted over the feast.

In the evening, the brides had to change their saris for what was called a reception. Prabhakara Rao's family had already boasted to one and all that Manjula had a "double M.A." To show off to the guests, they asked Manjula to say something in English. She was terrified, but thought fast and giggled and blurted out, "Thank you for your attendance." All the guests waited, but she said no more. She felt ashamed of not measuring up to the family's expectations and started to reproach herself. The correct word, she knew, was not *attendance*, but *presence*.

The next morning, Manjula observed a stream of neighbors and relatives knocking on the door of the Gidla household, asking back what they had lent the family for the wedding. One by one, right before her eyes, the furnishings that so impressed her disappeared: the chairs the guests had sat in, even the bed Manjula had slept in, belonged to someone else. The cups, saucers, and plates had come from the people who lived in the house behind. In the end, not even four plates were left for the four of them: Rathnamma, Percy Lawrence, Prabhakara Rao, and Manjula. The family had put on a show, and now the show was over. Despite their large, pukka house—which Manjula later learned belonged to Paul—they were as poor as her own family.

According to custom, after the reception the couple leaves for the bride's home.

Satyam, Maniamma, and Santhamma received them at Veeravalli. The celebration there was a simple prayer meeting with fifty people and a small feast.

The consummation ritual had to be postponed because Manjula was having her period, but her family allowed the couple to sit alone. They didn't talk much, and after a long silence he tentatively touched her hand. She became like a stone. It was a new feeling. She didn't respond or touch him back. After some time, they went to their separate beds.

The next day, despite Manjula's period, the couple was allowed to sleep together. As Uncle David had warned Manjula, it was painful.

In the morning, Manjula could not look her father or brothers in the eye. She avoided them now that she'd found out what a man is like and what he is equipped with.

During a stroll by the river the next day, Manjula found out her husband was seven and a half years older than her. Outraged, she stopped in the middle of the path. "What kind of nonsense is this! Why was I not told you were so old!" He told her to calm down. She saw he was embarrassed and did not pursue the matter, but it continued to bother her.

After a week in Veeravalli, the couple returned to Kakinada, where they were to live in Prabhakara Rao's family compound with the rest of his extended family. An upstairs room had been set aside for the two of them to sleep in. In the morning, as Prabhakara Rao descended, Uncle Paul asked him in English, "Ha, nephew, how did you fare?"

He blushed, yet replied, in English, "I did very well, thank you."

Prabhakara Rao's cousins on his father's side invited the couple to the nearby town of Rajahmundry, where Manjula went to sleep and the rest played cards. Prabhakara Rao, after losing awhile, came in to the bedroom, kissed his wife's foot for good luck, and went back to the game.

Manjula was not sure yet if her marriage was a good one, but after the first time sleeping with her husband she began to crave physical intimacy. She liked the feel of her husband. She didn't like to be apart from him, even for a second. Wherever he went, she would go; wherever he sat, she would sit; and if he was talking to someone, she would stand next to him, clinging to his side. When he left her alone to go hunting with his friends, she moped. She discovered that he loved going hunting more than anything else in the world.

After the monthlong wedding celebration, it was time for them to return to work. Prabhakara Rao went back to Anantapur and Manjula to Guntur, hopeful that they would soon manage to find jobs in the same city and live together.

Manjula's principal's wedding present to her was ousting orders: she would not be rehired for the coming academic year. Luckily she found another post as a lecturer in the night college in Vijayawada.

In a rickshaw on her way to the college one day, she looked at the furniture in the shop windows on Bunder Road and thought, "Whatever my life has been so far, my future is going to be fine. I have a husband. Soon I will set up a home. In that home—see those sofas in that shop—I will put such sofas in my house."

Four months after their marriage, Prabhakara Rao finally found a job for Manjula in Anantapur. A month later she was pregnant.

Her morning sickness was severe. She stopped going to the latrine because the filth made her nauseous. Nowhere in the whole city was there a clean lavatory. She developed constipation. When she tried a laxative, she began to miscarry. The doctors managed to save the pregnancy and confined her to bed rest for a few weeks. Prabhakara Rao could not help because he did not know how to make a cup of tea, let alone cook. They went hungry. The house was in shambles, strewn with trash and unwashed clothes.

Their first Christmas together, with Manjula two months pregnant, Carey visited, carrying presents. He took charge of the household, cleaned and cooked. As long as he stayed, they ate well. When the time came for him to leave, he took Prabhakara Rao aside and gave him valuable advice. "I saw how you treat my sister." Carey had seen her sitting cuddled up in Prabhakara Rao's lap for hours. "Women should never be treated so kindly. You need to treat them sternly; otherwise, they climb on your head and sit there."

Carey had to leave before the couple were able to look after themselves again. So Rathnamma came to stay with them. She not only cooked and cleaned but combed Manjula's hair and set out her own saris for Manjula to wear at work. She wanted her daughter-in-law to be healthy and look good. An ideal, loving relationship seemed to be forming between the two women.

During her morning sickness, Manjula always clung to her husband. Rathnamma, being old-fashioned, did not approve. She also feared that her new daughter-in-law, with her double M.A., would push her into a corner, usurping her authority as mistress of the household and relegating her to an insignificant position. Things soured between them.

Anantapur is a city in Rayalaseema, a region in Andhra known sardonically as Rallaseema—"terrain of rocks." The sun blazes down year-round on the dry, cracked earth strewn with boulders. One hot night, when Prabhakara Rao took a chair outside for Manjula to sleep on, Rathnamma could not believe her eyes. "You emasculated bugger, you carry chairs for your wife now?"

Right in front of Manjula's eyes, her husband transformed into a monster. He looked like a different person when enraged: face red, nostrils aflare, hair bristling. He had to restrain himself from attacking his mother. Instead he called her unmentionable names. Prabhakara Rao could not tolerate being called effeminate.

Rathnamma did not want to stay. Prabhakara Rao refused to take her back to Kakinada. Manjula, eight months pregnant, had to accompany her.

When Manjula returned, the heat was worse. There was no air inside. She asked her husband to set up a chair outside. He said no. She tried to set it up herself. He said, "No, you stay inside."

"I cannot breathe, please."

He shouted "No!"

She was scared to utter another word.

Manjula panicked. She, who prayed only in direst need, began to pray. "O Lord Jesus, what should I do, I cannot breathe. This man says I cannot sleep outside." Suddenly she started saying, "I am not going to live." She knew this was the end of her life, hers and her baby's. This was their last day on this earth.

At that moment, rain began to fall. The rain that visits Rayalaseema once in a decade. The earth cooled down.

Carey returned to take Manjula to Warangal for her delivery. There were no clean clothes to pack. He said, "We have no time." He gathered all the dirty clothes to wash in Warangal. When they left, Prabhakara Rao didn't say goodbye, let alone give her any money, even for her ticket.

In Khazipet, her brothers treated her as if she were a princess. When she went into labor, they took her to St. Ann's Hospital. By the time she delivered the baby—a tiny girl—Manjula desperately needed sleep. But she was filled with so much joy that sleep wouldn't come, and besides, she was afraid to miss a single, precious moment. Satyam's son Siddhartha, seven years old, came to look at the baby. He fell in love with the baby's feet, always touching, caressing, and kissing them, exclaiming delightedly all the while. Nancharayya came to see the baby. "Papa, your daughter is going to be a star. What a beautiful girl! Look at her fingers! She's going to be an artist, a pianist."

Carey sent their father a telegram. A month passed with no response. Maniamma looked after Manjula. For the first time, Manjula admitted to Satyam, "I should have believed you. You really did marry her for the sake of our family."

But the situation would soon be turned upside down when Satyam refused to allow Maniamma to accompany Manjula to Anantapur. Maniamma's heart was set on seeing the new city.

So Maniamma went on strike. She stopped cooking and taking care of her own children, including her six-month-old son. She climbed on a cot and covered her face with a sheet. It was chaos: a houseful of children wailing, unfed, unwashed. Carey had to take over. He was physically exhausted, and with Manjula's hospital bills the family was financially exhausted as well.

Maniamma's tantrums made Manjula feel unwanted. It was time to leave, but she had no money for the train. Nancharayya offered the money and Carey was ready to take them back, but the infant was not ready to travel. It had been raining continuously for days on end, and Satyam's house had no shutters on the windows. The cold wetness closed in upon the infant. Her lungs filled with moisture. She was gasping, her chest pumping spasmodically. They could not afford a doctor. An Anglo-Indian neighbor advised Manjula to drink two spoonfuls of whiskey before breast-feeding. "You can also dilute two drops with water and pour it in the baby's mouth," she said.

For the first and last time in her life, Manjula drank alcohol. She was aware that she was talking too much but could not stop herself. Nancharayya tried to calm her. "Papa, stop talking, amma, stop talking. Just stay calm." With his drunken sister and drunken infant niece, Carey got on the train.

Carey said, "Amma, please stop talking and go to sleep." He sat holding the month-old baby in his hands for sixteen hours straight. Whenever the train whistle blew, the sick infant woke up, startled. Carey held her tight against his chest.

They arrived in Anantapur station. They got into a *jetka* (horse buggy) and began the ride home. As they passed the town's clock tower, Manjula said to Carey, "Annayya, this baby, is she alive or dead?" When Manjula said that, Carey's heart stopped. He shook the infant.

She opened her puffy, toadlike eyes. Carey and Manjula were relieved.

The jetka stopped in front of the house. Prabhakara Rao was home. When he saw the baby, the callous husband she had left behind transformed at once into a loving father.

Manjula went back to work, teaching in a night college in Anantapur. Prabhakara Rao would sit holding the baby all night, never moving. Without having slept an hour, he would go to work in the morning.

Manjula had no one to teach her how to bathe the baby. She hired a woman. The woman boiled water. Manjula was expecting the woman would mix in some cold water to make it lukewarm. But the woman poured the boiling water on top of the infant's head. The baby screamed—Manjula could see her tongue, her uvula—and the infant's skin changed color like the flesh of a chicken when it's dropped into a sauté pan. Manjula grabbed her baby away.

Manjula tried to bathe her baby in such a way that she would have as pleasant an experience as possible. Manjula would put her nipple in her daughter's mouth and, while breast-feeding her, would slowly and carefully wash the baby in her arms, rinsing her with warm water from a tumbler.

When the baby was born, Manjula's niece had made a list of names and said, "I like Sujatha." Without a proper christening, they started calling her Suja.

But then a conflict arose. Rathnamma had been expecting them to name the child in her honor or at least to leave the choice of name to her. She said, "I want Grace." Rathnamma had had a daughter named Grace who died when she was eight.

Manjula was appalled. She didn't want an old-fashioned name like that. She justified her taste by saying she was secular and didn't want to give her child a Christian name.

Prabhakara Rao, who had to decide, would say nothing either way. The day of the christening, he, Manjula, and Rathnamma walked up the aisle to the pastor with Prabhakara Rao in the middle, carrying the child, flanked by the silently feuding women. When the moment came, they gazed helplessly at his lips. Were they forming *Gr* or *Su*? He said, "Sujatha."

When Sujatha was six months old, her head was shaved to remove the birth hair. When her parents brought her back to Anantapur, one of their students, a teenager, named her Nirupayoga Swami (Swami of Uselessness) and took to smacking her smooth little head.

Manjula cried, "Please, don't smack it!"

"But, madam, I can't resist, madam."

Suja had round everything: face, mouth, eyes. Prabhakara Rao was especially fond of her ass. "My daughter's ass is shaped like an apple." He brought an apple from the bazaar, held it up beside the ass. "See, right?" he asked his colleagues.

Nine months after Sujatha was born, Manjula got pregnant again and was let go from her job. Losing her job was a regular part of life for Manjula at this time. In government colleges she was only eligible for temporary positions, filling in for someone who was away on leave. It was easy for principals to fire her if for any reason they did not like her. Yet she could not qualify for a permanent post in a government college without taking the state lecturer selection exam. Because few positions were open in the state, this exam had not been held in years.

During summer holidays, Prabhakara Rao took the family to Kakinada. When Prabhakara Rao returned to Anantapur, Manjula stayed in Kakinada with her in-laws to look for work in town. She applied for a position at a women's college under the trusteeship of a wealthy Hindu temple—Annavaram Satyavathi Devi College—where, because it was a private college, she was eligible for a permanent job. She was interviewed by a group of old brahmin males, the three of them looking extremely orthodox with their heads totally shorn but for a tuft of white hair at the top and long, vertical red lines drawn down their foreheads. For an

235 I ANTS AMONG ELEPHANTS

untouchable young woman who desperately needed a job, a more daunting party of examiners could hardly be imagined. Manjula, intimidated, sat in front of them, her palms sweaty and cold, her knees pressed together.

"What is democracy?" one of them asked, peering over the top of his glasses.

"Umm . . . Democracy is a political system where the supreme power lies in the hands of the citizens. In democracy, it is the people who run the government through their elected representatives. In essence, democracy means a government of, by, and for the people."

The ancient brahmin males nodded approvingly and made check marks on the sheets in front of them. But she was not done.

"This is what they write in the textbooks. This is what the professors teach their students in colleges and universities. This is what students are forced to write in exams, and candidates to utter in job interviews. As I have just done."

The aged, conservative brahmin males looked up at her.

"But so far there has been not a single example of democracy in the world. Nowhere in the world, not in one single country, is there a rule of the people, let alone by the people or for the people. The British, the Americans, the French, and now the Indians—they may claim they have democracy in their countries. But it is all bogus. Hypocrisy. The very definition is wrong!"

In all their years as directors, those highly placed brahmins had never come across another candidate like her. An untouchable, at that!

She got the job.

At the women's college, the principal harassed her, constantly finding fault with her teaching methods. The filth of Elwin Peta exacerbated her morning sickness. It was mango season, and flies were everywhere. Suja had grown thin. Even with Manjula's job, the family could not afford milk powder, so they fed the baby rice, lentils, and vegetables. One day, Suja suffered a dangerously severe bout of diarrhea. She shat twenty-three times in one hour and was dehydrating fast. There was no money for the doctor.

Prabhakara Rao visited for a long weekend. Manjula begged him, "Please take me home. I cannot live here. We are going to die." Prabhakara

Rao simply said, "Let's go." Another temporary teaching job had opened in Anantapur. If she wanted to grab it, they had to start right away. In spite of a dangerous typhoon and flooding, they took their lives in their hands and left at once.

Manjula got the job. Three days later, she was ousted.

Prabhakara Rao and Manjula were dangerously in debt to the marwari moneylenders. Prabhakara Rao avoided telling his wife how bad their situation was. But he was drowning. When she was away in Khazipet, he had the desperate idea of treating one of his thug students to chicken meals in the hope of enlisting him to scare off the usurers who were after him. The plan came to nothing.

It wasn't just Prabhakara Rao. Most of his colleagues, on the first of the month, came out of the clerk's office with their salaries and handed the envelope over to the marwari waiting outside. Lecturers were special targets for marwaris, as they had a regular income.

Manjula blamed their situation on Prabhakara Rao's habit of smoking and having two cups of tea a day. "Imagine how much money you are wasting!"

Prabhakara Rao hated being called an *appulodu* (indebted man) even more than being called a sissy. It humiliated him. He carried on borrowing, paying back, borrowing, paying back.

Late one evening, he returned from work, got into bed. "Come here, lie next to me." He proposed a suicide pact. "Let us do it in a hotel."

Manjula did not ask him why he wanted to die. Perhaps he'd had a terrible encounter with a marwari who threatened him. She did not show the same sympathy that he did when she brought her fears to him, but self-righteously told him, "If you want, you go do it. I have no reason to kill myself."

Manjula constantly worried about the toddler. Little Suja turned out to be a danger magnet. One time she peeled off the masking tape her father had put over exposed electric wires; another time she stuck her hand in chili powder; and yet another she tried to reach for burning coals. She needed to be watched all the time.

Manjula had been out of work for some time. Her life was a series of

237 | ANTS AMONG ELEPHANTS

temporary jobs and oustings. During this particular hiatus, she swept the house every day. Every day she came across a stray envelope on the floor. Every day she brushed it aside. After a month went by, she finally grew curious enough to open it. It was a job offer. Yet again she started work.

For her second delivery Manjula decided to have Prabhakara Rao by her side and did not go to Khazipet. They wrote Rathnamma to come and help. In his mother's presence, Prabhakara Rao once again turned cold.

Rathnamma harassed Manjula day and night. She was a mere skeleton, yet her pregnant belly was huge. Prabhakara Rao asked her to make tea. She said, "Do you have to have two teas a day?" As she brought out the cup, she could see he was seething with anger. His mother was saying, "What a fuss just to make one cup of tea." Prabhakara Rao refused the tea. Manjula tried to pacify him. He got up from the chair, flew at her, and slapped her so hard that a big clot of blood fell on the floor.

Rathnamma said, "She has bad teeth. That's all."

Manjula knew that if she told her brothers about her situation, they would break up her marriage, probably beat her husband, too. She wanted to keep the marriage. She wanted social respect. She never said a word to anyone.

Early one winter morning, she went into labor. "We need to go to the hospital." Her mother-in-law began making tea for her son. Then she boiled water for him to take a bath. Then she made breakfast. Suja, who ate her food with hot mango pickle like an adult, had diarrhea. They had to wash her. Again another tea. All this while Manjula was moaning.

Finally, three hours after her pains had started, they got into a jetka and arrived at the hospital. When they reached the hospital veranda, the baby boy came out. Leaving Manjula at the hospital, her husband and mother-in-law turned around and went home.

Manjula's son was so beautiful. Big, fair-skinned.

But from the moment he was born, he was seriously ill. He cried and cried due to colic. A young nurse, to calm him down, mixed glucose powder in a spoonful of water taken directly from a rusty, moldy tap and poured it into his mouth. Immediately he began having diarrhea and vomiting. Manjula panicked.

The doctors saw that Manjula's son was choking on his own vomit. He was immediately taken to the ICU. Observing this drama, one of the visitors of the patient in the bed next to Manjula's ran after the doctors to see what would happen.

Manjula waited in tears. Hours passed. No one would tell her anything. While dozing off, she heard the patient next to her talking to someone. "The boy has gone."

Manjula screamed until the veins in her neck popped out. "My baby, my baby!"

The nurses came running and calmed her down. "What's the matter?"

Manjula screamed, "I want to see my baby."

They assured her he was going to be okay.

What the patient had actually said was, "The woman who went off with the baby has been gone a long time." Because Rayalaseema Telugu is different from the kind spoken in coastal Andhra, Manjula had misunderstood.

In India, the patient's family is responsible for helping the patient to the bathroom, bathing her, and feeding her. Manjula was hungry. No one sent food from home. She waited five hours before Prabhakara Rao arrived with something to eat. "Where were you?" Manjula asked.

On his way to the hospital, he had stopped to play a game or two of tennis. He took so much offense at Manjula's question that he turned around and left.

After a few days in the hospital, Manjula came home. Her husband was waiting at the door, blocking her way in. "I don't want you here. Take him and go wherever you want. You cannot come in."

Holding the infant, she waited outside for hours. Finally he let her in. She never asked him why he'd treated her like that.

The baby was christened Abraham, but at home he was always called Babu (little boy).

Babu's diarrhea, which began the day he was born, lasted thirteen months. Manjula grew sick with anxiety. Opportunistic as always when it came to faith, she turned to God. "Lord Jesus, save my son. I will in turn help the poor and the less fortunate."

Manjula feared for the lives of her children. She feared for her own

239 I ANTS AMONG ELEPHANTS

life. It occurred to her that her mother had died at twenty-seven, a year younger than Manjula was now. She tried to calm herself, thinking, "Just because my mother died at this age doesn't mean I will." She took her son to the pediatrician almost every day. He was kind to her. He always tried to assure her that her son was going to be okay.

The next time she went to see the pediatrician, the compounder (a peon in a doctor's office) informed her that the doctor had died. Some failure of a vital organ. He had only been twenty-eight, the same age as Manjula. Her efforts to assure herself that she was too young to die lost all meaning.

When the sun went down, her fear of death became impossible to bear. She would pester her husband. "Look, my hands are turning blue. I read in the *Indian Express* that is a sign of impending death." He would tell her again and again, "No, you are not going to die."

When she woke up in the morning, she would feel a little better, but as the day progressed, she was surer and surer that she and her children were going to die.

Her students hated her, too. They didn't want this anxious skeleton of a woman teaching them. Prabhakara Rao's students once went on a strike to have him appointed their permanent teacher. Manjula's students now did the same to have her replaced. The last straw for them came when she walked into the classroom and began to scream, "There are cracks in the ceiling. They are widening. This building is collapsing. We must run." There were no cracks in the ceiling.

When she walked on the sidewalk, she could feel the pavement moving, she could see the shops on either side of the street sliding in opposite directions. She tried to make sense of these experiences. She told herself she was crazy. She tried to assure herself that it was all in her head and to stop worrying, but time and again she would hear of some local tragedy that brought her fears back. A boy pissing on an electric pole electrocuted himself. A colleague was correcting exam papers at home and his son, the same age as Suja, interrupted him. "Daddy, come play with me." The father gave the little boy a shove. The boy's head hit the leg of a cot and it killed him.

Manjula knew death was around the corner. She wanted to save herself, her children. She did not care about her husband.

Finally, the crisis to which all these dark premonitions had been leading was upon her. She was attending a colleague's memorial service. Prabhakara Rao was sitting beside her, and on the other side was Ganga Raju. As the ceremony concluded, she let out a loud gasp and dropped to the floor. People came running.

She was actually dying. After all these months of feeling death approach but never being sure if it wasn't all in her head, she knew it was real and it was now.

Manjula looked around her, dazed. It was time to speak a few last words, to disburden herself of her earthly responsibilities. She reached for a trusted hand. Not Prabhakara Rao's. Ganga Raju's.

"Ganga Raju *garu*," she implored, adding an honorific suffix to show respect, "please take care of my children." Then her hand let go of his.

A few seconds later, Manjula came to. She was surrounded by the anxious faces of the lecturers.

Prabhakara Rao helped his wife back home. Just as they entered their home, their colleague Damodar walked in behind them. His face red with fury, he launched into a tirade against Prabhakara Rao. "What kind of a husband are you! Are you a man or a beast? Look at your wife. With two small children, she cooks, she cleans. And she has to correct the test papers. If not cooking and cleaning, can't you help her with preparing marks lists! *Tchee tchee tchee!* Shame on you!" Damodar stormed out.

In fact, these days it had been even harder for Manjula than usual. Prabhakara Rao sat up all night, night after night, to prepare for his M.A. exams. Manjula had to get out of bed in the middle of the night and spend forty-five minutes lighting the hearth to make him cups of tea.

He took the exams every year, failing each time. Manjula asked, "What's the point? You are only going to fail again. I know what your problem is. There will be five annotations and five essays. You love annotations and spend all three hours on one single annotation. Each annotation carries five marks. Even if you do all five, you only get twenty-five marks. Spend time on essays. And don't show off all your brilliance. No examiner likes a student more knowledgeable than himself."

He had to go to Aligarh (near Benares) for the exams.

"Don't leave me with these sick children."

He left.

"You will never pass!"

The Sunday after he'd gone to Aligarh, Manjula tried on a new blouse a tailor had just stitched for her. It was too tight around the biceps, and it made her vein swell as when a nurse ties a rubber band to draw blood. She could not throw the blouse away, as it had cost money, nor could she take it back to the tailor, who would take another three months to fix it.

Suja woke up crying. Manjula picked her up. Holding her on her hip with one arm, Manjula went about washing dishes, feeding Babu, cleaning him. When Manjula tried to set Suja down, even for a second, she started crying loudly. She would not even let her mother switch her to the other hip.

Manjula noticed a vein as long and thick and hard as a pencil sticking out of her upper arm. She knew at once it was abnormal. She left the chores and, taking the two children, right away went to see the doctor, who told her to rest immediately.

Manjula, having developed a kind of masochism in the face of her problems, went on with her chores, with Suja on her hip. By the evening, the vein had swelled up more. Manjula ran back to the clinic.

Dr. Nayanam was furious. "Do you have any brains? What did I tell you! You are educated. If you don't understand, then at least listen to the doctor! This is called thrombophlebitis. There is a blood clot forming. If it travels to your heart or your brain, it will mean immediate death. How about this? You go and die, for all I care. I gave you advice and you didn't listen. You deserve to die."

Manjula went home. She panicked. Her temples were throbbing. She sweated, grew dazed, and was overcome by a strange, crazy feeling.

Rathnamma woke up. Rathnamma, who never stepped out of her home, who knew nothing of the outside world, ran outside, calling for help. A neighbor rushed to the center, brought back a jetka, and helped the women into it. In the middle of the night, the jetka sped through the empty streets. At the general hospital, the doctors checked Manjula's blood pressure, which was dangerously high, and immediately took her to the ICU, gave her an injection, and laid her on a bed. On her fourth day in the hospital, a close colleague of hers who had come to visit his own relative looked straight at Manjula and walked right past her. She was unrecognizable. At twenty-eight, all her hair had turned gray.

Prabhakara Rao returned from exams. Manjula had returned from the hospital four days earlier. He listened to her story. He said nothing. Maybe he was sick of his sick wife. Maybe he was sick of the hospital bills.

"I was so ill. What if I had died? Why did you have to leave me and go away?"

The moment that last word left her mouth, Manjula saw the rapid change in Prabhakara Rao's features and realized what a mistake she had made. He bristled with rage.

"I want neither you nor this marriage!" he roared. He plucked off his wedding ring, ran to the front steps, and tossed it.

Manjula ran out looking for it, in the bushes, in the gutter. She was upset, not because it was their wedding ring, but because it was the most valuable thing they possessed. Hours later she found the band, but the most valuable part, the emerald, was missing.

The next year when Manjula, again pregnant unexpectedly, was due to deliver, Prabhakara Rao flew into a rage over some insignificant matter. He was listening to the BBC. He leaped from the chair, picked up the radio, still plugged into its socket, and threw it at her. She ducked. Electric sparks burst out of the socket.

Prabhakara Rao knew his pregnant wife needed nutrition. He could afford to buy vegetables but no eggs, no meat, no fish, no fruit. They had to stop giving milk to the children.

One peaceful Sunday afternoon, Prabhakara Rao asked Manjula to make him a cup of tea. She got up muttering, "What if you didn't have so many teas?" She went into the kitchen. When she returned with the tea, she could see her husband was angry. Rathnamma, throwing kerosene on the fire, added, "So what if he wants tea, why do you have to complain?"

Manjula was already well into regretting she had uttered a word. She began, "Okay, let us forget—"

Still sitting in his chair, her husband raised the hot cup and threw it through the open door at the houses on the other side. Suja and Babu were scared and began to cry pathetically, helpless little persons caught in a war. Manjula started crying, too.

"*Ayyo*, look out, Husband, the babies, our babies," she cried.

Prabhakara Rao was breathing laboriously. "We will see about your babies. I will lay you and your babies out in the street and hack you all to pieces."

This time Rathnamma tried to calm her son while continuing to blame Manjula for causing the fight. Almost every day the radio, the papers, had news of men who had too much debt killing their wives and children and then killing themselves.

◎

FIVE LONG YEARS AFTER MANJULA received her M.A., the government announced lecturer selection exams for history. This was a life-changing opportunity for Manjula. If she received a good rank and then passed the oral exam, she would finally escape the cycle of temporary employment. With a permanent government job, her livelihood would no longer depend on the whims of a principal.

As she came out of the exam hall, it was pouring. Her husband was waiting outside with an umbrella, holding their son. He was tense, like a strict father anxious about his daughter's performance. He scanned the question paper she handed him and asked her which topic she'd chosen for the essay. She showed him. He grunted, "Hmm. We will see."

Manjula came in tenth out of the tens of thousands of history graduates statewide who took the exam. But she had yet another hurdle to face: an oral interview with a panel of high-level academicians. Here test scores lost all value. Candidates relied on bribery or nepotism. Manjula had neither money nor connections.

So she went to appeal to Thomas Reddy, an MP from Anantapur and a Christian of reddy caste. Manjula and Prabhakara Rao hoped he would help them as fellow Christians. He said he would, but one could not expect much on such a flimsy basis.

In the interview, Manjula was asked every question she had anticipated and prepared for, and in the very order she had guessed. As she was leaving the interview room, one of the committee members, a highly respected mala professor named Bullayya, stopped her to ask one last question: "What is your opinion on apartheid?" It wasn't a test. He genuinely wanted to hear her views on that issue. Manjula just giggled stupidly and ran out, leaving Professor Bullayya confused. She did not have an opinion on apartheid, having never heard that term before.

A few days later, Prabhakara Rao received a telegram from one of his friends in Hyderabad: "Congratulations. Your wife has been selected."

Manjula and Prabhakara Rao went to thank Thomas Reddy. "Dear girl, no need to thank me. Thank our Lord Jesus. I did nothing. Your interviewers told me all about you."

After seven years of temporary positions, night jobs, and oustings, Manjula finally received posting orders from the university board to report to Tirupati College.

Tirupati was far away. But beggars cannot be choosers. Manjula resigned her job in Anantapur and took a train to Tirupati.

The principal there, a brahmin woman named Rajeswari, took one look at Manjula and said, "You have no job here. I won't let you report."

Manjula could not believe what she was hearing. In tears, she left the principal's office.

The clerk saw what had happened. He had nothing but pity for Manjula's situation. "Look, amma, it would be no use going to the board. If that woman says no, then it is no." What hurt most was that Manjula had left the job she had.

Prabhakara Rao, who had accompanied her to Tirupati, sympathized but was helpless to defend his wife. They did not sleep that night.

She would have to rush back, see her principal in Anantapur, and beg for her job back. By six-thirty the next morning, she and her husband were at his doorstep. Mr. Habibullah simply said, "Write a sick-leave application for the two days you were away. I will rip up your resignation letter." Then he called his wife and he told her in Urdu to bring tiffin and coffee for the couple, their first meal since the debacle in Tirupati.

◎

RATHNAMMA'S HEALTH WAS POOR. HER heart was enlarged. Her feet were always swollen. She suffered exhaustion and shortness of breath while doing household chores. But she kept on working by sheer habit, by sheer force of tradition. Her so-called educated sons could not care less. Prabhakara Rao only defended his mother's "authority" against Manjula. Other than that, he never did anything for her. He never brought her things she liked to eat, never walked her to church, never even talked with her much. Yet he chased and beat up his wife to champion his mother.

Rathnamma asked her son to take her to a famous Christian hospital in Tamil Nadu for a medical checkup. But Prabhakara Rao, fearing the prospect of more debt, remained silent.

Manjula, without telling her husband, sold the gold chain that Prabhakara Rao's family had given her for her engagement to the owners of the restaurant opposite the house. She gave the money to Prabhakara Rao. "Take your mother to Vellore." The doctors did the tests, gave Rathnamma prescriptions and advice, and sent her home.

In Anantapur the family bought the medicines. The doctors had said that Rathnamma should go on a special diet and take bed rest. Manjula took care of everything.

But she had selfish motives in doing all this for her mother-in-law. Manjula observed that her husband was a loving man when they were alone, yet turned into a monster in the presence of his mother. She knew that Rathnamma wanted to go back to her family in Kakinada. She had only been waiting to get the medical checkup and medicines she wanted. Once she got all that, she left.

Manjula took Babu with her and went to Khazipet for her third delivery. Carey was not there to receive her at the station. He had married a Telangana girl in a simple ceremony in Seetharamayya's house, and the couple had gone to Nirmal to visit the bride's mother.

It pained Satyam to see his sister in this condition. She was nothing but bones, pale and weak. If she wanted to sit, she needed to be helped down. If she was sitting, someone had to put his hands in her armpits and lift her up.

Satyam was busy. Every night after supper he left home, walking in the dark across fields and hillocks to avoid police, and went to Warangal. He would have meetings with mill workers, students, railway workers, peasant youths. He was organizing teachers. He was fully immersed in his activity. Coming back at four or five in the morning, he would go to Nancharayya's house, and without disturbing his friend's family, he would sleep on the bare floor of their porch, leaving before they woke up. Sometimes they would get up early and find him there. Manjula wondered how this brother of hers, who behaved like a prince at home, was able to work so hard for his ideals.

One night at two, when Satyam was out doing his clandestine organization, Manjula began having contractions. Maniamma locked the five sleeping children, including her two-and-half-year-old boy, inside the house and took Manjula to St. Ann's. As the nurse was taking down the patient information, Maniamma remembered what Satyam had said to her. "My sister is too weak. If she has a fourth pregnancy, she is sure to die." Without telling Manjula, Maniamma told the nurse to arrange for a tubectomy after delivery. At that, the hospital turned Manjula away. As Catholics, they did not approve of birth control.

In the dead of the night, Maniamma took Manjula to the government hospital in Hanamkonda, two hours away by rickshaw.

No one knew why, but during delivery Manjula started to bleed uncontrollably. A doctor told Maniamma to go out and buy an injection to stop the bleeding. It cost seventy-five paisa, which she didn't have. She had spent all the cash they had between them to hire the rickshaws. And the medical stores would not open for hours. A thoughtful nurse used an injection that was meant for another patient whose life was not in danger.

After the baby was born, Satyam arrived at the hospital. The doctors were waiting for him. "Her condition is very poor," he was told. "We strongly urge that she have a tubectomy."

Manjula hesitated.

Satyam was furious. "You are going to do as I say."

In a few minutes the very same doctor who had told Manjula she must have the operation returned to inform Satyam that the hospital could not operate on her. "We need a signed permission from her husband."

But that husband, once she left Anantapur, never wrote, never phoned. To get in touch with him, they would have to write a letter. The going-and-coming of those two letters would take at least ten days, and the operation needed to be performed within two or three days of the delivery.

For the second time, Satyam committed forgery for the sake of his sister. Posing as her husband, he signed the permission.

The doctors prepared Manjula for surgery. After the anesthesia was administered, the surgeon had to leave her on the table to fill out some papers. The last thing Manjula heard was "I will be right back."

The next thing she felt was excruciating pain. Her belly was being cut open. The doctor, having returned well after Manjula's anesthesia had worn off, performed the surgery as she lay awake.

After the operation, they did not give her penicillin, because her family had yet to find the money to buy it. The doctors simply stitched her up and went away. Modern thinking was Manjula's curse. She knew the importance of antibiotics. She was sure she was going to die.

The next morning, Manjula woke up screaming. The janitor, a rude paki woman, had come to clean her. Perhaps out of some psychological reaction to their own horrible oppression, the pakis working as janitors in government hospitals often behave cruelly toward patients who are poor. This woman was irate to find Manjula still asleep after sunrise. "Hey, you! Why are you sleeping day and night? Get up!" She violently pulled off Manjula's sheet.

For hours, blood had been oozing out at her incision, soaking the sheet, and as the blood dried, the sheet got stuck to the stitches. Tearing off that sheet, this woman ripped the incision open.

Maniamma, asleep by the bed, woke up and, catching the janitor by her bun, yanked her neck back and punched her in the mouth. Maniamma was the girl all the other girls, including Manjula, had been scared of back when they went to high school together. When she got angry, she was the incarnation of the goddess of wrath.

But the janitor was not afraid of Maniamma. The two women, one wilder than the other, wrestled on the floor.

Maniamma had set upon the janitor to defend her helpless sister-in-law, but once the fighting started, Maniamma forgot all about Manjula. Locked in each other's arms, the two combatants crashed down on top of Manjula and tore open more stitches. Visiting relatives of other patients in the ward, who had been watching the spectacle, stepped in to separate the two women. Manjula, losing blood, was taken away by nurses to get her stitches repaired.

By afternoon, the janitors' union had called a strike. They wanted Maniamma to apologize. As she was the wife of a Communist leader, the situation was delicate. The party tried to intervene, but the union refused to back down, and finally Satyam had to force Maniamma to apologize.

The ordeal of the delivery and the surgery had one important effect on Manjula. She had tasted death, gone through it, knew now what it was like.

She lost her fear.

NINE

◉ ◉ ◉

IN FEBRUARY 1966, WHEN MANJULA came to stay with Satyam's family in Khazipet to deliver her third child, she rarely saw her brother at home. He was busy leading, from behind the scenes, an agitation in Warangal around the grievances of the native Telangana people.

Ever since Andhra and Telangana had merged into one state, sentiment within Telangana had been turning against the Andhra migrants flooding into the region. Telangana people complained they could not compete with Andhras in any field. In the countryside, rich Andhra settlers were buying up all the farmland. In the urban areas, Andhra doctors, teachers, professors, and administrators were taking all the jobs. Andhra students filled the medical and engineering colleges. Telanganas, held back culturally and economically under the rule of the Nizam, were being pushed aside.

A disgruntled Telangana Congress leader had called on the people of Telangana to fight to separate from Andhra. So then sporadic attacks on Andhras living in Telangana turned into systematic, government-funded, police-aided anti-Andhra pogroms—looting, rape, arson, murders. Everywhere the cry was raised "Andhras, go back!"

Carey was relatively safe. Not only had he married a Telangana woman, but also many of the Telangana thugs leading the anti-Andhra violence were his friends. Satyam had no such security. He was forced to temporarily move his family out of their home into a place near the Railway Workers Colony, where friends and supporters would protect them.

Seeing that Telangana people were indeed losing out to Andhra people in every field, Satyam took up the cause. He wrote leaflets setting out these just grievances, had them printed, and littered Warangal's main square of Hanamkonda Chowrastha with them overnight. Every morning fresh ones would appear. They were unsigned. These writings struck a chord with the Telangana public. People looked forward to the new one that would be left each day and argued over the mystery of who the author was.

Satyam also organized meetings of supporters in the Azam Jahi mills in Warangal and the Khazipet Railway Colony. These workers had been taking part in the looting of Andhra-owned businesses. He told them, "Okay, there is injustice done to you. But what did the ordinary Andhra man, a clerk, a teacher, do to deserve to be attacked? Why humiliate his wife, his daughter?" He told them they should instead fight against the landlords, exploiters of both Andhras and Telanganas:

Kadupu chetto pattukoni vacchina vadini kadayya,
Kadupu kottataniki.

(Attack those who deprive your stomach,
Not those who came here for their stomachs' sake.)

It is not Andhra versus Telangana, he said. It is exploiter versus the exploited. He organized looting of shops selling grain or clothes regardless of the regional identity of their owners.

In Warangal and Khazipet, the mill and railway workers were incredulous to see this Andhra chap championing their movement. Satyam and his squads successfully defended themselves as well as ordinary Andhra families and students against the well-funded militias backed by the police. Since Satyam's side was disadvantaged, his idea was "we should be the ones to attack first." Whenever he got the slightest clue that an anti-Andhra pogrom was being organized, his squads took the hooligans by surprise. Satyam called this strategy "offensive defense." He revised the teachings of the Sermon on the Mount: "Blessed is he who attacks first, for he shall inherit the earth."

At a time when Andhras across the region were fleeing or hiding, Maniamma calmly went out to shop for groceries. The shop owner joked with her, "Amma, all your Andhra people are leaving everything and running away. You must have guts to be walking around in the streets!"

She replied, "Andhras may be fleeing, but *we* Andhras here have the business of organizing the Telangana agitation. If not for *us* Andhras, where would *you* be? This whole movement is ours, *my* old man is working for it day and night. Why would we flee?" The shop owner didn't know what she was talking about, but he remembered her words, and years later, people in Khazipet were still talking about this incident.

Seetharamayya visited every ten days. He would listen to Satyam's reports with excitement, with joy, and with a hint of envy. Seetharamayya, whose family was among those buying up Telangana farmland, could hardly take a leading role in this agitation.

As long as Telanganas were killing and raping Andhras, government officials and police were content to join in the violence. But once these mobs were driven away under Satyam's direction and poor and working people started making off with food and clothes, the authorities suddenly became alert to the "law and order" situation. Indira Gandhi, who had been elected prime minister in January 1966, ordered the Central Reserve Police Force (CRPF) deployed to Telangana. Shootings occurred in the streets, and all the known leaders of the agitation were rounded up and taken to the Central Jail in Warangal. Satyam, who had been operating clandestinely, was not among them.

So the agitation continued full force. The public at large as well as the police were puzzled. Who was the invisible leader behind this unrest?

◎

IN THE SUMMER OF THE same year, Satyam roused the deeply dormant discontent in the Catholic community in Khazipet. He stirred up this population that religiosity had long rendered servile and incapable of confronting the religious authorities who controlled all the public institutions.

Fatima Nagar, the center of the Catholic community in Khazipet, had not existed seventy years earlier. When Father Rolla, an Italian missionary sent by the Pontificium Institutum Missionum Exterarum, arrived there, it was a thick jungle. No people, except for Lambadi tribals.

With his own hands and with the help of the Lambadis, the Father cleared the forest and established the Cathedral of Our Lady of Fatima. Around the church grew Fatima Nagar, the largest neighborhood in Khazipet. Fatima Nagar was a Catholic *nagar* (neighborhood), all of it owned by the Catholic mission. There the missionaries built two big and prestigious schools: St. Gabriel for boys and Fatima for girls. They also built St. Ann's Hospital to rival the big government hospital in Warangal and the one in Hanamkonda. The Catholic mission was the biggest private employer in the town of Khazipet.

The families in Fatima Nagar formed an extremely close-knit community of Catholics whose lives revolved around the Church. They went to mass in the cathedral, were educated in the two schools, and worked in either the schools or the hospital. The church leaders had the final say in everyone's personal affairs: who married whom, what they named their children, what careers they pursued.

In the summer of 1967, Satyam disturbed the calm surface of this nagar when he instigated his colleagues to unionize.

Until Satyam came along, it had never occurred to the teachers to cross the Church authorities. When Satyam first proposed the idea, they covered their ears and ran away. *Union* was a blasphemous word.

But by and by, furtively, the female teachers began to listen to him. They wanted better salaries but were afraid to upset the Fathers. So they asked Satyam to negotiate for them.

When Satyam first started teaching at St. Gabriel, the Catholic authorities, seeing him as an asset to their institution, had given him benefits no other teacher had. Now he went to the negotiating table as his colleagues' representative.

The Mother Superior asked him, "Why are you interested in all this? We gave you everything."

He looked directly at her. "Consider it my madness."

First came the protest against the predatory Fathers abusing the boys. Then the Khazipet police informed the Fathers that their prize teacher Satyam might have been the one inciting the REC students to strike. This union business was the final straw. The Fathers decided to get rid of him.

But if they were to fire him, he was sure to tell the newspapers about the teachers' union drive. They were afraid the Church would lose respect if the salaries and working conditions in their institutions were revealed.

Father John was brought back from retirement to handle the situation. His first move was to meet with the teachers, not as a group but in small batches. "Okay, tell me, what are your problems? I will take care of them." No need to unionize.

Soon a rumor started circulating in Fatima Nagar. People said that Satyam had declared it his mission to convert the Cathedral of Our Lady of Fatima into a union office. "We shall see how this god can hold out here!" This report shocked all who heard it, including Satyam's colleagues.

Late one evening, Satyam returned from out of town to find Maniamma in distress. A great commotion had occurred in Fatima Nagar that day. It seemed that a teacher had organized a gang to beat up a student, and the students were planning to go on a strike to demand action against that teacher. That teacher, the student had charged, was none other than Satyam.

The entire population of Fatima Nagar united with the students of the two convent schools to call for the firing of this godless, student-abusing teacher. "We have no protection from this monster unless he is removed from Khazipet!" The Khazipet police joined in.

Satyam's family was ostracized. When they stepped out of their house, they were met with angry glares, with spitting and snarling. No one would speak to them. Shop owners ignored them. The three children were scared.

Satyam went to see Omkar, the CPI(M) leader in Warangal. When Satyam had started organizing teachers, Omkar had encouraged him, thinking it would help win votes in future elections. But when Omkar heard about the situation Satyam found himself in, he was not happy. "You are butting heads with the Catholic management! Do you know how mad that is?"

"Well, what has happened has happened. What am I to do about it now?"

With his feet up on the table and leaning way back in his chair with a cigar in his mouth, Omkar gave a simple order: "Withdraaaaw!"

Denied the party's support, Satyam returned home. Satyam and Maniamma stayed up all night, fearing an attack on their house.

The next day Satyam left for Secunderabad to meet Iyer, the state secretary of the Telangana Private Schools Union. Iyer was a Communist who had also left the old party. When Satyam explained his predicament, Iyer gave Satyam his assurance. "They cannot touch you."

While Satyam was visiting Iyer, Carey received word of the trouble his brother was in. He got together with his friend Kumar, who was a big *dada* (muscleman). They got drunk and rode a borrowed motorcycle to Fatima Nagar. When they arrived, it was already dark. Carey and Kumar strutted through the streets, stopping in front of the bishop's lodge and calling out, "Hey, you bastards! Come on out of your holes. Let's see who has the guts to lay hands on my brother. Come on! I challenge you to pluck a single hair from my brother's crotch."

The lights came on in every house in Fatima Nagar. People stood at their windows to gawk. The drill teacher at St. Gabriel, a well-built man named Marianna, came out, walked up to Carey, and punched him in the face. Carey, already unstable on his feet, went down. His nose was broken and there was a lot of blood.

As he struggled to get to his feet, Carey spotted Satyam returning home. *"Anna* [big brother], I challenged those buggers. They don't know how to fight honorably. They punched me, I fell down, I am bleeding."

All the assurance Iyer had offered evaporated in an instant. Here was an aggravating circumstance.

When the word got out that the Catholics were harassing Satyam, the people he had organized for the sake of the new party—railway workers and young agricultural laborers—came to his aid.

The following night some fifteen of them paid a visit to drill teacher Marianna's house. He was not home, so they beat up his brother and left. In the morning, news of the assault on Marianna's brother spread. Satyam realized the danger he was in. He could not approach the police. It was no longer safe to remain in Khazipet. In the dark of night, the family left Fatima Nagar and went to stay with Carey in Warangal.

At school the next morning no one—no one—would talk to Satyam.

In the evening he went back to Warangal. As he entered the house, Maniamma was waiting for him outside. "Let us go back to our own place. I'd rather die there than stay here."

While Satyam had been at school, Carey's wife had returned home in her nurse's uniform, mad as fire. At the hospital everyone was talking about a badly beaten patient brought in from Fatima Nagar. The story was that he was a Catholic and the brother of a teacher at St. Gabriel, and was mercilessly beaten on the orders of an Andhra. And that Andhra was a Communist.

Carey's wife, Premalatha, was furious with her husband. "Is this true? Is your brother behind this? Do you know how difficult it is for me already as the wife of an Andhra? Now your brother has to go and do this? What happened? I am sure you had something to do with this! Tell me, did you go there with your useless bastard friend Pratap? Did you two start this nonsense?"

When Premalatha lost her temper, she was hell's fury. And when a woman acted insolently, Carey showed no tolerance. She punched him, he threw a kitchen knife at her. Maniamma got in the way. The knife gashed her hand. She said nothing and waited quietly for her husband, pressing a cloth on her wound.

Satyam decided to take his family back to Fatima Nagar. The party once again refused to help him. Neither would his neighbors. He stood accused of "swearing to depose God in the church" and of beating up a student and now the drill teacher's brother. He found no sympathy anywhere.

At school the students surrounded him, shouting slogans and shoving him. Even small children joined in and threw punches at him. As he went home along Fatima Nagar Road, a group of students came at him with iron chains and lashed at him, tearing his shirt, his skin. He was drenched in blood. Maniamma and the kids stood watching from the house. Satyam walked a little distance to a cigarette kiosk, bought a soda, and lit a cigarette.

When he came home, six-year-old Sri Devi asked her father, "What is this, *Nanna*? They came to beat you up and you didn't try to run away."

Maniamma cried, "Masteroo!" (O Teacher!)

"Array, are you a madwoman or a sane woman?" Satyam asked. "What is there to cry about? This is nothing."

The next day he was given a dismissal letter. In the evening, police came to his house, handcuffed him, and loaded him into their van. Inside, he met three other teachers who had actively supported the union.

As soon as the news of Satyam's arrest reached the capital, the teachers in every Catholic school in the twin cities went on strike. It lasted six weeks. Manikya Rao, still a member of the old party (whose leaders were now advisers to Indira Gandhi), had been elected a member of the Legislative Council and in that role worked closely with the department of education. He brought pressure on the school to take Satyam back.

Finally the Catholic management yielded. They revoked Satyam's dismissal but refused to allow him to return to St. Gabriel. "If you want your job, go to Nalgonda"—a district in Telangana where the church had a school.

Satyam was still weighing his options when some engineering college students barged into his house one morning and woke him up. Standing around his bed, they told him what they had heard on the news.

ON JULY 5, 1967, AN editorial in the *People's Daily*, the newspaper of the Chinese Communist Party, declared:

> *A peal of spring thunder has crashed over the land of India. Revolutionary peasants in the Darjeeling area have risen in rebellion. Under the leadership of a revolutionary group of the Indian Communist Party, a red area of rural revolutionary armed struggle has been established in India. . . . The Chinese people joyfully applaud this revolutionary storm.*

A week earlier, a broadcast on Radio Peking had described this uprising of poor tribal peasants in the northernmost Darjeeling district of West Bengal, centered in the village of Naxalbari, as "the front paw of the revolutionary armed struggle launched by the Indian people."

Satyam's sense of the CPI(M)'s betrayal was complete when, like the CPI, it had renounced armed struggle in favor of a parliamentary path. He was not alone. In West Bengal, where CPI(M) was strongest, a man named Charu Majumdar organized a faction opposing this revisionism.

Satyam was disgusted when the party stooped to a new low by allying with bourgeois parties to win elections in West Bengal. And they won, making West Bengal the second state in India where Communists captured the legislature (Kerala was the first, in 1957).

Satyam's cothinkers in Calcutta, the capital of West Bengal, challenged the new government: "Now you are in power. You control the police force. If there were to be a peasant revolt, to whose aid would you send your police? The landless or the landowners?"

As if to put the party to the test, poor peasants rose up under the leadership of two men, Kanu Sanyal and Jangal Santhal, based in a village called Naxalbari. Tea workers from all over Darjeeling launched a strike in support. Charu Majumdar joined the revolt, supporting it from the city.

Sure enough, the CPI(M) government massacred the peasants. In a matter of weeks, the Naxalbari revolt was stamped out.

Declaring "Naxalbari will never die! From its embers will rise a thousand Naxalbaris," Charu Majumdar went underground to organize a new movement.

The REC students came at once to see Satyam. He was still in bed. "Wake up, wake up!" they said. "Our time has come. We must begin."

They couldn't wait to abandon their bright futures, to pick up weapons and go into the jungles. All the engineering and medical students, the mill workers and railway workers and peasant youth Satyam had organized in Warangal for the CPI(M) became Naxalites—adherents of the peasant-guerrilla line put in practice in Naxalbari—that morning.

Various Communists, veterans of the Telangana revolt who had come to Warangal with their followers waiting for an opportunity to start an armed revolt, were jump-started by the news of Naxalbari. They joined together in the Revolutionary Communist Party (RCP).

Meanwhile, in Srikakulam district, on the northern border of Andhra, Satyam's university friends Panchadi and Tejeswara Rao were way ahead. They convened the Naxalbari Solidarity Committee. They sent a representative off to Calcutta to ask Charu Majumdar to be their leader and seek his guidance for their plan to start an armed revolt in Srikakulam district. They also sent a message to Satyam: "There will be a meeting soon." He was ready to put all else aside as soon as this connection with the Calcutta comrades was made.

As Satyam waited, Seetharamayya's daughter Karuna and his son-in-law Ramesh, who had both recently finished medical school, would come to Satyam's house three, four times a day and pester him. "Where is the armed struggle? Naxalbari happened in Bengal, but there is no movement here." The delay was unbearable for them.

"Soon, soon," Satyam told them. "We are waiting for a message."

A nineteen-year-old brahmin REC student named Mallikarjuna Sharma, who had already quit his studies, sulked and pouted. He harassed Satyam day and night, not letting him sleep. "Sundarayya promised armed struggle. He betrayed us, and now you, too? When do we start?"

"O my husband!" Satyam told him fondly. "Just because you and I want it, it is not going to happen this minute."

The RCP called an emergency meeting in Warangal. The meeting was held at midnight in a village far away from Warangal city called Ped-dammagadda. There, inside a large thatched meetinghouse in the madiga goodem, students, railway workers, mill workers, and laborers gathered in secret.

While they all supported Naxalbari, many were opposed to the launching of an immediate armed revolt in Srikakulam. Satyam and Seetharamayya were the only two leaders who disagreed.

Representing the majority was Chandra Pulla Reddy. He arrived fashionably late, flanked by two glamorous girls who looked like cinema stars. As a respected veteran of the Telangana revolt, he spoke first, giving a long, repetitious speech. When the first rays of daylight appeared in the sky, he was still talking. "We cannot fight in the rain, we must have training, we must first occupy land and then arm ourselves, this is our Telangana experience."

When he finished, Satyam had only a few minutes to say a few carefully chosen words in favor of taking up arms immediately.

Pulla Reddy was annoyed. "All right, then. If the daughter-in-law needs to pop the baby, what can the mother-in-law do? Go ahead and start your insurrection!" The cinema stars giggled. Pulla Reddy was alluding to the traditional authority of the mother-in-law (*attha*) over her daughter-in-law. The attha can stop her daughter-in-law from eating, from sleeping, from relaxing, but how can she stop her from going into labor?

Satyam was ready with his reply: "The relation between a comrade like Pulla Reddy and the revolution cannot and should not be that between mother-in-law and daughter-in-law. Pulla Reddy is not that attha. He must lead, he must support, he must encourage."

After that meeting, the RCP split into two splinters, each one claiming the same name: CPI(M-L)—M-L for "Marxist-Leninist." They were distinguished by two additional letters, the initials of their respective leader's name.

Satyam became the leader of the CPI(M-L)-CM—for Charu Majumdar—in Warangal. Their slogan was "Come one, come all. Join the struggle in Srikakulam!"

As they waited for word from the West Bengal comrades, Satyam's house was filled with feverish activity: writing propaganda, mimeographing leaflets, translating Mao. Satyam never tired, never longed for rest. He and his followers didn't wait for Naxalbari to come to them. Warangal was their Naxalbari.

In the meantime, representatives of the Andhra people were traveling to Calcutta, the base of Satyam's new party, to show support and seek direction. But they were not returning. The courier Dushyant was shot. Tejeswara Rao was arrested. All except Panchadi, who had managed to meet Charu Majumdar.

Two days later a courier informed Satyam that he, along with Seetharamayya and his eighteen-year-old son, Chandu, were invited to a secret meeting. Calcutta was too dangerous, so a meeting was being set up in Andhra. A top leader of Naxalbari was making the trip to talk to them. The identity of that top leader was withheld.

"We will send a courier to tell you the time and place." They were to wait for instructions and in the meantime not leave Khazipet. So Seetharamayya left his old parents to fend off the murderous Telangana reddys by themselves and came to Khazipet to wait.

Satyam gathered his wife and children. "I am leaving you. You must go away. Go back to Krishna district. Go to your grandfather's. I don't know what you will do, but you must leave. My time has come."

In marrying Satyam, Maniamma had counted herself lucky. When she saw the railway workers, teachers, and engineering and medical students coming to their house to talk with her husband, looking up to him, she was proud. She liked living amid all this important activity. Several of the students, Chandu among them, spent all their time at Satyam's house. They ate there, slept there, and Maniamma looked after them. She thought, "This man, what happiness is he getting from his teacher job? All his happiness comes from his party work. Twenty-four hours a day, the same preoccupation."

Poor Maniamma, a nearly illiterate girl from a remote speck of a village of half-naked untouchables, never thought that some people in this world were not satisfied to have decent, comfortable family lives. However much her husband had explained his ideas, his passions, to her, she had never expected this day would come. Poor Maniamma, how could she protest now? She had agreed to all his conditions before marrying him.

Now that armed struggle was around the corner, many people who previously couldn't wait to join lost their nerve. The president of the Naxalbari Solidarity Committee, Dr. Venkateswara Rao, bought a ticket for America and left. Scores of others with wealthy parents followed him.

Karuna and her husband, Ramesh, who once couldn't wait for the armed struggle to start, suddenly longed to get as far away from it as possible. They both went to work as doctors in a hospital in faraway Bastar.

"Array, what happened?"

"We are too sensitive. We cannot bear to watch our comrades killed by police."

Karuna's father, Seetharamayya, would be making the trip with them.

Satyam was not pleased. "What about the meeting?"

"I have to accompany my daughter. They cannot carry all the luggage themselves. They don't know Hindi. They need my help." Seetharamayya, upon getting the news of the secret meeting, had gone to Rajeswara Rao, the leader of the old revisionist party, and begged him to use his influence with Indira Gandhi to help his daughter and son-in-law get positions elsewhere.

Seetharamayya gave Satyam his Bastar address and told him to send a telegram as soon as he got the meeting details. "I will start right away."

"How you will start right away? It is at least two days' journey to Bastar."

Seetharamayya departed, and as soon as he had gone, the courier from Srikakulam arrived. "Okay, let's go," he said.

Satyam told him they had to send a telegram to Seetharamayya.

"No telegrams. We want no trace."

Caution was necessary. By then the Communist government in Calcutta had launched a full-scale attack on the Naxalites. The streets of the city were wet with the blood of young students, most of whom came from privileged and even aristocratic families. Their families' social status could not save their lives.

"What is the agenda of the meeting?" Satyam asked.

Don't ask.

Who is going to be at the meeting?

Don't ask.

Where is the meeting?

Don't ask.

When is the meeting?

Don't ask.

Who are you?

Don't ask.

They went.

The delegates were taken to a room. At exactly four o'clock, they were taken to another house. There they saw all the delegates from all the districts in the state who had been invited to the meeting along with Satyam. Panchadi and his wife, Nirmala, were there. So were Y. Koteswara Rao and others from Satyam's old circle at Andhra University. Nineteen people in all.

After it fell dark, five cars arrived at the doorstep. Each car seated four passengers plus the driver. The drivers were all Naxalite supporters from Vijayawada.

Before they got in, someone came up to Satyam, limping with a stick, with smiles all over his handsome face. It was Satyam's brother-in-arms, his bosom friend Rama Rao. He said in English, "Everything is set."

This was the dream they had shared for fifteen years.

A man who looked to be a hundred years old joined the meeting. A man so frail he couldn't breathe without effort. He was—could it be? It was none other than Comrade CM, as he was known in party circles: Charu Majumdar.

Satyam was delighted. "Array, Charu Saru himself!"

"Yes, it's him you're meeting," Rama Rao confirmed, unable to conceal his pride.

CM, a Bengali, didn't speak Telugu. He said the word *hello* to everyone in English.

The delegates all got into the cars and drove a long, long way into Guntur district. Five cars going one after the other in the middle of the night at high speed. Anyone who caught sight of them would wonder what was going on.

Sometime after daybreak, the drivers stopped at the side of the road. From there the delegates would have to continue on foot.

Panchadi lifted CM up and carried the old man on his shoulders. The summer sun was strong. Panchadi had a big towel that he used every so often to wipe himself and the older comrade. Each time he wrung it out, large quantities of sweat poured out. But he wouldn't let anyone else carry Comrade CM. Panchadi could not trust anyone but himself to ensure the old man's safety.

"Array, how can you carry him so far? You'll get exhausted."

"Once you want to do revolution, how can carrying our leader be a burden?"

They all laughed.

They walked until they came to a hill. Steps led up to a *bilam*, a natural passage in the rock. Inside the bilam was a pool fed by a little stream where they bathed and refreshed themselves. They saw a temple in front of them.

A month ago an important man from the neighboring village (a supporter of the Naxalites) informed the priest of this temple that the fame of the bilam had suddenly grown and spread far and wide. He knew of a party of several devotees from different states who were planning to visit it soon. "They want to come and worship and stay several days, cooking and sleeping and talking among themselves inside the bilam."

The priest was so happy. It had been a long time since his neglected temple had attracted visitors from such faraway places.

The delegates approached the sanctuary bearing coconuts as offerings to the god. To make the delegates look like genuine devotees, six had been told to bring their wives. A large group of single men descending on a temple would raise eyebrows. They broke their coconuts in front of the image of the god and then sat down to start the meeting.

First, Comrade CM gave a report on the struggle in Bengal. Then Satyam reported on the RCP faction fight in Warangal. They discussed their plans for the future struggle in Srikakulam and the rest of the state. They elected a state committee.

All of this was accomplished in three days. With CM in poor health, they couldn't take any more time. CM spoke little. In four words he would reveal a great truth. They all listened to him keenly and never questioned him. They had no experience of revolution and wanted to learn. This man had led the Naxalbari uprising two and half years earlier. Whatever he spoke, it was a word from the scriptures.

At the meeting it was unanimously decided to launch the Srikakulam armed struggle immediately. They all vowed to support the revolt by any means necessary.

Panchadi was elected secretary of the Srikakulam Struggle Committee. He argued that every single supporter from every village, town, and city should move at once to Srikakulam.

Satyam disagreed. "We have to initiate struggle in every district. That way we spread the enemy thin. We must make the army run here and there madly in every direction. Haven't we all read this in books on strategy?"

Satyam's argument was approved. A resolution was passed to inaugurate the armed struggle by simultaneously taking an action against one or two landlords—robbing them of money or arms or burning the debt papers that kept the peasants at their mercy—in every district in the state of Andhra.

They discussed whether to grant membership to Seetharamayya. One after another delegate spoke out in opposition. Seetharamayya's son Chandu was the most vehement. "No, sir, my father is not a trustworthy man. He says one thing and does something else. He betrayed our family. We cannot have in our party a man who lies." Chandu became emotional, shed tears. Others also said, "Communists of all kinds have rejected him. There is no reason for us to take him now."

CM was bewildered. "Who is this man?"

"He couldn't make it to the meeting."

Satyam alone insisted, "We must have Seetharamayya. He is the only one among us with Telangana experience. Without him, we will be lost."

Chandu shouted, "He is a liar!" That Chandu's father had lied to the party before he was expelled about his relations with Anasooyamma was well known.

Satyam tried to calm Chandu. "Yes, he lied and that was wrong, but the fact is we need him. All our rivals are now setting up camps in the forests, organizing men, training them, collecting funds, getting ready to launch their own actions. They all have experience as guerrillas. Which of us has that? Only Seetharamayya. Only he can lead our struggle. I can't do it, you can't do it. You must understand the situation. We don't even know what it is to live underground. What do people living underground even look like? Should we wear false mustaches, false beards? Wear a wig? A turban? These very fundamental things we don't know. In any case, he repents his mistakes, he is begging us to give him a chance to serve the people."

Chandu refused to give way. "You tell me one thousand things, but I'm not convinced. He ruined my family, he is going to ruin the party."

As moralistic as Satyam could be, in this case he felt the others had no decency or culture for condemning Seetharamayya over personal matters. "Anasooyamma and Seetharamayya have been together like wife and husband for ten years. Koteswaramma has settled as a single woman. She is no longer complaining. Why bring it up now?"

Panchadi began to see Satyam's argument. To Panchadi, all that mattered was Srikakulam. To defend Srikakulam, they needed to create unrest in Telangana. To create unrest in Telangana, they would need a man like Seetharamayya.

CM resolved the whole debate quite simply, speaking in English in his drawling manner: "Yesss. The real problem eees, the revisionist leaders, CPI, CPI(M), RCP, expelled Seetharamayya from their parties. And we revolutionaries invite him. Fineeesh."

After the meeting, Panchadi again carried CM on his shoulders for the return trip. The older comrade was only fifty-one, but he was shockingly thin and in poor health.

By the time they reached the bottom of the steps, the one who was carried also needed to rest. CM went off a little way alone to stand in the shade of a tree. Satyam thought, "He must be communicating with the Chinese party by some invisible wireless device to inform them that the meeting was a success." Satyam cautioned the others, "The man will be away for a bit. Don't disturb him."

They all shared these exaggerated impressions. They surmised that this man was acting under the very guidance of Chairman Mao and according to his plan. That behind Charu Majumdar there was a huge machine. And that this movement they were forming would enjoy unlimited political, material, and military support. "We may not have anything now, but wait four days, we'll get everything."

⊚

FULL OF NERVOUS ENERGY, SATYAM returned to Khazipet. As he climbed off the train, he saw the familiar faces of his friends and supporters among the railway workers and others who worked there. One of them, a tea vendor, waved and called out, "Hey, saar, come get your chai!"

"How are you, brother? How is the family?"

"Saar, we don't see you these days anymore," complained the tea vendor.

As Satyam reached for the cup, a dozen police fell on him and dragged him away.

Satyam's revolutionary future was cut short before it had even begun. For the resolutions passed in the cave he could be charged with sedition and hanged. Shackled to the wire grill inside a police van, he was transported to the Central Jail in Warangal.

The police in Warangal had finally figured out that the invisible hand behind the Separate Telangana Agitation in Warangal was one K. G. Satyamurthy, a teacher at St. Gabriel. Their informer, the vendor, fingered him getting off a train at Khazipet station.

When Satyam found he was being booked for leading the Telangana agitation and not for his part in a conspiracy to violently overthrow the state, he let out a sigh of immense relief.

Those who had been jailed for the Telangana agitation were called détenus; they were not ordinary prisoners, they were political prisoners. It was prestigious because the agitation had been called for by a Congress leader, a member of the Legislative Assembly.

In jail, Satyam was surprised to see the luxury in which the détenus were living. They were given a 150-rupee allowance per day. Since they had to spend it or lose it, they bought cigarettes, snacks, sweets, fruits, ice cream. Each of them was given expensive bedding, mosquito nets, and bathroom sandals.

The leaders welcomed Satyam. "So you were the one behind the agitation!"

A few weeks later, the High Court of Andhra Pradesh ordered the release of the Telangana détenus. Each détenu was given a certificate saying, "It is hereby certified that so-and-so is a political sufferer," which could be profitable in the future. They were allowed to take with them the expensive things given to them in jail. Satyam refused both the certificate and the luxury items.

People thronged to greet the leaders outside the jail. Satyam had to attend to the business of Srikakulam upon his release. He had already sent instructions to Carey, who arrived on a motorcycle. Satyam hopped on behind him.

Satyam knew the police had been watching him in prison. They could see he was not like the other détenus. He was the only Andhra, the only one who wasn't a member of the Congress Party, who didn't hold political office or have a criminal record in Warangal. He knew the police would try to follow him to see where he would go, who he would meet, and what he would do.

Avoiding the main streets, weaving through the narrow back lanes, the motorcycle arrived at the less-used entrance of Warangal railway station. Carey's wife, Premalatha, stepped out of a dark corner and handed Satyam a ticket to Vizag and some cash.

Carey and Premalatha did everything exactly as instructed. Satyam slipped into the station. The platform was crowded with people pushing each other to squeeze onto the train. Police were everywhere. He got on the train. But inside the train, too, he saw them walking up and down, pushing people aside, looking for him. He got out and waited.

When the train stirred, he jumped into a bogie and immediately jumped out on the other side. A freight train was on the adjacent track. He walked quickly toward it. The motorman, who admired Satyam, saw him through the corner of his eye. With his sight still trained directly in front of him, he slowed the train. Satyam jumped on and the train picked up speed.

That would always be the way the man who could not run escaped. Satyam, born with high-arched feet, was never able to run. Not at the age of eleven when the golla boy chased him through the buffalo-grazing fields for wearing knickers instead of a loincloth, and not now.

◎

SATYAM ARRIVED IN VIZAG JUST in time to attend the meeting at which the decision to launch the armed revolt was taken. A resolution was passed that comrades in each district should carry out an action to loot the class enemy and expropriate funds for use in the struggle. A date was set for a status meeting where each section was to report on the results of its action. Later in the evening a public meeting was held. Ten thousand people attended, mainly tribals organized by Panchadi and his friends in Srikakulam.

Immediately after, Satyam rushed back to Khazipet, where Seetharamayya was waiting, upset that he hadn't been informed of the meeting. "Why did I have to find out about it from the papers?"

Satyam and Seetharamayya organized a squad to carry out their action. Youth from the villages surrounding Warangal and Jangaon joined along with mill workers and railway workers and a couple of engineering students.

Unfortunately, the squad hadn't managed to launch the action by the time Satyam had to set off for the status meeting. Seetharamayya said he would stay behind with the squad and make sure the action was accomplished before the end of the meeting, which was scheduled to go on for three days. "You go ahead and we will send you a telegram when the job is done."

On the third day of the meeting, Satyam was still waiting anxiously for news. The Srikakulam cadre were not pleased. "What is this, comrades? How can we make a revolution like this?"

"I am expecting word any minute."

Satyam's turn came to give his report. Just as he rose to speak, he was handed a telegram. He looked at it and smiled. It said simply, "Done."

The Warangal squad's action had been carried out under the guidance of a man named Iliaiah, who'd been a Communist since the days of the old party.

The squad decided to loot the house of a rich *komati* (moneylender/ trader) in Jangaon, a small town near Warangal, since Iliaiah was from Jangaon and knew everyone there.

Iliaiah knocked at the komati's door. It was opened without hesitation, as Iliaiah was a well-respected man. The rest of the squad members forced their way in behind him to storm the house. Finding the iron safe where the komati kept his cash, they surrounded him and demanded the key. But the komati pretended to be confused, insisting that he couldn't think where it was. The looters then turned to the komati's wife, hoping to make off with her jewelry. But most of her gold was locked up in the safe, and despite the looters' threats, her husband refused to produce the key. So the looters set to breaking it. But the iron safe wouldn't break. What to do?

The noise and commotion woke up the komati's three-year-old daughter. Startled, she began to cry. One of the Naxalites, the nineteen-year-old brahmin engineering student Mallikarjuna Sharma, couldn't stand to see her tears. He left the safe and ran over to take her in his arms, pressing the little girl gently against his breast. "Oh, don't cry, little one, don't cry," he cajoled her, gently patting her back. "Shhh, shhh. This class war is not against you."

When they saw this display of tenderness, the komati couple relaxed and started screaming for help. The neighbors came running. Iliaiah answered the door and told them, "Don't worry, it's me. I joined the Naxalites. Go bring something to help open the safe." The villagers went off and came back with axes and spades.

The Warangal squad hacked away at the komati's safe, but it proved too strong to crack open and was too heavy to carry away with them. It had been hours already since they started the action. At last they gave up, grabbed some clothes, and took whatever cash they found outside the safe, along with a battery-operated transistor radio and a few pieces of gold from the person of the komati's wife. They warned the couple not to call the police.

With their meager loot, the squad trekked across the surrounding fields. When it got dark, they stopped at a hillock to take rest. As they spread the komati's clothes on the ground to lie down on to sleep, a bunch of keys fell to the ground.

"*Humma nee*, this clever komati! Look where he hid his safe keys!"

For a while they debated going back to the house. In the end they sent one man back to see if the situation was clear. But by then the police had come and moved the iron safe to the Jangaon police station.

Little though they had to show for it, their action was technically accomplished. They sent off their telegram and proceeded to Adilabad according to plan.

From the meeting in Vizag, Satyam would go directly to Adilabad without stopping at Warangal. Seetharamayya would meet everyone at a place called Ranga Samudaram. There they would cross the river Godavari and enter the forests of Adilabad to begin setting up their guerrilla operations.

On the way back from the meeting, Satyam took a train and got off at Eluru. He had arranged for Maniamma to meet him there and see him one last time. They checked into a lodge together. He took her to the cinema, bought her jasmines, sweets.

On the second night, he told her.

"Maniamma, this is my last visit."

Maniamma said nothing. She had no words for what was inside her, no capacity to articulate her feelings. She couldn't even grasp that she had been wronged in this marriage.

"Do you want to come with me, Maniamma?"

Now she knew what to say, and she said it clearly. "The country and its problems—your responsibility. Your children are my responsibility. You take care of your business of liberating the country, and I will raise your children, protect them, and educate them."

He warned her to destroy every photo of him and every piece of paper that bore his handwriting.

She came to see him off at the station. As the train pulled away, she stood under a lamp in a blue sari with the flowers he'd bought her in her hair. Under the dim light she waved to him with a smile on her lips.

"What courage, what strength, that woman has!" thought Satyam, sitting back in his seat as his train left the station. "She is sending her husband off to the jungles of Adilabad with a reassuring smile."

A comrade named Goru Madhava Rao had told Satyam and others about his own wife's reaction. "She fell to the ground in front of me and grabbed hold of my ankles and wouldn't let go. She cried and cried. Abba, that daughter of a widow stood in my way. I kicked her aside and came here."

Satyam reached Jannaram by train and started for Adilabad.

◎

THE PLAN WAS TO TRAVEL in pairs and arrive at Adilabad from different directions. The time was deemed so ripe for armed revolution that all they needed to do was set out and throngs of youth would join them on their way into the jungles.

Iliaiah and another comrade started from Karimnagar. At Luxettipet they stopped at his favorite tea stall, where the teenaged Muslim server complained as always, "I hate this job."

"Come with me, then."

The boy followed them.

An aged brahmin with bad legs, a nostalgia for the Telangana Armed Struggle, and a wish for rejuvenation also joined the youthful Naxalites.

They were joined as well by a young man named Nagi Reddy, the idealistic son of a rich farmer who had long been waiting for the Naxalites to come to town. Before leaving, Nagi Reddy quarreled with his father and made off with forty thousand rupees for the armed struggle. In addition to that large sum, he brought with him a stack of maps. He was going to be the map expert.

News of the movement spread across Telangana. Everywhere people talked of the Naxalites. "They are here, they are here." "What do they look like?" "Seems they look like students." In the villages, people talked of the tender concern displayed by the young engineering student Mallikarjuna Sharma for the scared little girl during the Jangaon action. This became the popular image of the Naxalite.

But when the comrades met at Dharmapuri, Mallikarjuna Sharma and his mate did not make it. In their student clothes, wearing conspicuous sunglasses to hide their faces and carrying suspiciously heavy bags, they immediately attracted the attention of the villagers. The police were called. Before they laid a finger on the two, the students told all.

Y. Koteswara Rao hitched a ride on a lorry that was intercepted by the highway patrol. As soon as the lorry stopped, YK jumped out and began running into the shrubs on the side. The police were bewildered. They had stopped the lorry only to check if the driver had proper papers. When they caught up to the fleeing revolutionary, he told them everything before they had even asked him why he was running.

Satyam had foreseen that some of the comrades might be caught and might talk. That was the reason for traveling in pairs and letting no one know from which direction the others would be traveling. Still, he was not pleased. "Who told them to wear student clothes and sunglasses in a village?"

A few miles farther on, the old man with bad legs declared, "I am going back home. I did not know revolution involved so much walking."

Every time they stopped to rest, Nagi Reddy spread out his maps. "Here, if we take this road, then we have the cover of this hillock, then on the other side, we have a dirt path." They were in awe of his knowledge but could not follow what he said and did not need this level of expertise. Not just yet, anyway.

The men arrived on the banks of the Godavari River. They bathed in it and rested. In the early hours they boarded a bus to Ranga Samudaram. There, a poor washer-caste man joined.

As they approached the Lambadi *thunda* (colony), the Lambadis wept with joy: "Sons, where have you been? We have waited for you fifteen years!" They remembered the Telangana Armed Struggle.

Two Lambadi youths joined: Bhoomayya and Kishtha Gowda.

In the afternoon, the comrades gave some money to the washerman and sent him into the village to buy rice, lentils, oil, and salt at the komati shop.

The komati stared at the washerman, who all his life had wrung his hands, bent his waist, speckled his speech with "I am your slave, sir" while talking to powerful villagers like the komati. The washerman said, "Hey, son, what are you looking at? Tell your friend, that *munsub* [head of the village], that son of a whore who raped my wife, tell him he is finished tonight."

The washerman comrade returned with the groceries. The comrades cooked and ate and went into the Godavari to bathe.

Meanwhile in the village the komati locked up his store and ran to the munsub's house to report what the washerman had said. The nearest police station was far away; the munsub would not have time to get there. But luckily a CRPF battalion was nearby in Jagtial because of the Separate Telangana Agitation. The munsub dispatched a manservant to the camp.

As the men were bathing in the river and enjoying themselves, they heard a huge commotion. As they struggled to figure out what was happening, the would-be guerrillas found themselves surrounded by CRPF forces pointing rifles in their direction.

Satyam saw some of his comrades swimming and others running away. He could do neither. He was dazed. He could see the two Lambadi youths swimming away fast, bobbing like jockeys galloping away on horseback, their white turbans blazing in the sun.

Satyam let out a grunt and fell to the ground. A CRPF man used his rifle to knock Satyam hard in the back.

When presented to the police chief, Satyam was naked but for his underwear. "Wrap some clothes around this man. I am embarrassed to look at the sad spectacle that his body is."

"There is no shame in being rendered naked. There is shame only if I abandon the revolution."

Along with hundreds of men arrested for their participation in the Separate Telangana Agitation, Satyam was thrown into a camp. Half-naked and hungry, he squatted on the filthy ground.

On the third night after his arrest, when everyone was asleep, Satyam got up on his tiptoes and slipped away. He walked through the fields, stopping to hide behind shrubs to check if he was safe. He was hungry. Exhausted. Alone. His heart was pounding. He didn't know what had happened to his friends. Where was he going to go? He was hundreds of miles away from any place he knew, with no proper clothes, no footwear. No one was likely to help him.

It was jungle all around. No human beings. Strange howlings of animals and flappings of birds. He was scared to death when a twig broke under his foot. Sometimes something would scurry in the dried leaves. He would stop still, holding his breath. Hours passed. He kept walking. In the dark he suddenly began to see eerie creatures. He could not see their figures. They were there, stout, squat, dark, features unrecognizable. They were staring at him. They stood surrounding him, their eyes burning in the dark, darting here and there. "Why are they not coming after me? Why do they just stare?" Exhausted, he gave up and fell to the ground.

Waking, he realized the stout figures were young palm trees, the burning eyes fireflies. After two days, Satyam reached the safety of a friend's house.

◎

ON MAY 27, 1969, SIX months after the cave meeting, as they returned from a meeting with Charu Majumdar in Calcutta, Panchadi Krishnamurthy and six comrades were caught getting off the train at Sompeta. They were taken into the woods and shot dead.

Soon after, in the hills of Rangamatia, Krishnamurthy's wife, Panchadi Nirmala, along with Subba Rao Panigrahi—a key leader of Srikakulam Armed Revolt—and four others were arrested, taken to a police station, tortured, and killed. Their bodies were tossed onto the roadside.

Eighteen-year-old Chandu's mutilated body was found hanging in a hotel room, staged to look like a suicide.

Between March 1970 and August 1971, 1,783 young supporters of the CPI(M-L) were murdered, according to police records. The actual toll was likely higher. On August 21, 1971, up to a thousand were killed on a single day in one neighborhood in Calcutta.

This was the period when the word *encounter* entered the Indian English lexicon to refer to police killings of unarmed Naxalites, who were always said to have died in an exchange of fire between the police and the Naxalites.

With the killing of Panchadi, Satyam took over the task of meeting

Charu Majumdar in Calcutta. He was the only one to take on this role and survive.

However, the meetings came to an end when a courier, succumbing to police torture, gave away Charu Majumdar's hideout in Calcutta. He was arrested on July 16, 1972. No one was allowed to see him in the jail, not even a lawyer. Twelve days later, at 4:00 a.m., he died in the same Lal Bazar lockup, which was notorious for torture. His body was not released to his family. As the police took his body to a crematorium, the whole area was cordoned off.

In 1975, Bhoomayya and Kishtha Gowda were hanged.

The movement in Calcutta was snuffed out. The Srikakulam revolt was crushed as soon as it was launched.

The two survivors, Satyam and Seetharamayya, would escape to Hyderabad, where they prepared to launch a new movement, the People's War Group, the most notorious, famous, and successful Naxalite party, a thorn in the side of the Indian rulers. Thenceforth the duo would be known by their noms de guerre: SM and KS.

Twenty-five years later, two of their old recruits from Warangal, both students, one who studied electrical engineering at REC and the other who was getting a master's in science at Kakatiya University, took the reins of the party. They shifted the base of their guerrilla operations from Telangana to Chhattisgarh in Madhya Pradesh and changed the party's name from People's War Group to Communist Party of India (Maoist) and their class base from peasants in the countryside to tribals in jungles. They are now engaged in a bitter struggle against the Indian government and some of the world's most powerful corporations, which are after the trillions of dollars' worth of mineral wealth lying under the lands and habitations of the tribals.

Today if you visit the site of the temple in the hills around Guntur where the famous cave meeting took place, you will find a monument erected in memory of Charu Majumdar and the martyrs of the armed struggle in Srikakulam.

TEN

◎ ◎ ◎

MANJULA NEVER BOTHERED TO CHRISTEN her third child. Ganga Raju
came to see the new baby. Somehow they began talking about Italy and the
Risorgimento. He said, "Why not call her Anita," after Giuseppe Garibaldi's
wife. So they gave her that name, spelled the Indian way: Anitha.

Christened or not, Anitha brought good luck to the family. Prabhakara Rao finally passed his M.A.—not only passed it, but stood first. This
time, he admitted, he had taken his wife's advice. He received five marks
more than the university gold medalist, but because he was not enrolled
as a student, having prepared for the degree on his own and simply paid
the fee to sit for the exam, he was not eligible for medals. With the high
demand for English lecturers, he immediately found a post.

Manjula also received a job offer. Leaving her family in Anantapur, she reported to the Women's College in Nellore, in the south of Andhra.

Manjula didn't know anyone there, so she asked help from a Christian colleague of hers, Sunandamma. Sunandamma and her three spinster sisters, all of whose names started with *Su*, helped Manjula find a house right next door to them in James Garden, an untouchable colony.

It was a huge house, and though the rooms were small, they were surrounded by a large veranda. In front of the house was a well with a pulley and a bucket. A large front yard full of green trees shaded the house from the sun. Best of all, if Manjula needed anything, Sunandamma's sisters were right there.

In Dussehra (harvest festival) holidays, Manjula went back to Anantapur to fetch her children. They were happy to see her. They clung to her calves, clamoring, "Amma! Amma! Amma!"

Rathnamma came, too, bringing pots and pans and sheets. The children liked the new house. They ran across the veranda. The family had no cots and slept on the floor, Suja with her *nayanamma* (father's mother) and Babu and Anitha with their mother.

Rathnamma, waking early to set up the kitchen, found monkeys had broken into it overnight. She ran out screaming onto the veranda. The house was surrounded by thirty or forty monkeys. They were sitting on the branches of the trees, on the roof, on the veranda itself. Big ones, smaller ones, babies, black-assed and red-assed. They seemed angry that their territory had been invaded.

Rathnamma and Manjula grabbed the children and locked the doors. Like animals in a zoo, they gazed out at the monkeys looking in through the windows. The monkeys started dancing and screeching and strutting about. After two hours, Manjula ventured out to get help from the neighbors. "No one can stop them. You just have to manage somehow." Hindus would not allow the monkeys to be killed because one of their gods is a monkey.

The family stayed in for days. Then Manjula borrowed a large stick from the neighbors and went out to buy groceries. On her way back, the monkeys launched a surprise attack and made off with the groceries, screeching triumphantly. In time Manjula learned to wait until after dark, when the monkeys went off to other trees to sleep, to bring groceries home. Another time Rathnamma, cutting vegetables, was set upon and robbed of the produce. The family had to cook with doors and windows closed and latched. The back and front yards and great big verandas that were the house's best feature were useless, as the children had to stay indoors at all times.

Manjula consoled herself. The ordeal would soon be over. When both husband and wife are lecturers, a government rule says that they have a right to work in the same place. Prabhakara Rao had already started looking into getting Manjula transferred.

Manjula enrolled Suja in the American Baptist Mission School, a pleasant, spacious, peaceful school. In missionary schools, where the staff are all untouchables, the untouchable children aren't made to feel out of place. Manjula paid the fees, had Suja's uniform tailored, and hired a rickshaw man to take her daughter to school. Babu and Anitha, three and two years old, respectively, stayed home with their nayanamma. Rathnamma didn't seem happy to be there, but the children needed someone at home.

The principal of the college where Manjula taught was a despotic little spinster named Sivagami. For some reason, as soon as she met Manjula, Sivagami took a visceral dislike to her, recoiling from her physically. In the first month Manjula was in Nellore, Sivagami marked Manjula late five times, though she was never late by more than two or three minutes. She tried to leave early, but every morning the monkeys delayed her.

Because Manjula was on her own in Nellore, she did not have to hand her salary over to her husband. She was surprised to find how much better the family finances could be managed. She had neither savings nor debts. She wanted nothing more than for things to continue in this way. Someday soon she would be allowed to transfer, and the family would be reunited.

One time when she used her lunch hour to visit Suja's school, she was amazed to find that her daughter's teachers had so far taught her only the *ka gunintham*, the first one that is taught to children learning to read. A gunintham is the set of different ways that each consonant in the Telugu script can be written in combination with the twelve vowel marks. Telugu has thirty-six guninthams, so learning the first one—for the consonant *ka*—is something like learning the first letter of the alphabet. Manjula had assumed that Suja had already been taught all thirty-six guninthams because she was writing and reading them at home. She had made out the pattern from the one she was taught and picked up the rest on her own.

Manjula was pleased to find an old acquaintance of hers in Nellore, her AU batchmate Nessy, the Christian girl. Manjula took her children to pay a visit to Nessy. Nessy bragged on and on about her children. Finally, Manjula also felt as if she should tell Nessy a cute thing that one of her children had done: "My son sometimes becomes so adamant. When I make squash, he demands okra, or he won't eat."

Nessy cut her short. "Boys like that grow up to become *nara hanthakulu*," she said, using a biblical word for "murderers."

Another lesson for Manjula: Never talk about your own children. Neither brag about nor belittle them.

Some years later, Nessy would bring a small boy, the son of a poor family in Kakinada, into her household to work as her servant. After he left home, his parents never heard anything from Nessy or their son. They were too poor to travel to Nellore to find out what happened. When someone who knew Nessy in Nellore visited Kakinada, she told Manjula the word in that town was that Nessy had beaten the boy to death.

At Nessy's house, her own children were given some kind of snacks to eat, but she didn't offer any to Manjula's, who looked at them with curiosity. They had no notion of what snacks were.

It made Manjula deeply sad to see this. On the way home, she had the impulse to take them to an ice cream parlor. She explained to her children that ice cream was a nice thing to eat. To them it was like a scoop of paradise. Watching them eat it, Manjula made a vow. Every month, the day she got paid, she would take them for ice cream before the money got spent on other things.

◎

IN NELLORE, ALL THREE OF Manjula's children contracted some terrible skin disease that produced boils. Babu got a few on the forehead, while the girls had such big ones, and so many of them, on their bottoms that they couldn't sit. At one stage in the life cycle of these eruptions her daughters' little globular asses looked like pink-brown breasts with multiple pus-colored nipples. Suja had to stop going to school and couldn't be restrained from scratching.

Manjula took the children to a doctor and did all he told her to do. She changed their *cheddis* (underpants) often, washed them after they wet themselves, kept their sheets clean. But nothing helped. That James Garden was a filthy, filthy slum. The sooner they moved out, the better. Manjula prayed to God for her transfer to be approved.

Rathnamma, an uneducated woman who never stepped out on her own even to go next door, never understood the problems of her employed daughter-in-law. As Rathnamma hated Manjula more and more, Manjula grew more and more depressed, making Rathnamma hate her more and more. Neither of them had any concept of stress or mental illness.

Rathnamma would discuss her daughter-in-law with the neighbors: "Always complains of headaches."

"Why is she like that?"

"A trick to lie in bed and do nothing."

"Maybe she is possessed. Why don't you take her to Priscilla's husband?" Priscilla—a name that everyone, herself included, pronounced "Priss-killah"—and her husband were household servants in a sheikh's house in Kuwait. They were in Nellore on vacation. Priscilla's husband had lately earned a name for himself by performing exorcisms, ridding possessed women of Satan.

Manjula hated the idea. A lowly servant, a former slum dweller! The audacity of these people to suggest such a thing.

She didn't refuse, though, because she knew the preacher had already told Rathnamma that the devil would refuse. Refusing to undergo an exorcism was the surest sign that one is possessed.

Manjula already knew what the ceremony involved. Priscilla's husband would have the possessed woman kneel on the floor with her hands folded in prayer. He would then ask her to close her eyes as he started a prayer.

He would hold a Bible in one hand, and the other he would place on the head of the possessed. He would talk to God, ask Him to drive the devil out. He would pray and pray, he would talk and talk. His pitch would go up as he talked faster and faster, louder and louder, until he was speaking in tongues. Then suddenly he would smack the poor woman's head with the Bible in his hand. With eyes closed, the possessed wouldn't see it coming. She would pass out and fall to the ground. When she came to, he would declare the devil had been driven out.

Manjula knelt on the ground as Sunandamma's mother and Rathnamma watched. Manjula closed her eyes as she was told, but kept all her other senses sharp. She had to be ready. Right when the Bible was only an inch from her head, she ducked. This was not an outcome the exorcist was prepared for.

On his summer vacation, Prabhakara Rao came to Nellore. In the two months her husband was there, Manjula's carefully balanced finances were ruined by his cigarettes, his three teas a day. He took his mother's and Manjula's own gold chains and pawned them to the marwaris. The women consoled themselves for the loss of their meager jewelry with the hope that as soon as they had the money to spare they could get it back from the pawnshop. Of course this never happened.

Manjula, who had been praying for a transfer, began to have doubts about this plan. If she lived together with Prabhakara Rao, she would have to give her salary to him, and he would use it up. The children would have nothing.

While he was there, Rathnamma told him many things about Manjula, complaining that she didn't want to live with her. But if Rathnamma left, Manjula would have no one to look after her two toddlers.

To please Rathnamma, Manjula began waking up early in the morning to fetch water out of the well and wash the dishes and the clothes. One day, slicing vegetables, she cut her thumb badly. But for a long time a combination of self-denial and self-pity kept her from seeing a doctor. She went on fetching water, cleaning dishes, and washing clothes with a gashed thumb. Finally, she consulted a doctor, who told her to stop using that thumb until it healed. Manjula reluctantly hired a maid to do the dishes.

That Sunday, Manjula stayed in bed a little longer.

"Why are you asleep still?"

"It's okay, *atthamma*. The maid is coming in to do the dishes."

"The maid is here. Get up and put out the dishes!"

Manjula was annoyed at Rathnamma. "Let me sleep, will you?"

A hand grabbed Manjula by her hair, lifting her right out of bed and onto her feet. Prabhakara Rao was standing there like a dragon spewing fire. Then he slapped her face. Manjula screamed. The children woke up.

The scene that day is burned into Sujatha's—into my—memory. The terrified woman—her mother—disheveled, her hand wounded, utterly naked, running to save herself. The man—Sujatha's father, her beloved father—chasing after her mother, who, desperate, ran out of the house. Her father went after her. Sujatha's mother ran around to the other side of the well. Her father followed. He pretended to start chasing her mother in one direction, and when she tried to run away, he turned around and caught her from the other side. The children's grandmother stood looking on with pride at her son's display of manliness.

The three children, startled out of their slumber, with crusts in their eyes, dried saliva on their cheeks, and boils on their asses, their underwear soaked in piss, stood there wailing, scared out of their minds.

The adults were too busy to notice. One running for her life, the other trying to take that life, and the third watching the hunt.

The monkeys sitting on the veranda, startled, ran up to watch the spectacle from the rooftop. The neighbors, too, came out and watched. Sunandamma's mother and sisters came by to pick up Rathnamma to go to church. They watched the scene for a while and left without interfering.

◎

AT THE END OF THE summer Rathnamma went away with her son. Manjula had to leave her children alone at home to go to work at the college. When she returned, Babu had three scratch marks close to his eye from a monkey's claw.

She took the three of them in her arms and consoled them, telling them that soon she would get a transfer to Kakinada.

"Amma, what is *transfer*?"

"We are all going to go to your nayanamma's town and live together with your father, uncle, and nayanamma, and nayanamma is going to take care of you while I am gone to college."

The children started to think *transfer* meant something exciting.

"Amma, when is the transfer coming?"

"Soon, soon."

Sorting out her problems, Manjula decided the first step was to move out of James Garden and closer to the college. She found a room in Moolapeta, a neighborhood that was just beginning to develop. The surroundings were so unpleasant that no one else wanted to live there, so the caste-Hindu owners agreed to rent it to Manjula. Even though Anitha and Babu were still too young, they would have to go to school. She got uniforms stitched, paid the school fees, and hired a rickshaw to take them.

After Manjula had spent all that money, Anitha, just three years old, told her mother that she didn't want to go to school. She organized her sister and brother, and the three of them stood their ground. Their mother could do nothing. A lot of money went to waste, but Manjula was delighted with her youngest's leadership qualities. She told herself, "Anyway, after the transfer they would have to go to a new school."

Their new living quarters were a portion of a house built to be independently accessible. Construction wasn't finished. The floor was still waiting to be plastered, and the walls were just bare bricks. There were no windows, just holes, and the doors were raw wood. They had just one small, damp room and a dark kitchen, which was also the bathroom. There were no steps in front: the floor of their rooms was level with the street. And the street was not paved, but just loose dirt. Centipedes and scorpions crawled in through the cracks between the bricks. But it was going to be temporary because Manjula had heard from Prabhakara Rao that he was going to get a transfer to Kakinada and soon her own transfer there would be arranged. There was no question of his joining her in Nellore, even if that was possible—which it wasn't, as there was only a women's college there. She wanted to flee that town, to get as far away as possible.

The children wouldn't go to school, but Manjula decided to try at least to take care of their nutrition. She got the idea to give them corn-flakes as they do in England and America. She went to a high-class store that had recently opened in town and bought a package. If anyone found out, her relatives or colleagues or friends, they would be sure to ridicule her for her fancy ideas. She explained to her children what cornflakes were, and when she told them that was what they eat "in foreign," Babu and Anitha were unimpressed, but Suja's eyes widened in wonder. Manjula sat on the low stool in front of her little hearth and lit a fire. She put the milk on the hearth and fanned and fanned and fanned it for half an hour until the milk boiled. Then she put the cornflakes in a big tumbler that she used to make *charu* (mulligatawny). She poured the hot milk in and added a heap of sugar. Sujatha watched in awe while the other two were suspicious. When the meal was ready, the eldest child put a spoonful in her mouth and felt dizzy and nauseated.

Manjula tried patiently for three days to get her children to eat the corn-flakes. But they didn't like them, and it took too much time and too much effort to light the fire and keep fanning it until the milk boiled. For months she couldn't get herself to throw away the package. So much money down the drain. She kept the box as a souvenir and token of modernity.

One evening Manjula came home and saw her eldest daughter's hair all sticking up in a swirl on top of her head with a small cropped circle at the crown. She questioned her daughter as to where she had been. Had someone come into the house? Suja said no to everything. She was five and a half years old and felt too ashamed to tell anyone the neighbor boy and his friends had made her stand still while they spun their tops on her head—heavy wooden tops with sharp carpenter's nails at their base. The nails made a small bloody hole in her scalp, and the hair was snarled and cut short. The boy and his friends had bullied the three children while Manjula was away teaching.

Whenever she could, Manjula would leave the children in someone's care. She discovered that a very, very, very distant relative of Prasanna Rao's—a Mr. Neelambaram—lived in Nellore. He had a son in his late teens who suffered from TB and stayed home. It was safer to leave the children with a TB patient than with no supervision at all.

The children spent the sweltering afternoons running around outside. Mr. Neelambaram's son was nicest to Suja. One afternoon he put his hands in her armpits and lifted her up, standing her up on the cot. He opened his lungi and pulled out his *jujji* (Manjula's made-up word for "genitals"). Suja had never seen a jujji like that before. It wasn't small and mouselike. It was hard like wood and big. It was burning hot with fever. She felt bad for that *anna* (big brother) that this thing was hurting him, which is why he was asking her to caress it. He moaned and whispered. Somehow she knew that this also must be something to never tell anyone.

Manjula could only hope for her transfer to come and their nightmare to end. She rushed home from college each day and spent all her time with her children. She fed them, bathed them. The four of them slept on a thin sheet on the bare rough floor. She told them stories. They fought among themselves to be at her side with their knees in her ribs or their legs on her belly.

One night it rained and rained. It was cold, and the damp, absorbed by the concrete, rose up from the floor. The children and their mother, scared of the thunder, huddled against one another. They couldn't sleep. Every time there was a peal of thunder they all screamed.

Then they saw it. The bloody head of a snake. Just the head. It came in through the space under the door and went crawling across the floor. They saw it crawl silently, purposely, relentlessly, making a drawing in blood on the floor. It crawled and crawled. They were scared to breathe. At last, they saw it go out through the kitchen.

In the morning, the Hindus told them that when it rained, all the snakes from the swamps came out and swarmed around the slightly higher grounds of the house. Some animal must have eaten most of the snake, leaving the living head to crawl off and die.

The next day, Manjula moved out. She rented a portion in a Christian house. It had three rooms and was way too expensive for Manjula. She approached a colleague of hers, Margaret, an unmarried zoology lecturer who was also looking for a place. Even though Manjula had found the place and paid the major portion of the rent, Margaret took the best, most private room for herself, leaving Manjula and her children in the open room in front with holes in the roof. They used the charu bowl and the water pitcher to catch the rain. Margaret saw the children sitting on the floor in a row while their mother made rice balls and put them in their mouths. Margaret was touched by the scene. "Look at that, three pairs of *ali chippalu* [mother of pearl], their eyes are just like ali chippalu. So wide and big." These tender feelings lasted but a moment. Ever after, Margaret did her best to keep the children from coming near her.

The house owners were a short, gray-skinned couple in their late forties. Manjula's children called their sixteen-year-old daughter *akka* (big sister).

Manjula did not know what her children got up to when she was at work. She did not know that Suja became an accomplice in the neighbor akka's schemes. Suja adored the older girl. She was pretty, with a long, long braid reaching down below her waist. When she walked, that braid bounced from one buttock to the other. She had big eyes, which she adorned with eyeliner. Akka's parents wouldn't let her go out to see "friends" because they suspected her friends were boys. But if akka took Suja with her, they allowed her to go, little thinking she would be so shameless as to make out with boys in front of a little girl. Suja saw akka touching and holding different annas in ways that were not familiar to her. She knew this, too, must be kept secret.

Akka liked to invite Suja to piss together in the alley between the house and the compound wall. When they did, Suja was filled with a sweet, breathless, restless sensation. The whooshing sound of the teenager's pissing intrigued her. Suja longed to know how it was different between the akka's legs and her own, what it was that made her piss whoosh while her own only tinkled.

Manjula had no time to watch out for her children. At college Principal Sivagami tortured Manjula. Puny and cold in a stiff sari, Sivagami walked around like Napoleon. When Manjula taught, Sivagami would come and stand at the door. She had made it her goal in life to bring down Manjula.

When Suja had a fever, Manjula went to college to ask Sivagami if she could take the day off.

"Respected madam, I need one day casual leave, as my child is ill."

"How old is this 'child' of yours?"

"Five, madam."

Sivagami laughed until her ribs hurt. "She is five and you still call her a child? Come off it, will you?"

Manjula was forced to stay.

In winter, Manjula and the children went to Anantapur on a surprise visit. Their eyes shining with mischief and joy, they knocked on the door of Prabhakara Rao's house. They waited a long time. Prabhakara Rao finally opened the door. "Array, it's you!"

"Why didn't you come to the door?" Manjula asked.

He mumbled that he'd been in the lavatory.

Later the house owner called Manjula over and told her that her husband's behavior had not been irreproachable. "The maid is always there. Sometimes he shuts the door while she's inside." When Manjula questioned Prabhakara Rao about this, his face became red. His hair stood on end. He put on clothes and sandals and went off somewhere.

In her absence he had become as indigent as a beggar. Instead of giving him money, she brought groceries from Nellore. There was nothing left over for treats. She had to renege on her ice cream promise after only one time.

When she returned to the college, Sivagami summoned her to her office and ordered her to testify against a colleague of hers, Padmavathi, whom Sivagami hated.

Someone had told Sivagami that Padmavathi had bragged in the staff room, "Within a week I will have Sivagami transferred to a remote place. If not, my name is not Padmavathi."

As scared as she was of Sivagami, Manjula politely refused. "She may not like you, madam, but she never said anything about getting you transferred."

"I want you to testify!"

"Then why don't you ask Mrs. Kanakamma to testify?" Manjula suggested. Kanakamma was Sivagami's friend.

"How dare you tell me what I should do! I want *you* to testify, and you *are* going to testify."

Sivagami locked the door to her office from inside and made Manjula stand in front of her. For two hours, Sivagami prodded and threatened her.

Manjula knew that this meant the end of her hard-won government job. Sivagami had her in a stranglehold.

Manjula went home. She thought of going to the telephone exchange and calling her husband to see how the transfer efforts were coming along. "O Lord, just get me out of Nellore, emancipate me from Sivagami."

Nessy paid a visit to pressure Manjula on Sivagami's behalf. Sivagami set up spies everywhere to report on Manjula. She went to the bathroom, she got written up. She was thirty seconds late, she got written up. She dictated notes to her students. "You didn't spend the whole hour on the lesson, you wasted time on notes." Write-up. Manjula brought this all upon herself. She had no fondness for Padmavathi, who, like Sivagami, was highly contemptuous of Manjula for being poor and untouchable.

One day Manjula was summoned to meet some visitors to the college from out of town. It was Manikya Rao and Niranjanamma. Manikya Rao was powerful in the department of education at this time, and he and his wife were in Nellore for a meeting. They couldn't believe that this person standing before them was Manjula. "Papa, you look so old! You look like a mother of ten children!"

The annual college fete was coming. Sivagami instituted a new rule that year. "We have invited Nellore's prominent people. You are not allowed to bring your children to the fete. They are a nuisance." No one dared say anything except a mild-mannered physics lecturer, Sarojini. "Madam, this is our college, we work here, this is our fete, and you want to ban our children?" The lecturers stood strong. They formed a line outside Sivagami's office, and one after another, they went in to protest. She rescinded the memo. But on the day of the fete no lecturer dared to bring her children.

Manjula had wanted to. She was afraid to leave them alone after her usual hours. And it would have been a chance to show them where their mother worked. But she left them at home. Their clothes were torn and faded. They had no shoes.

Manjula couldn't wait for the function to be over. There were speeches, praises, prizes. Her children were home alone. She asked someone,

"What's the time, madam?" Six o'clock. She had never stayed at the college so late.

There were patriotic songs, mythological dramas, traditional dances. Her children were home alone. What's the time, madam? Seven o'clock.

There were sweets, soft drinks. Her children would have loved to eat those sweets. But they were home alone. What's the time, madam? Eight o'clock. There were rustling silk saris, jingling bangles, fragrant flowers, glittering lights. But her children were home alone. What's the time, madam? Half past eight.

The neighbors were away. Margaret was at college, too. Manjula's children would be scared.

As soon as she was allowed to go, Manjula ran out. The house was not far, but the distance stretched out before her, uncrossable. It was dark out. Her children would be missing their mother.

As she ran along, she saw a small crowd of people by the side of the road, gathered around some spectacle. She had not a moment to stop; she merely threw a glance. When she did, it felt as if someone had taken her heart in his fist and squeezed hard. She saw them. Their eyes, three pairs of ali chippalu eyes, peeked out at her from under a filthy sheet on the roadside. It was January, the coldest month, and her three children were variously naked under that sheet, crouching there in the dirt, beside the sewer, in the middle of the deserted bazaar, silent and inscrutable, drawing a concerned but passive crowd.

Manjula gathered herself, walked over, and whispered, "Come." She took Anitha on her hip, held Babu with her other hand, told Suja to hang on to her sari. With the soiled, tattered sheet under her arm, she brought them home.

In the semidark, her three abandoned children had ventured out, nearly naked, with nothing on their feet, into the streets, dragging their favorite, well-worn purple sheet with little black diamond shapes, looking for their mother.

She bathed them, fed them, put them to bed. She couldn't sleep. What was she to do? Leave the job? Leave Nellore? Have their father come to Nellore, leaving his job? She had to choose. Tomorrow. It couldn't wait.

The next day she got a letter from Prabhakara Rao that their transfers were being arranged.

She was lucky. Despite the rule that husband and wife were to be posted in the same town, because of corruption such transfers were seldom implemented without huge bribes. The going rate was eight thousand rupees. Many women were in Manjula's situation, women who struggled with small children in a society with no concept of organized day care.

As she waited for her transfer to come through, Manjula took the children to Anantapur and left them with their father. She bought groceries and asked one of Prabhakara Rao's poor students whom he had helped with civil service exams to act as housewife because her husband could not even make tea, let alone wipe his children's noses and behinds.

Manjula missed her children. She missed her little boy, who, when she wouldn't let him put on his favorite knickers because they were still drying, would sit sulking on the doorstep, holding them against his face, and grieve ever so quietly with his mouth a quivering upended smile and his eyes two brimming pools of tears.

And Anitha, the most delightful of all. She ate well, played vigorously, loved her mother's stories, wouldn't go to sleep. Every night, to get her to bed, Manjula had to threaten that a police uncle would come and get her. For some reason, Anitha feared police more than anything else in the world. One night, the same routine. "Shh, it's night. We all go to sleep." They were to sleep outside in the open in front of the house, all of them, on their newly acquired folding cot. Anitha wouldn't come.

"Look! The police uncle."

"Where?"

A man in khaki shorts and a nightstick materialized in front of them and roared, "Go to sleep, little girl! Or I will drag you off to jail," startling Manjula. Anitha quickly shinned up onto the cot and shut her eyes tight.

The policeman, on his way to night shift, had overheard her mother's warning.

When the transfer came, it read, "Manjulabai is hereby transferred to Kakinada Women's College upon relief." That "upon relief" was the key. The woman who was supposed to relieve her was posted in Hyderabad.

No one working in the big city would ever agree to leave it to come to Nellore.

Sivagami called Manjula to her office. "Now is your last chance. Are you going to testify against Padmavathi or do you want to be written up for insubordination?"

Manjula knew that she was going to lose her job one way or another. It was better to quit.

The next day she came to college with her resignation letter in hand. A peon was waiting for her at the college gates. He took her straight to Sivagami's office. Some high-ranking police officials were sitting in front of Sivagami, waiting to question Manjula.

"Are you Kambham Mary Manjulabai?"

"Yes."

"Do you have a brother named K. G. Satyamurthy?"

Her brother must have been shot dead. "Yes, yes!"

"Do you know his whereabouts?"

Relief. "No."

They asked if he had written her, when was the last time she'd seen him. Did he visit her in Nellore? Where did she live? Who all lived in her house? Where was her husband? Why was he in Anantapur?

She wasn't told directly, but she could guess. Her brother had gone underground. Become a hunted outlaw. She had lost him forever.

When the police left, Manjula was given new transfer papers. Unexpectedly, the lecturer from Hyderabad was coming to relieve her.

◎

TRANSFER DID NOT EMANCIPATE MANJULA from Sivagami. She, too, was transferred the same week to the same college. She would stay there until her retirement three years later, subjecting Manjula to continual abuse.

Because Manjula's salary was garnished to pay back old debts incurred in Anantapur, she was not eligible for promotion according to the government rules. While all her contemporaries and juniors went on to become principals, she remained a lecturer to the end of her career.

Since she and her husband now both had permanent jobs and regular incomes, Manjula had entertained a hope that their financial troubles would finally go away. But that, too, never happened. In Kakinada, she lived as married women commonly do, not only with her husband and his mother and brother, but also his uncles, aunts, cousins, and their spouses and children. At any given time some twenty to twenty-five people lived in two adjoining houses, and as no one else except her, her husband, and her husband's brother, Percy, was educated and employed, the others all lived off those three salaries. Although the cooking was done by each family separately, when Manjula was at work, the other families would come and pillage her kitchen for rice, lentils, tamarind, chili powder, cooking oil, and kerosene. If they couldn't find what they wanted, they went to the grocer's and put it under her account. They stole her saris and bedsheets from the clothesline.

While in Anantapur, Manjula had noticed that Prabhakara Rao was kind and generous except when his mother or another relative was around. Now that they lived in a joint family, the two of them were never alone.

For twenty-one years they lived like that. After the three children had finished school, with two having just left home to go abroad and one about to, Rathnamma died at the age of eighty.

Manjula was alone with Prabhakara Rao at last. She finally enjoyed a harmonious, loving relationship with him. It lasted until his death three years later.

AFTERWORD

⊙ ⊙ ⊙

I GREW UP IN THE untouchable slum of Elwin Peta in Kakinada. All around me was abject poverty. When you are surrounded by so much misery, you don't see it as anything extraordinary. I remember when one of my friends in the neighborhood told me she'd had roast venison for dinner three days in a row. I laughed along with her, knowing that was her ironic way of saying she'd gone without eating. I was thinking of the joke she was making and not that some people don't have anything to eat.

Yet two things I witnessed when I was seven or eight years old especially horrified me. Whenever I think of Elwin Peta, these moments come back to me. They will haunt me until I die.

A woman named Santoshamma with her two gaunt teenage sons lived across the street from our house under a thatch supported by four posts. She was only in her late thirties or early forties, but her body was so ravaged by starvation that she couldn't walk anymore. She lay on rags under the thatch, moaning day and night, hungry and in pain. One day she just wanted something to eat. She sat up. But she couldn't stand up. She put her hands on the ground behind her. Propping herself up on the heels of her palms, she lifted her ass up and propelled herself forward. Then she lowered herself to the ground again and stretched out her legs. Repeating these steps, she crawled all the way across the street and through our front gate.

I was skipping rope in front of our house. When I saw her come through the gate, I stopped and stared wide-eyed at the sight of her in her rags, her wrinkled skin hanging from her skeletal frame, her hair wild and dry like straw, with tears pooling in the folds around her eyes, desperate, crawling like some crushed and oozing creature.

She continued around the side of the house toward the kitchen in back to beg for some food from my grandmother. My grandmother, catching sight of her, was shocked and started weeping with helpless compassion and yelling at her in a trembling voice, abusing the poor woman for presenting us with such a bizarre and pitiful spectacle.

My mother would hire another woman, named Ruthamma, to do chores in our house. She was washing dishes in a bucket on the kitchen floor when I walked in, eating a piece of apple. It was the day after Christmas. We could afford apples only at Christmas. A couple of apples for the whole family. Ruthamma looked at the piece of apple in my hand with such a stupid, lustful grin, salivating openly, that I could not eat it anymore. I knew that she had never in her life tasted an apple. I can't remember if I gave it to her.

Experiences like this made me wish there were no poor people in the world. But how could that be achieved?

Growing up, I heard about my uncle through my mother. She told us he had sacrificed everything, left his family, and gone off to help the poor. How did he help them? He had a gun. He would threaten rich people, take their money, and give it to those who had nothing. My uncle was like a cinema hero to me. I wanted so much to be like him. But we were never going to see him, my mother said, because the police were secretly watching our house. If he tried to visit us, he would be arrested and put in jail. All this made my uncle seem like a mysterious star shining in the sky high above.

My mother also told us that he never kept any of the money that he took for himself. He lived a hard life in the jungles. I practiced sleeping on the bare cement floor to prepare myself for the future when I'd have to sleep on the hard ground. I told my friends that I was going to be a Naxalite when I grew up.

One summer afternoon when I was fourteen years old, I was riding my bicycle home from my maths tutor's house when I spotted a group of teenagers singing to a small crowd gathered on a street corner. Fascinated, I got off my bicycle. They were singing about poor peasants and workers, how unjust it is that they suffer from want because they are the ones producing the wealth, not the owners of the land and the factories. Never had I heard a song like this before. "Come on, peasant brothers," they sang, "come on, all you exploited and impoverished, join the party of the peasants and the poor and let us all stand up to the landlords."

I walked through the crowd right into the midst of the singers and declared, "I want to join."

They were delighted to have won a recruit. I invited them home with me. My family was surprised but also curious. Sitting on our bed, they sang for us, filling the small, asbestos-ceilinged room with revolutionary passion. We were enthralled. When my mother started talking to them and asking them questions, we learned they belonged to a party founded by none other than my uncle.

That day I became a Radical—a member of the Radical Students Union (RSU), the student wing of the People's War Group (PWG).

It was all informal. Whenever the party needed me to take part in some activity such as distributing leaflets, they met me at home or in school and asked me. I was always ready to do what they wanted. I joined a street-theater group like the one I had met and went around singing about unemployment, the rising prices of basic commodities, corruption in government hospitals, the evils of the education system. When student strikes were organized by the party, I would make speeches asking people to support them. On summer holidays, I joined "village campaigns." Ten or fifteen of us would spend a few weeks traveling from village to village in the vicinity of Kakinada, stopping for a day or two in each one to learn about the lives and aspirations of the poor peasants and to tell them their lives needn't be so hard, that in China a people's government had been established. For a couple of years I was the youngest member.

We were aware that someday we would be called on to take part in other forms of struggle. When I was sixteen years old and weighed about seventy-five or eighty pounds, I was attending a conference and a man my father's age came up to me and shook my hand so vigorously that my whole body shook. He said to me fondly, "You are so frail, you must eat, put on weight! Else how are you going to carry your rifle?"

The party stood for people's war: an armed struggle against the landlords to seize their estates and distribute the land to the poor peasants who actually worked on it. We Radicals looked forward to this future phase of struggle that we were helping to prepare for by winning mass support for the party.

In the meantime, we were very much on the receiving end of violence at the hands of the landlords and the police. Hundreds of PWG members and sympathizers were arrested. Torture in custody was routine. Every month I would hear of comrades being shot dead, including many students.

We were aware of these dangers. But they did not frighten us. We knew they were part of a revolutionary's life. In fact, we dreamed of how heroic it would be to face repression without betraying the party or losing our revolutionary zeal.

Then I myself faced it.

When I was nineteen, I left home to enroll in a master's program at the Regional Engineering College in Warangal. It was the same REC where my uncle did political work while teaching at nearby St. Gabriel. Thanks to him, by the time I got there student life was dominated by the Radicals, and many faculty were Naxalite sympathizers.

When I was in second year, it was brought to our attention that an uppercaste professor in the electronics engineering department was passing all the students of his own caste with high marks and failing his low-caste students. We warned the professor to stop this practice, but he did not listen. Then we took the matter to the principal. To our surprise, the principal, who never used to disagree with us, sided with the professor. So we called a strike. All the students left except those leading the strike. Not being on the strike committee, I went home.

A few days later, a large police van stopped in front of my house, and a number of police got out. The sub-inspector came inside and told my parents he was arresting me and transporting me to Warangal. Then he took me away.

I was one of dozens of students and workers (including the physician at the campus medical center) to be thrown in jail in retaliation for the strike. I was the only girl among them. The police made it impossible for our families to find us by continually moving us from one precinct to another. We were deprived of food and water and sanitary facilities for long periods and tortured. They beat us with sticks, with ropes. I heard a deputy superintendent of police tell two female cops, "Beat her until I can see the welts on her." They stuck pins under our nails. We did not know how long this was going to go on. Weeks went by.

Not knowing where I was or even what the charges against me were, my mother went to the state capital of Hyderabad to find a famous civil rights lawyer named Kannabiran and ask him to file a habeas corpus.

In response, the police finally moved me to the Central Jail—the same one where my uncle had spent some time. My parents had to fight hard to get me out on bail. I'd been locked up for three months. During this time, I contracted tuberculosis.

Although no charges had been filed, the police issued a warning that if I wanted them to leave me alone, I must get out of Warangal and never return. I had no particular reaction—since the day I'd been arrested my mind had gone blank and I'd just let things happen to me—but my parents were upset that I wouldn't be allowed to finish my master's program. They got an appointment with the assistant superintendent of police to make a special plea to let me finish. The ASP was reluctant. He made my parents promise that I would not talk to anyone—anyone at all—while I finished my degree, and that once I did, I would leave. The principal, professors, students, administrative staff, and campus workers were all warned not to talk to me.

I lost one year. When I went back to school, I was still recovering from tuberculosis. My father came to stay with me for five months, taking care of me and himself contracting the disease. Under close surveillance and constant harassment by the Warangal police, I finished my master of science in technology and left Warangal.

My arrest had an indelible effect on my family. We were socially ostracized. Christians, especially, avoided us. There was little chance any-one would want to marry me or my siblings. Even those who sympathized with us kept away for fear of police harassment. Of all of us, my sister, Anitha, a twenty-year-old first-year medical student at the time, suffered most. But none in the family, including my beloved grandmother, re-proached me for my radical activities or my mother for having steered me in that direction.

All the Radicals had been arrested. Because I was held in women's jails, I did not know what had happened to my friends, but my mother found out while she was running around from precinct to precinct searching for me. Ashok, Johnayya, Satyam, and others from impoverished untouch-able families with illiterate parents were not so lucky as me. They spent even more time in police custody, where they continued to be subjected to torture. They had no one to file habeas corpus or post bail on their behalf. Later I heard that one of them had a heart attack and died soon after his release and another hanged himself. Worse still was the fate of some young tribal dishwashers in the REC messes who were friendly with the Radicals. They were arrested at the same time as us, but not taken to any jail. They were never heard from again, and it was presumed they had been shot dead.

The party stayed away from me while I was under surveillance, but after I graduated and came back home, the district organizers started coming by my house again to talk to me. My parents told them they didn't think it was a good idea, but they ignored them. Once when my parents were not around, one party representative asked me, "Now that you've finished your education, what about going full-time?" This would have meant going underground to become a full-time party worker. Once a person goes underground, he or she will be wanted by the police.

Before my arrest, I would have accepted immediately. But after all my parents had been through, I said I wanted to think about it.

The party representative took me to a house in a nearby town where a man was waiting for me in a small room. The representative left me with this man, who introduced himself by his party name, Exiled Sun. I could tell he was a top underground leader. He sat with me for eight hours continuously and explained how ennobling it was to dedicate one's life to the revolution. I just listened and said nothing. It became clear to Exiled Sun that I wasn't interested. The party representative returned to take me home.

Shortly after this episode, the same party representative came to our house one evening when everyone was home. He told us in a quiet voice that he had some important news: the party had expelled SM.

The news was shocking because to everyone I knew, SM *was* the party. He was the one who drew intellectuals and students to PWG politics and, with his slogans and poems and songs and the people's theater troupe he inspired, invested the party's program with a romantic aura. It would be no exaggeration to say that because of him the PWG had become the most successful guerrilla party in the subcontinent, except perhaps for the Tamil Tigers in Sri Lanka.

He was expelled, we were told, because he had turned traitor and tried to divide the party. I instantly spat out, "That traitor!" Despite my decision not to go underground, I was still staunchly loyal to the party. I made sure to be firm in my denunciation to show I was not swayed by the family relation. My mother, on the other hand, wanted to know exactly what he had done. They could only say that things would become clearer in time. When my mother asked if there were any documents, they said they would try to get her some.

Soon after, I got a job as a research assistant in the Indian Institute of Technology (IIT) in Madras. There was no RSU or PWG in Madras, but that didn't matter to me. I was twenty-two years old. I wasn't thinking of revolution or even of my own future. I made new friends and went out in the city with them. We went shopping or to movies, restaurants, the beach. I had boyfriends and loved to stay up late either in the Precision Engineering and Instrumentation Lab with Hegde as he did his M.S. or in the Holography Lab with Masalkar as he did his Ph.D. I listened to Western music and read novels.

After I had been in Madras for a year, the attendant at the hostel announced one Sunday that I had a visitor. This man, in his late twenties, introduced himself as Usa and told me in a whisper, "I'm a friend of your uncle's." SM had sent him to explain why he had been expelled, Usa said, so that I could tell the world.

In 1984, KS had been arrested while waiting for a train and thrown in prison. During that time SM, who had been second-in-command, took over as general secretary of the PWG. Seizing the opportunity, a group of young untouchable members approached him and complained of casteist practices in the underground functioning of the party. They pointed out that when members were recruited, they were assigned duties according to their caste. Barber-caste members were told to shave their comrades' chins, and washer-caste members to wash their comrades' clothes. Untouchables, of course, were made to sweep and mop the floors and clean the lavatories.

Talk of caste feeling inside the party had always been taboo. But the political climate had changed in the wake of a shocking massacre that year in the village of Karamchedu, where an entire madiga settlement was brutally attacked by a mob of two thousand kamma men, killing eleven, after a madiga woman complained that the kammas were washing their buffaloes in the madiga drinking-water tank. Awareness of casteism as a political question was spreading among untouchables. The college-educated young untouchable members who spoke to SM had joined the party precisely because they saw it as the best way to fight against the system that bred such injustices. When they joined, they were not given a gun. Instead they were handed a broom and told to sweep the floors. They called on SM to raise this question.

SM himself had received his share of casteist insults from uppercaste

303 | ANTS AMONG ELEPHANTS

members who were close to him. They were known to leave small amounts of money in the bathroom to see if he would pocket it. He had brushed this behavior aside as the product of backward social attitudes that had inevitably seeped into the party from outside and would surely wither away as it grew in strength. But now he could no longer close his eyes.

After KS escaped in an ambush organized by SM, he returned as party leader. Once he was back, SM called a Central Committee meeting to discuss the complaints the young members had aired. SM barely had a chance to finish presenting his document. The reaction of the other leaders was swift and ruthless. He was expelled on the spot for "conspiring to divide the party."

After his expulsion SM and his companion, a young woman named Parvathi, went on the run. Their lives were in danger from both the police and the PWG.

I didn't know what to do with this information and didn't take the mission I was given seriously. But when I went home on vacation some time later, I learned my mother, too, had been contacted and told the same thing. She showed me a letter she had written to the widely read daily newspaper *Udayam*, exposing, first, that SM had been expelled from the PWG, and, second, the real story behind his expulsion. But she was not sure what good it would do or who would care.

I insisted that we take the letter in person to the *Udayam* office. There we met with a subeditor named Vasanta Lakshmi, who took it upon herself to see that it was printed. When the letter came out, it sent shock waves through Andhra.

A few months later Vasanta Lakshmi's lover, a young journalist named Tripuraneni Srinivas, managed to contact my uncle and conduct a series of interviews with him, which, when they were published in *Udayam*, gave wide publicity to the casteism inside a so-called communist party. Until that time, the general public had not been aware that SM was an untouchable. He was known only as a founder and leader of the PWG and a great poet.

As this drama was unfolding, I was preparing to take the GRE, as everyone in every IIT does in his or her final year. I was accepted into a graduate program in America and came here to enroll, leaving everything behind.

After four years on the run with a price on his head, SM made a bold move and appeared unexpectedly in front of thousands of people in a public meeting held by the Revolutionary Writers' Association as part of their annual conference. The organizers were stunned when he climbed up onstage, took the microphone, and began addressing everyone present, including reporters and police. He announced that he was unarmed, that he had been expelled from the PWG, and that he was surrendering to the police. He made clear he was surrendering only legally, not politically. With this statement, he bound the hands of the police because they could no longer claim he was killed in an encounter. He explained why he had been expelled. Some PWG members present then tried to remove him from the podium by force, but several young untouchables in the audience rose silently in his defense, rolling up their sleeves. The support he attracted from untouchables was to save his life. The PWG could not harm him without alienating the largest section of their base. And despite his surrender, he was never arrested.

My uncle's expulsion came at a time of sharpening conflict between the landed castes and landless untouchables. Due to economic changes over the previous decades, untouchable laborers had started seeing themselves as wage workers rather than servants of the landlord. The landlords reacted with murderous violence. In 1991, six years after Karamchedu, eight malas were massacred by reddy landlords in the village of Tsundur. The bodies were chopped up and tossed into an irrigation canal.

SM went and settled in that village, leading the agitation from there. With the help of several civil rights lawyers, including a young brahmin named Chandra Sekhar, SM conducted an investigation of the incident. While other untouchable leaders were calling solely for legal recourse against the accused, SM sought to organize untouchables in self-defense. Fifty-six men were charged with murder. SM did not live to see the end of the case, but through his participation in this struggle he established himself as a leader of the untouchable masses of Andhra.

Two years later, he started an agitation to commute the death sentences of two untouchable youths who were waiting to be hanged. Although there had been movements worldwide against capital punishment, the cause was not popular in India. When the youths were spared, SM became a legend in the districts of Guntur and Ongole.

All throughout his career in the Communist movement, my uncle had avoided talking too much about caste. He shared the view that the toilers should only be organized to fight for the demands of the whole class, not for those of particular groups. After his expulsion, he took the opposite position. He decided that uppercaste peasants and toilers couldn't be won to a truly revolutionary program. He tried to organize untouchable and low-caste peasants on a caste basis as a revolutionary vanguard. Others would be allowed to join but not to serve as leaders. To the end of his life, when he was barely able to walk and had to rely on his supporters to carry him on their backs through the jungles, he was trying to start such a party.

On April 17, 2012, two days after I finished writing the introduction at the start of this book, I woke to find my uncle's death was national news in India. Thousands thronged to get a last glimpse of him. Even his worst political rivals showed up. For days all the TV channels in Andhra ran nothing but programs on his life and legacy. The newspapers were full of his poetry. Processions in his memory went on for weeks afterward in cities, towns, and villages across the state. It all came as a great surprise to his family. We never realized he was loved by so many, and so much.

I still look forward to a day when there are no poor people in the world, and I agree with my uncle that it will take a revolution to achieve this. But I disagree with the programs and tactics he espoused both before his expulsion and afterward, including his different views on the strategic role of the struggle against caste oppression.

In 1928, a major strike wave in the textile mills in Bombay under the leadership of the Communist Party threatened to turn into a general strike against colonial rule. But the strike failed because the workers were divided in several ways, including on caste lines. For many years, the caste workers organized by the Communists refused to work alongside untouchables in the weaving department, demanding that untouchables be confined to the lowest-paid jobs, in the spinning department. During the strike, at the urging of their leader Ambedkar, who argued that they had the most to lose and nothing to gain, the untouchable workers crossed picket lines. When finally toward the end of the strike, as the workers were already starving, the union agreed to include a demand to open the weaving department to untouchable workers, the management said that if keeping them out was an injustice, it was entirely the doing of the caste workers themselves. Had the union fought for the rights of untouchable workers from the start, the struggle might have turned out differently.

ACKNOWLEDGMENTS

⊙ ⊙ ⊙

The author would like to thank Alan Horn, Laird Gallagher, Ken Alper, Professor Kontham Purushotham, and Stephany Evans.